WRITING FOR
CHILDREN & TEENAGERS

WRITING FOR
CHILDREN &
TEENAGERS

Lee Wyndham
Revised by Arnold Madison

Cincinnati, Ohio

First printing 1968
Second printing 1969
Revised by Lee Wyndham 1972
Second printing of revised edition 1974
Third printing of revised edition 1976
Fourth printing of revised edition 1977
Fifth printing of revised edition 1978
Sixth printing of revised edition 1979
Revised by Arnold Madison 1980
Second printing of 1980 revised edition 1982
Third printing of 1980 revised edition 1983
Fourth printing of 1980 revised edition 1983
First paperback printing 1984
Second paperback printing 1985
Third paperback printing 1986
Revised by Arnold Madison 1988

Other fine Writer's Digest Books are available from your local bookstore or direct from the publisher.

03   02   01   00   99   15   14   13   12   11

Library of Congress Cataloging-in-Publication Data

Wyndham, Lee.
    Writing for children and teenagers.

    Bibliography: p.
    Includes index.
    1. Children's literature—Authorship.I. Madison, Arnold.II.
Title

PN147.5.W9   1980   808'.068   79-24459
ISBN 0-89879-347-5 paperback
ISBN 0-89879-585-0

To Phyllis A. Whitney
Whose torch has helped
to light so many candles.

L. W.
A. M.

BOOKS BY LEE WYNDHAM

Candy Stripers (Messner)
Beth Hilton, Model (Messner)
The Timid Dragon (Lothrop)
Mourka, the Mighty Cat (Parents')
The Winter Child (Parents')
Russian Tales of Fabulous Beasts and Marvels (Parents')
Tales the People Tell in Russia (Messner)
Sizzling Pan Ranch (Crowell)
Silver Yankee (Winston-Holt)
Slipper Under Glass (Longmans-McKay)
Golden Slippers (Longmans-McKay)
Showboat Holiday (Winston-Holt)
A Dance for Susie (Dodd)
Susie and the Dancing Cat (Dodd)
Susie and the Ballet Family (Dodd)
On Your Toes, Susie (Dodd)
Susie and the Ballet Horse (Dodd)
Camel Bird Ranch (Dodd)
Binkie's Billions (Knopf)
Ballet Teacher (Messner)
Lady Architect (Messner)
Dance to My Measure (Messner)
The Lost Birthday Present (Dodd)
Ballet for You (Grosset)
Bonnie (Doubleday)
Chip Nelson and the Contrary Indians (Watts)
The How and Why Wonder Book of Ballet (Grosset)
Family at Seven Chimneys House (Watts)
Thanksgiving (Garrard)
Florence Nightingale, Nurse to the World (World Pub. Co.)
The Lady with the Lamp (Scholastic)
Holidays in Scandinavia (Garrard)
The Little Wise Man — with Robert Wyndham (Bobbs)
First Steps in Ballet — with Thalia Mara (Doubleday)
Buttons and Beaux — with Louise Barnes Gallagher (Dodd)
Anthology — *Dancers, Dancers, Dancers* (Watts)
Anthology — *Acting, Acting, Acting* (Watts)
Adaptation — *Folk Tales of India* (Bobbs)
Adaptation — *Folk Tales of China* (Bobbs)
Adaptation — *Tales from the Arabian Nights* (Whitman)
Adaptation — *Mark Twain's The Prince and the Pauper, from Walt Disney's screenplay* (Whitman)

BOOKS BY ARNOLD MADISON

Danger Beats the Drum (Holt, Rinehart & Winston)
Think Wild! (Holt, Rinehart & Winston)
The Secret of the Carved Whale Bone (McKay)
Vandalism (Clarion)
Drugs and You (Messner)
Fast Break to Danger (Pyramid)
Vigilantism in America (Clarion)
Treasure Hunting (Hawthorne)
Smoking and You (Messner)
American Global Diplomacy (Watts)
Carry Nation (Lodestar)
Aviation Careers (Watts)
Lost Treasures of America (Rand McNally)
Suicide and Young People (Clarion)
Pocket Calculators (Lodestar)
Don't Be a Victim (Messner)
Great Unsolved Cases (Watts)
Arson! (Watts)
Lacrosse (McKay)
Runaway Teens (Lodestar)
Surfing (McKay)
Mummies in Fact and Fiction (Watts)
How the Colonists Lived (McKay)
Polish Greats (McKay)
How to Play Girls' Softball (Messner)
It Can't Happen to Me (Scholastic)
Transplanted and Artificial Body Organs (Beautfort)
But This Girl Is Different (Scholastic)

CONTENTS

PART I
A PRACTICAL GUIDE TO PUBLICATION

PART II
SPECIAL WRITING PROBLEMS AND PROJECTS

fiction • Magazine articles • Selecting a topic • Lists of subjects • Market study is necessary • Samples of writing style • Query letters • Nonfiction books • Categories of books • How to find book ideas • Preparing a proposal • How to outline • The importance of back matter • Selecting the sample chapters • Openings — statement, question and answer, anecdotal • The body of the article or chapter • Keep your nonfiction non-sexist • How to avoid unintentional racism or religious prejudice • How to insert quotations into the text • Endings.

Opening night • Overlooked market • Writers' insecurities • The market • Plays written for children to be acted by children • Plays written for children to be acted by adults • Plays written for teenagers and/or adults to be acted by teenagers and/or adults • The creation of a play • Ideas • Characters • Plot • Scenario • Segments and beats • Quoted play segments.

Reference items on my bookshelves • Books about children's books • Some textbooks from my shelves • For that stamp of professionalism • Magazines for writers • Market lists.

Writing is heady stuff • Happiness is the chief product.

Illustrations

PART I
**A PRACTICAL GUIDE
TO PUBLICATION**

1
Readers, Readers Everywhere . . .

A writer must have readers—for reading is the other half of writing. A writer whose work is not read might as well be keeping a diary. Fortunately, there is a clamor for books and magazines all over the world. Never have so many been published, imported, exported, reprinted, reissued, translated, and put in paperbacks. In the United States, between two and three thousand children's books are brought out annually by some one hundred sixty publishers; our children's magazines have a combined circulation of more than thirty-five million copies.

Library circulation of books for children has increased phenomenally in many areas. There is no dearth of readers. From the age of three and up, we have at least sixty million boys and girls and *each one is a potential reader of what you write!*

Government activities and subsidies for book purchases, the efforts of teachers and librarians, and high-powered private promotions have made people increasingly aware of the fact that reading is the primary tool of learning. Today, publishing is "big business." Its chief product is books; its major need, authors.

Editors are constantly on the lookout for authors. At the same time, authors are in search of markets for their work. Editorial safes, filing cabinets, and windowsills groan under the weight of manuscripts. However, most unsolicited manuscripts submitted to juvenile departments return to their authors, often because the writers did not realize they were competing in a highly *specialized* field.

The primary purpose of this book is to help you achieve publication. The chapters are arranged in the order that I have found most effective in class teaching. The Table of Contents headings outline the course; listed under each chapter are the topics covered. A comprehensive index at the back of the book is designed to simplify your search for specific items.

Emphasis throughout is on practical guidance to professional competence, which will not only help make you a better writer but will also furnish much professional know-how that might otherwise take you years to acquire. Even if you have achieved publication on your own, you will find valuable pointers, drawn from a wide writing, publishing, and lecturing experience.

WHAT IT TAKES TO BE A WRITER FOR CHILDREN

You already have the first requirement—you want to be a successful writer—or you would not be reading this book.

The second is that you must *know* and *like* children. If in your secret heart you think they are little monsters and potential juvenile offenders, then writing for juniors is not for you. You must respect your audience, whether it be three-year-olds or fifteen-year-olds.

If you do not have children in your own family circle, make friends with your neighbor children—especially in the age range for which you'd like to write.

Books *about* children and teenagers will help you to understand the younger generation. These will be discussed more fully in other chapters and listed in the bibliography.

In preparing to write, study material already published for the specific age group you have in mind. Such reading will put you into the proper mood for your own effort, and also indicate how to handle subject matter, sentence structure, vocabulary, and length of story. Throughout this text, titles of specific books are suggested as outstanding examples. The important thing to keep in mind is that the books are only that—suggestions. All libraries do not have all books. Should you not find a certain title or if it is not available through an inter-library loan system, check with the children's librarian who should have become your friend by now. He or she will be able to guide you to other appropriate readings in the various categories.

Reading is the other half of writing — not *merely* for entertainment, now that you're studying the craft of writing, but for research, general knowledge, and object lessons in how professional writers deal with their material. Every magazine article, story, or book that you read will be dissected to see what is the subject, who is the viewpoint character, and what is the message of the story. Why did the author use first person? Or third person? Judgments went into those decisions, and you, the writer, will want to trace that reasoning. We learn from those who have gone before us.

Writing for young people is a great responsibility, because their minds are impressionable and what they read can affect not only their current lives but their future ones as well. Writing for them should be approached with a serious regard for the possible influence of your words. Do not plan to write for children because you think it is easy, or the writing does not need to be as good as that in books for adults. Requirements for good juvenile writing are far more strict than they are for adult fiction, and there are many dedicated people watching out to see that they are observed, for the very reasons mentioned above.

There is much to learn about this special field. But if you have the qualifications, really love to write, and have the necessary talent, learn you can.

And the rewards — the heartlifting ones will emerge as you turn these pages and learn the how's and why's of writing for young people. As for financial returns, few authors write only for the money. There are much easier and more dependable ways of earning a living. And yet — well, you may not ever make twenty thousand dollars a year — but on the other hand, with new market possibilities for children's books opening up, you just might! If you become a prolific and popular writer, after a few years a backlog of books can provide sufficient royalties for a comfortable living — or at the very least, a nice supplementary income.

LIFE SPANS OF JUNIOR BOOKS

A number of children's books have achieved such popularity that they continue to sell years after their first publication. *Mike Mulligan and His Steam Shovel* has been selling since 1939; *Dr. Doolittle* and his adventures, since 1922; *Johnny Tremain,* since 1943; *Mary Poppins,* since 1939 — and look what's happened to her! *Understood Betsy* charmed today's grandmothers in 1917 — and their granddaughters love her, too.

Many favorites outlast the life spans of their authors. Glance over the classic titles available in multiple editions in the bookstores; *Black Beauty* has been selling steadily since 1877; *Heidi* was published in 1880; *Treasure Island* in 1883; and the beloved *Little Women* — forever new to girls who first discover it — was published in 1868! From a child's point of view, a "new" book is one he or she has not read before — even though the author may be long dead. Enthusiastic fan letters are still penned to Daniel Defoe, Robert Louis Stevenson, and Louisa May Alcott.

Who's to say that you won't write a best-selling classic that will live forever! But even if you don't write deathless prose, there is a place for you if your work catches the popular fancy. Look at the *Bobbsey Twins* — 1904 (continued in an updated version today); and *Tarzan* — who's been swinging through the trees since 1914. *There are all kinds of readers in the world, with all kinds of tastes; it takes all kinds of writers to please them.*

There is also such a thing as the "serviceable" book, written with professional competence and grace, if not with resounding literary style. It, too, can enjoy an extraordinary long life as a children's favorite in our ever-expanding world of readers. And there are many niches where a capable writer can fit. Let's look them over in the next chapter.

**2
A General Survey of the Junior Magazine
and Book Fields**

According to the most recent lists in *Writer's Market,* a Writer's Digest Books publication, there are over one hundred juvenile and teen magazines and story papers buying fiction and freelance articles. Most of these are church affiliated, published once a week for Sunday school distribution. Because of their frequency of publication, they use a great deal of material. With a few notable exceptions, the rates paid are generally low. However, to the beginner, *publication* means more than money at this stage. Writers whose work is published get a definite psychological lift. They begin to feel, act, and write like professionals.

THE JUVENILE SHORT STORY FIELD

In the church magazines, material should be helpful and practical, designed to aid young people to meet and solve the problems they face daily. The stories must encourage, inspire, build honest, loyal, clear-thinking, moral young people.

Although "lesson stories," they still must serve the primary function of fiction; *they must entertain the reader.* The valuable lesson — kindness, understanding, brotherhood, honesty — must be slipped into the plot through the actions and reactions of the story characters. Readers, however young, must not suspect that they are being taught anything through a fictionalized sermon. If they do, they'll stop reading.

Some denominational magazines look first of all for *entertaining* stories that do not flout the rules of ethical conduct.

In a sense, the stories are bait to catch the reader's attention with something that's fun to read; and as the youngster turns the pages, the hope is that the specially prepared spiritual messages usually written by the staff will be read and absorbed.

TABOOS

The "don'ts" are getting fewer, but they still exist, and you'll save postage, wear and tear on your manuscripts and your nerves, if you become aware of what these taboos are and where they apply, both in denominational and secular markets.

In books you'll have a much broader scope in which to work. Magazines, however, depend on subscriptions, and so controversial material, such as religious bias, politics, situations involving unethical conduct (without retribution), or the casting of aspersions on a particular geographic area or cultural or ethnic group, which might offend a substantial number of subscribers and/or advertisers, is generally avoided. Slang, swearing, and bad taste are not wanted, even as horrible examples. Rampant crime and youngsters chasing adult bandits are usually frowned upon in most—but not all—quality publications. Some magazines do not want any adolescent love themes, others welcome romance.

Taboos, like everything else in publishing, change, and the only way to keep up with what they are is to study market reports and lists—and these will be discussed later on. A study of sample issues of the various magazines will indicate the position taken on all such matters. In addition, many publishers supply writers with "Editorial Requirements" leaflets on request. Be sure to enclose a stamped, self-addressed envelope to get yours.

Except in rare instances, an author cannot write for the three-year-old and the ten-year-old in the same story, or reach the six-year-old as well as the sophisticated teenager. Although age groups do not bind the reader hard and fast, there have to be arbitrary divisions in a publishing program. To send your winged horses to the right stables you must be aware of the age ranges into which reading matter for juniors is divided. There are small but important differences between the groupings used by the magazines and by book publishers. Magazines separate into three groups.

Primary

Material for six-, seven-, and eight-year-olds must be simply presented, in easy-to-understand language. Stories should have a single idea, and everything that happens in the story should contribute to this idea. A simple plot is required to hold the reader's interest. Lengths are from 300 to 500 words, sometimes 700, but seldom over 900. Some of these magazines include material that will interest even the youngest members of the family—the two- to five-year-olds. For samples of the different publications you can write to denominational houses. For nondenominational magazines, check your local newsstands for *Humpty Dumpty's Magazine, Jack and Jill,* or send for sample copies of *Child Life, Highlights for Children,* and *Cricket.* There is always a need for publishable material for this age.

Intermediate and Middle School

The nine- to thirteen-year-olds want lots of action set in the framework of an exciting, unified plot. The stories should be centered around their own interests, contemporary problems and experiences. Since the appeal should be to both boys and girls, it is wise to use boy and girl characters in your stories.

The writing must be subjective, narrated from the viewpoint of the main character. Everything should be presented through the character's eyes, senses, and emotions. Get in drama and suspense, and good brisk pace. Lengths are 700 to 1,500 words, with 1,000 to 1,200 considered most desirable. Serials may have from two to four parts each with the same word lengths just mentioned.

High School

Stories for thirteen- to seventeen-year-olds must become more complex. Teenagers demand all the elements of good fiction technique: plot, characterization, conflict, complications, suspense, drama, and the satisfying solution.

Story backgrounds should be of interest to high school youth: school life, part-time jobs, sports, camp life, adventure, foreign backgrounds. Problems might involve getting along with others, tolerance of other people and other ways, finding a job, personal and business ethics, sportsmanship. Some of the magazines for this age are designed for girls or for boys only, but most have to please both. So again, you have a better chance of making a sale if you use boy and girl characters in your stories, although one or the other plays the leading role.

Generally stories for the high school group range from 1,200 to 3,500 words, with 1,600-1,800 preferred. Serials run in the same lengths for each installment. For samples of this kind of writing, look for *Seventeen, 'Teen,* and other magazines for teens on the stands. Write for samples in the denominational and educational fields.

THE JUVENILE AND YOUNG ADULT BOOK FIELD

Here the publishers' age divisions are so varied that for practical purposes in my book reviews and lectures, I have found it more useful to divide the books into seven main groups.

1. *Picture books* — ages one through six. On the surface, this classification might seem to be one solid division. However, it is a complex grouping. There are books written for the child one to three years old, three to five, and others for the five- to seven-year-old. In Part II of this text, I shall deal more fully with the particular requirements of this multi-faceted group.

In general, however, there are a few lines of text and a picture on every page. The illustrations are expected to carry fully half of the story — if not more — supplying descriptions and character details. If your story is accepted, your editor will arrange for all the art work. Unless you are a professional artist, fully adept at creating color overlays and art of the highest caliber, do not send art work or even suggestions as to what the illustrations should depict. Doing so will kill an editor's interest in your story. The text of a picture book may run from 25 to 1,500 words.

2. *Ages seven to ten* — More text, fewer pictures, lots of action in the story. A definite plot line, which leads the main character to a desired goal, is usually developed and makes this "a real story." The book is still a "two-lap" affair, with an adult reading to the child, so the vocabulary need not be oversimplified. However, the story should be easily understood by the child, so erudite words have no place here. Keep out adult whimsy, too—plays on words or situations that will be over the head of the child-listener. The text of the picture story may run from 1,000 to 10,000 words.

3. *Easy-to-read*—ages six to nine (grades one to three). These stories are for children to read on their own with their newly acquired reading skills. The plots should be lively, featuring humor, mystery, or adventure. They should be *fun* to read. Manuscript length ranges from 500 words to about 2,000, with 1,000 to 1,500 preferred.

To be published, a story with even the most severely controlled vocabulary must be told in rhythmic, natural style. This is difficult, and many an author has grown gray in the process or given up altogether. But the struggle is well worth the rewards, for easy-to-reads are one of the strongest trends in juvenile literature today. The techniques will be discussed more fully in Part II.

4. *The eight-to-twelve* readers compose the biggest reading group, the "Golden Age" of reading. The interests of the boys and girls are limitless. Stories of today, yesterday, tomorrow, all are read avidly; funny situations—and grim ones, too—mysteries, stories about families, sports, adventure, animals, stories about conservation, ecology, air pollution, our fantastic space explorations—fact and fiction about people and places, all are popular. Books definitely for girls and definitely for boys appear now, but mixed groups of characters are very welcome. Best lengths for manuscripts are 20,000 to 40,000 words.

5. *The teens*— Although theoretically "teens" means readers of twelve to sixteen, actually they can be from ten to fifteen, seldom older. Yet these young people of today are reading more serious books, often dealing with themes and experiences unheard of in junior fiction a few years ago. Heroes and heroines strive to understand themselves and others, the new morality, politics, and civil disturbances. They struggle with issues such as idealistic new worlds, the raising of the underprivileged in an egalitarian society, and rights for women. These book and story characters explore, experiment, and come to grief with the shattering realism of their real-life counterparts.

Suspense tales are always popular, and so are science

fiction and biographies. All these will be dealt with more fully in the following chapters and in Part II.

6. *Teenage romances* — For a number of years, this type novel had fallen into disfavor with editors. The reasons are obvious when reading the older novels of the genre. The characterizations were weak, the plots unrealistic, and the world they described had vanished by the early 1960s. Recently, there has been a resurgence of teen romances, but with stories based on today's world.

7. *Hi/lo* — The name of this category tells the whole story: high interest/low reading level. The novels and nonfiction books are aimed at readers from the intermediate grades up through high school who have reading problems and cannot cope with material written at the usual reading level for their grades. The stories must be fast-paced, contain plenty of dialogue, and deal with realistic, contemporary problems. The nonfiction subjects should also be ones that the readers would definitely want to read about. The writing techniques needed for this type of book will be discussed more fully in Part II.

In each age group children like to read about youngsters in the leading roles who are as old or older than themselves — almost never younger. In your writing avoid diminutives for the heroes ("little Dick," "tiny Sally"). The usual aim of these readers is to be "bigger," "older," "stronger," than they are at the moment, so they do not take kindly to "littleness" in the characters with whom they are to identify.

Adults in the stories should be kept to an absolute minimum. Introduced upon a scene they have an annoying way of taking over — just as in real life. Keep your stories for children *about* children, working out problems suitable to their years, with as little grownup help as possible.

WHAT DO EDITORS WANT?

Very often they don't know *exactly*. But an editor is like a roving reporter: neither knows precisely what he or she is looking for, yet recognizes it at once when confronted with it.

Primarily, editors want stories that are fun to read. The chief business of fiction is to entertain the reader, whether the writing be for children or grownups. In addition, your story should have some plus values, such as an interesting background, information — a message perhaps — something that will make the editor feel your story or book is worth publishing.

Most wanted are stories about today's children in American settings, working out contemporary problems suitable to their years. Urban settings are especially welcome. With today's emphasis on getting along with people of different races, cultures, and beliefs, stories featuring young characters of various backgrounds are welcome.

In historical background stories, the young people must figure as main characters. Stories of courage, daring, or exploration are always popular.

TRENDS IN SUBJECTS AND PROBLEMS

Times are changing, and our fiction should reflect contemporary life. A basic fact of life for writers is that there is fierce editorial resistance against any material that perpetuates tired, stereotypical images.

If you have a story in which Mom is in the kitchen while Dad is repairing the car, and Betsy has just returned from her ballet lessons at the same time Rob has come home from a rough and tumble game of football — you can be certain that the story will be rejected. Every woman does not spend all her time in the kitchen, nor does every man have facility with mechanical problems. Girls are not necessarily interested in gentle activities or boys eager to participate in contact sports. Break the mold somewhere. Let at least one of the characters reflect today's thinking. Dad might do the cooking because Mom's job does not permit her to get home in time. Don't become absurd by going overboard. We don't want Dad cooking, Mom repairing the car, Betsy playing football, and Rob taking ballet lessons!

As narrow minded as sexual stereotyping is, traditional age depiction may be even more distorted. Gone are the white-haired grandmothers who always wear aprons and cook turkeys on Thanksgiving while Grandpa sits in the living room, smoking a pipe and showering his family with a supreme knowledge of how to live one's life. More likely, widower Grandpa might be shuttled off to a nursing home because his presence is making life difficult in the home, or else Grandma has no time to bake because every Monday she takes her disco dancing lessons.

People no longer want to be cast in predetermined roles, and our characters should display a drive for individuality, too.

In subject matter, trends reflect whatever currently concerns large numbers of people. That which makes headlines and thoughtful articles in the magazines, and leads to discussions in the PTAs, civic groups, and lecture halls is a guide to those concerns—and can suggest what *you* might write about, if you too feel strongly on the given subject(s). Just hope this "concern" won't fizzle out before your book is published. A sense of timing is a valuable asset for the author—and I've sometimes wondered if a dependable crystal ball might not be a good investment.

Editors (for all ages) are always on the lookout for current themes, with authentic, realistic treatment. When they were made acutely aware of the lack of books and stories about black children—in the middle class and among the disadvantaged and deprived—editors eagerly sought to correct the situation. In their initial enthusiasm to fill a void, almost anything went. Now there is no lack for such books, and the editors have become stringently selective both in subject and quality of what they accept for publication. It is no longer a catch-penny get-on-the-bandwagon market, and the examples cited in the note below should make clear the quality that will be expected in current submissions.* (Incidentally, many of the titles mentioned here and elsewhere in the text are available in paperback editions. Check

---

*Read: Mildred Taylor's *Roll of Thunder, Hear My Cry,* 1977 Newbery Award winner, for a cross between *Roots* and the television show "The Waltons." The love and affection of the family is crystal clear. For humor, see Bette Greene's *Philip Hall Likes Me, I Reckon Maybe,* Newbery Honor Book 1975. Read Judy Blume's *Iggie's House* and Mimi Brodsky's *The House at 12 Rose Street;* Laurence Yep's *Child of the Owl* and *Dragonwings,* Newbery Honor Book, 1976. Bedoukian's *Some of Us Survived* is a terse but heart-wrenching account of an Armenian boy's blighted years as part of a victimized minority in Turkey. Read Sebestyen's *Words by Heart* for a compelling portrait of one black family in a midwestern town. Virginia Hamilton's *The House at Dies Drear* is a real thriller, and her *Zeely* is poignant and beautiful. The same author's *Justice and Her Brothers* is a powerful story, displaying rare sensitivity.

a bookstore or library copy of *Paperbound Books in Print.*)

Other ethnic groups are pressing for recognition, and there has been a healthy spate of stories of Spanish-Americans (sometimes in dual-language, so if you speak and write in Spanish, you might check what has been published and see what you can add to it). The Oriental-Americans also want recognition for their contribution to our society, so books of the past and present, if well done, would be welcome.

Experience has shown that it is difficult for the middle-class, white writer to portray authentically, realistically, the life style, thought, and viewpoint of the black person — the black child — especially in the ghetto or otherwise disadvantaged situation. Unless you can *think black,* or for that matter, Latino, Native American, or whatever, do not attempt such writing. The errors, the false notes in your presentation, will be pointed out to you in short order by groups who stand ready to spot and pounce upon misrepresentations, real or imagined "racism" and what not.

Characters in all these stories must be presented as *individuals,* not stereotypes — the black with the great sense of rhythm, the "lazy" Mexican, the stoic Native American, the gesticulating Italian, the bowing Chinese. Neither satires nor ethnic caricatures are wanted in literature for the young.

Stories of adolescence, the physical and emotional changes that come with it, and the anchors young people need to keep from drifting aimlessly, are certainly of interest to the older youngsters and teens. So, if you feel strongly about some topic, wrap it around a set of interesting characters, place them in a human situation, and write about their actions and reactions, out of your own convictions and sense of need. If a bit of controversy does result, it will only boost the sales!

MODERN FANTASY

For any age, fantasy is the hardest material to write, and even harder to sell. So much of it that is simply dreadful has been submitted to hapless editors that many of them have declared flatly in the market guides: *No fantasy.* Yet recent publishers' lists reveal that more fantasy is published today than has been in years. Pressed for an explanation, the editors admit that what they really mean is that they don't want to see rehashed old classics, like latter-day Alices, and tales modeled on the bones of easily recognizable fairy tales told so well by Andersen and the Brothers Grimm.

Fantasy for today must be sparkling fresh and original and clearly recognizable as such. What is more, the excellence of the writing required can be achieved only when the author is thoroughly familiar with his craft and all the techniques that enable him to tell a gripping story.

My heartfelt advice to all my students has been to learn their craft first, through the writing of here-and-now stories, and then zoom off into fantasy or science fiction or whatever their hearts desire. By then they will be able to make the fantastic come off with the necessary special logic and skill which will give the imaginary and bizarre the illusion of reality, the conviction and believability, which is a must for the genre.

Alas, the fantasy-prone seldom heed this advice and put their flat-wheeled apprentice carts before their wingless, plodding horses. If you plan to do likewise, at least study examples of some of the best *modern* fantasies before you dash off your own.*

Picture book fantasy will be dealt with in Part II of this text.

YOU AND THE GENERAL SURVEY

You have been shown the characteristics of the various subdivisions of fiction for children and young adults through-

---

*Read the works of Susan Cooper beginning with *The Dark is Rising;* George Seldon's trilogy *The Cricket on Times Square, Tucker's Country Side,* and the hilarious *Harry Cat's Pet Puppy.* Reread *Charlotte's Web* by E. B. White, as fresh today as when it was written in 1952. Read Beverly Cleary's *The Mouse and the Motorcycle* and *Runaway Ralph* and compare them to the humorous situation in Roger Brury's *The Champion of Merrimack Valley. Freaky Friday* by Mary Rodgers is exaggerated, funny, and revealing to both Annabel and her mother. The sequel *A Billion for Boris* will make you wish for such a television set. Read Alpha Keatly Snyder's *Below the Root* and *Until the Celebration.* All of her books are worth studying. Madeline L'Engle's *Wrinkle in Time* is a classic of good against evil. Read the sequel *A Wind in the Door* and the continuation of the story written sixteen years later in *A Swiftly Tilting Planet.*

For science fiction, read Dale Carlson's *The Plant People* with its very realistic photographs; *Is There Life on a Plastic Planet?* by Mildred Ames, and Daniel Pinkwater's *Lizard Music* and *Fat Man from Space.* Robert Westfall's *The Devil on the Road* contains an intriguing blend of history and the supernatural.

out this chapter. (Nonfiction will be dealt with more comprehensively in Part II.) In a way, the facts should say to you, "This is what you will need to provide if you write for a particular age group." But that is not where your creative thinking should begin.

First, let your main character and his or her problem take shape in your mind. Certain problems are intrinsic to particular age groups. Once you have zeroed in on the age of your hero or heroine, you have the age group for which you wish to write. Editors determine recommended levels by the age of the main character. All experts in young people's literature know that children don't want to read about persons younger than themselves. The reader feels he or she has "lived through all that stuff." The person wants to share a literary experience with a fictional individual his or her age or a year older. Adults wallow in nostalgia; young people look to the future. Thus—the reader is in effect dictating to you the age level for which you wish to write.

Once you've selected the youngster who will carry your story, then check back to the criteria given in the last pages to see what qualities your story or book will have to possess.

Now let's talk about you and your work habits, and how to make the most of your potential.

3
You and Your Work Habits

Having read the previous chapters, you now know something of what's involved in writing for young people. It is a specialty, it demands the best you have to offer, and it can be a rewarding vocation.

You may be one of the fortunate few with all the time in the world to write, but what is more likely is that you have a job, are the family breadwinner, or the keeper of the hearth. There's just no time to write! Remember, however, that we can always make time for the things we really want to do.

HOW TO MAKE TIME
TO WRITE

You have a job? Some writers get up two hours earlier and go straight to their typewriters. Then there's time after supper, on weekends, and holidays.

Everything has its own price, even *time*. To get time to write, you may have to give up something, perhaps social life. While you don't need to become a recluse, you'll have to strike a balance that will favor your writing time.

You're a homemaker with young children and a husband? Then you must organize yourself and your work. Your routine *can* be changed. No one is going to die if you become a less perfect housekeeper—and let a bit of ironing slide till next week. Moreover, somewhere in your day there must be times when the children go to school or nap or amuse themselves in the playpen.

During one semester, after I had expounded on this subject at NYU, a student who had previously bewailed her lack of time suddenly began to turn in a story a week for criticism. Before the end of that fifteen-week session she had begun to write a book, which was accepted for publication upon completion. Betty learned how to *make* time to write. And so can you.

You are also "writing" when you are thinking out a story or turning over ideas that might be developed into one. And "think-writing" you can do anywhere, at any time. Routine jobs — dusting, vacuuming, mowing the lawn — can be productive "think-times" while the hours you spend waiting for buses and riding on commuter trains can provide you with note-making time, and even writing time.

DISCIPLINING YOURSELF
TO WRITE — REGULARLY

Self-discipline is something else again, and not easy, for there are always siren voices calling: attractive social engagements, inviting books to read, and even self-deluding reasons why you can't write now. Writers become past-masters at inventing alibis for procrastination. The reluctance to write is a peculiar phenomenon of the professional author as well as the beginner. What causes it? Perhaps it is the overwhelming knowledge that there are so many ways in which to tell your story — and the disquieting thought that you may start (or continue) on the wrong track. But we revise to correct our mistakes. You are not working in marble, but on paper — and the words can be easily changed. So get busy!

The one thing a writer must be is a self-starter. In the final analysis there is no one who can make you write but *you*. *Writers are self-made.*

Make it a rule to spend at least two consecutive hours in actual writing *every day*. It is difficult to be productive in less time because it actually takes about half an hour to warm up to your subject each time you come back to it. Try to establish regular working hours in your daily schedule, but if this is not possible, don't despair. You can train yourself to write even in the snippets of time available — and under almost any circumstances. I know.

You don't *need* a book-lined, air-conditioned study, either. I have one now, but my first eight books were written in an all-purpose room filled with two children, a big black and white collie, two cats, and a TV set. I wrote right through the most gripping episodes of the Lone Ranger and Captain Video. My "desk" was a rickety typing table and my typewriter an aged portable. My husband was a recording engineer then, and many of his sessions were run at night. So I wrote at night, too, and lullabyed the children with the sound of my tapping keys.

I had to adapt myself to my husband's odd hours until we were both able to work at home; to the children's needs (with one foot on the gas pedal); to what seemed to be overwhelming problems at times. And I know many other writers who managed to work in spite of unfavorable conditions. Successful books and stories have been written laboriously in bed by ailing men and women; and in attics and jails, concentration camps, and at the bottom of the sea in submarines. They have been written at kitchen tables on brown paper sacks. There's no such thing as "no place to write" just as there is no such thing as "no time to write."

WHAT YOU HAVE TO GIVE

What can you bring to this particular field of writing? Can you remember what it was like to be a teenager, an intermediate-grade youngster, a small child? I hope you can, because it will give you greater kinship with your readers, a deeper understanding of the lights and shadows of childhood. Take yourself back a few years at a time. What happened in your life five years ago? . . . ten? . . . and before that? When you get to the teen years, remember more carefully—and don't shut out the emotions, the triumphs, the disappointments, and the tears. Slip down the years to the earliest things you remember.

When you have *felt* yourself a child again, you will have a deeper insight into what it's like to be young and vulnerable, with no mature philosophies with which to cushion the bumps of life. I say "you" because in writing a story, *you* become the character you're writing about, just as an actor becomes the person he or she portrays.

There is the lighter side, too. Everyone likes to laugh. Humor is a great leavener, so cultivate your own sense of fun and inject it into your stories when you can.

Develop enthusiasm and a sense of wonder; to a child the whole world is *new*. Nothing about it is tired, or worn, or hopeless (for very long). And children are seldom nostalgic. They do not look back, nor do they spend much time peering into the future. Anything promised for "tomorrow" seems forever away. Because they live in the present, stories written for them should have the urgent quality of "something happening — *now*."

APPRENTICESHIP

Everyone knows that in order to become a doctor, a nurse, a carpenter, a musician, or a magician, one must serve a period of apprenticeship, of intensive study. But people often expect their very first efforts at writing to be masterpieces worthy of instant publication. This is seldom the case.

Although I now prefer to write books, I broke into the juvenile writing field as a short-story writer — and I'm glad I did. In writing short fiction you can learn all the fundamentals of the writing craft and at the same time sharpen your ability to tell a story in relatively few words. The brisk pace becomes such a habit that when you graduate to book lengths, you will have overcome the tendency to ramble and will instead leap right into your plot and carry it along with lively action.

Grownups, more patient than children, will bear with a slowpaced author who does not really begin the tale until page 50. But a child's story must begin immediately — and never at any point slow down. Once you have learned to tell a story in 2,000 words — or less — you have also learned to free yourself of unnecessary details. Your stories will move ahead in the manner the modern reader has come to expect. In the course of a year you can write a great many short stories — and very possibly start to earn even as you learn how to write for children.

A full-length book, on the other hand, may be from 20,000 to 40,000 words long. It requires much more preparation and time to write and, for a beginner, is just too much to tackle.

In short stories you can also experiment with different age groups and different styles of writing. Where do you fit best? Now is the time to find out — not through 200-page books but through 1,000- to 3,000-word stories. Brief — and expendable.

One of my students suddenly discovered after struggling for weeks with stories for the very young that she could write first-rate teen fiction. You might discover that you are sufficiently versatile to write fiction, or even nonfiction, for several age groups. The change of pace each group requires is refreshing and stimulating for the next effort.

I had fifty shorts and serials published before my first book was accepted. *This first book had ten rejections before it found a buyer on the eleventh submission.* It sold also as a five-part first-rights serial, made a book club, and was re-sold for second serial rights to another magazine.

However, if I had not already had the short-story and three- and four-part serial training — and a baptism in rejection slips — I doubt if I'd have had the courage to continue submitting this book. So the short stories serve another purpose: they help to toughen a writer's skin.

To get the most out of your apprenticeship, cultivate a professional attitude toward your work. One of the marks of the professional is *continual output*. You must learn to be ready to start on a new story the moment the old one is on its way to market. Once you drop it in the mail, it should cease to be your topmost concern, because you should now be involved with the new idea you're ready to work out. Such an attitude not only serves to maintain your output, but it also becomes a shield against the disappointments of rejection slips. Keep a number of stories circulating and you will become known among editors as a *producer*. And that is what editors want: people they can count on for repeat performances, not one-shot geniuses.

To avoid dry spells between stories, keep a stock of ideas on tap. Where to get them and how to keep track of them is discussed in the following chapter.

4
Ideas and You

Workable ideas are the result of careful preparation. For a storehouse of ideas, notebooks and card files are invaluable to the professional as well as to the beginner. So is a sure knowledge of oneself.

GETTING TO KNOW YOU

Before you can know others — real people and characters — well enough to write about them, you must know yourself, because all emotion and experience that you write about is first filtered through *you:* the kind of person you are, the personal values you hold dear. In this lies the secret of your individuality — and your writing style.

Are you an optimist or a pessimist? Does a partly filled jar of honey look half-full or half-empty to you? You'll do better at writing for young people if your outlook is bright. This does not mean that you can deal only in sweetness and light. Juvenile literature — even for the youngest readers — can tackle realistic problems.

It would be ridiculous to think that children are not aware of the seamy side of life and that they are not affected emotionally by this awareness — whether it comes from exposure to TV, movies, radio news, photojournalism, or newspapers; not to mention what they hear and see when grownups forget or ignore the fact that they are nearby. Maybe in a bygone era there was such a thing as an overprotected child. I doubt that such innocence is possible today. So, if you want to write about alcoholism, divorce, integration, prejudice, drug addiction, street gangs, or girls and boys in deep trouble — you may — *if* you can handle such subjects skillfully. Your job as a writer for the young is to resolve this type of plot action in such a way that your story evolves on a hopeful note, though not necessarily in outright happiness.

Your characters should be willing to fight for their goals without whining or pitying themselves over failures. Even in stories written "just for fun," the enduring human values should be very much in evidence.

The point is that your writing must say something to your readers. You will be saying what *you* believe. Be sure you know what that is — and that it reflects sound, healthy philosophies.

And what are those philosophies? This is where a notebook comes in. It should have several sections, so be sure to use index tabs or dividers. In order to be useful to you, all of your reference material must be easy to locate when you need it.

Section One:
How do you want to head this section? "Me in Depth"? This book is just for you. No one else is supposed to see it. But you may want to leave it to posterity after you become famous! The important thing is to put in it exactly what you think, your real opinions, what makes your mental or physical hackles rise.

Whatever you believe, like, or dislike deep down inside yourself will come to the surface, because all writing is in a sense autobiographical. You can't help but inject your way of looking at life into your work. That is why it is so important for you to know about *you.*

Section Two:
"What I Know." Anything you know can be adapted to stories for the young, so it is valuable source material. *Professions* — teaching, engineering, science. *Jobs* — secretary, machinist, sales clerk, delivery man, coal miner, lumberjack, scout leader, oil driller, baby-sitter, telephone operator. *Skills* — jewelry making, skiing, deep sea fishing, carpentry, mountain climbing.

A good place to prospect for ideas is in your own field of interest. What are your hobbies? Do you collect or make things? Does art or music have a special meaning in your life? Are you an expert at anything?

What do you like to read? Romance, travel, history, biography, science, mystery? Your reading interests may indicate the type of things you can write, too.

How about *Backgrounds, Regional and Local*? Do you know Mouse Hollow, U.S.A., or East 88th Street, New York? Paris, Rome, Bombay, Johannesburg? Small town, big town, urban, suburban, rural; north, south, east, west; desert, lake region; farm life, college life, or island living? Make a note of whatever is familiar to you.

Perhaps you know *Periods in History*—ancient Egypt, Greece, our own Old West, the Civil War period, or Colonial times. Of course you know life as it is lived this minute, wherever you are.

In your search for story material, do not overlook your own backyard. Don't discard the too-familiar because it does not seem exciting enough to you. To someone else it may be brand new and remarkable! Do you live on a farm in North Dakota? A condominium in Santa Barbara, California? Use that home for a story setting. And small events in everyday life have potential. Did your son find an injured bird and nurse the creature back to life? Was your daughter the first girl on the middle school's football team? Train yourself to look at the familiar through the eyes of a stranger. You may be surprised at how many ideas are just waiting to be molded into stories.

Suppose a letter were found with mysterious instructions; or a paper, with just the word "Help!" were blown through your living room window from the house next door? Or a skeleton were found in your attic?

The familiar can produce a convincing background and lifelike characters, and you'll be following the tried and true precept of *writing what you know.* But you'll add a special ingredient, your writer's imagination, and the familiar and unusual (the plot stuff you dream up) will fuse into a story.

Section Three:
"What I'd Like to Know About." *Interesting Jobs and Professions*—Did you ever long to be an actress, an adventurer, a detective, a nurse, a doctor, a model, a dress designer, or a lawyer? Might you like to be a ballet dancer, a scuba diver, an astronaut, a submariner, a fireman, a band leader? The list of other people's businesses can be a never-ending, fas-

cinating source of story possibilities. Add to it *Places and Backgrounds* — anywhere in the world — that you'd like to know well enough to be able to write about.

A sure way to get your material noticed is to use some unusual subject in your story, or a background that's really different, or a hero who is a real individualist. In one of my short stories, "Rajah and the Sacred Tooth," I used a Ceylon setting, with a celebration honoring Buddha's Tooth. The facts were researched, while the human situation was my own invention. This story sold at once to *Junior Scholastic,* was later reprinted in a collection of stories, and included in a school reader.

One of the musts for a writer for juniors is a big bump of curiosity, because youngsters are curious about everything. Any subject that intrigues you can be a story possibility — if you're willing to do some research on it. (The how-and-where of research is detailed in Part II of this text.)

OTHER SOURCES FOR IDEAS

Leave your desk now and then and explore the world around you. Take a trip — I don't mean a little jaunt to Spain or up the Amazon. Around the corner, downtown, or to the zoo will do. Or, you can travel armchair style, with a book or magazine; but do so with a mind open to ideas. A word, a name, a background, a picture — any and all of these can be the seeds that sprout into stories.

Names for characters are very important. A card file will make these easily available. Collect girls' names, boys' names, and possible last names. Nicknames are also useful. Collect foreign names and nicknames, properly tabbed as to nationality, so you can find them when you need them.

Don't overlook names for pets. My lists include names in English and in foreign groups. Lists of street names, town, and place names are also helpful.

Newspapers, magazines, books, and the telephone directory are splendid sources for names. Or, you might buy yourself a "Name the Baby" book. I find name dictionaries immensely helpful because they give derivation and meaning of names.

Some writers keep lists of possible *titles.* These, too, can spark story ideas. Books of quotations are dependable title and theme sources. Be sure, however, to keep titles simple and indicative of what the story is about. You'll catch more readers that way.

THE IDEA FILE

Jot your ideas down on 3-by-5- or 5-by-8-inch file cards. Don't depend on remembering them; they can vanish all too easily. When you are ready to start on a new story, your idea may very well come from this file. In any event, *having* the idea there, on tap, gives you a nice sense of security. You know you won't need to cast about frantically for something to write about.

But, to carry out a story idea—many story ideas—the writer must create a set of characters through whom the story happens.

5
Characters Who Make Your Story—
Techniques That Tell the Tale

There is nothing more important in fiction writing than your characters. They are the center of your story. Each story stems from the main character's problem or goal and his or her way of solving the one or reaching the other against great odds—with suspense woven in to keep the reader reading. In capsule form, these are the elements of plot—for the short story, for the book, and for any age reader you may have in mind.

HOW CHARACTERS
CAN HELP YOU

Everything that happens in your story springs from character action and reaction. Therefore characters *are* plot. Or, to put it another way: Plots are not possible without characters.

If your story actors become real people to *you*, with human qualities, emotions, and desires—whatever their age—they'll help you devise the plot. Their ideas, hopes, motives, and antagonisms—charged with your technical know-how—will create the situations, the problems, the complications, the climax, and the solutions you will need. Of course, when I say "real people," I mean characters to whom you have given the *illusion* of reality.

Actual children and grownups, just as they are, have no place in fiction. Their real characteristics and traits would be a hindrance rather than a help because they would not blend with the action and reaction necessary to your story plot. At some critical point your inner voice might whisper, "Aunt Helen, or Joanie, or young Mark simply wouldn't do this!'' and how do you get past a block like that?

Story actors must be built to order, to fit the needs of the tale to be told. For this reason real people are good material only when they are used as composites from which the *needed* fictional characters are created.

Story characters must not be mere types or caricatures such as are sometimes found on our TV screens: silly gum-chomping "juveniles" who seem afflicted with some kind of nerve disease and squeaky vocal chords or precocious children who talk like miniature adults. Hackneyed characterizations are found in adult actors too: "hard-boiled" reporters and slick, trench-coated detectives. Avoid stock characters in your writing. They're sure to bring rejection slips. Enrich your characterizing skill with study of the more truthful examples from fine literature and from personal observation.

And absolutely do not use characters from films, TV, published works, or commercially sold toys. At the very least, you'll be justly accused of a total lack of imagination, and on an economic level, you could be sued for copyright infringement. But things wouldn't go that far because no editor will touch any story or novel featuring another person's characters. Remember—you are the artist. Don't expect someone else to do your thinking. After all, one reason we write is to see *our* creations take life, forged by our personal perceptions.

HOW TO "COLLECT" CHARACTERS

Carrying a small notebook with you always, in your pocket or purse, along with a reliable ballpoint pen will enable you to jot down spot observations and quick character sketches before the first sharp impressions fade away. You'll need all kinds of story actors, because even picture books can include a wide range of ages, relationships, occupations, and nationalities. Learn to observe and analyze swiftly, wherever you are.

"Characters" are all around you. You have been looking at them all your life, but it may be that until now you have not really *seen* them as story material. This is what you should look for in people—that first impression they create, then the individual features that contribute to that impression. The way they talk, gesture, walk, and even smell. All sensory details are important reflections of character. Note facial expressions under varying circumstances, tone of voice, ways people of all ages move under different conditions or disabilities.

Note differences among people in the same occupation social groups and in family relationships. Being aware of human variety will help you to make individuals of your characters instead of stock types. Grandmothers come short, tall, thin, fat. Some are loving, some are doting, some are full of chuckles, and some are not. Store clerks are different from each other. How are they different? Janitors, too, differ from one another, as do doctors, judges, school principals, ladies next door, teachers, librarians, little boys, big and little sisters. Real people are individuals—and so must your story people be.

Your brief notations, legibly transferred into your loose leaf notebook or card file, under suitable headings, will then be at your fingertips whenever you need them for character composites. They serve the writer as sketchbooks serve the artist.

CHARACTERIZATION FOR DIFFERENT AGE LEVELS

Characterization in books for very young children is, of course, the very simplest. The child is named, the age is given, or more likely, indicated in pictures.

Books for the six to nine age group continue with the lively character who undergoes a change that is significant for that age child. A boy may overcome a fear, or a girl's doubts that she is as much loved as her younger brother might be eased as she learns that she is indeed important in the family unit. Whatever the learning or growth, the main character is changed by the events of the story.

In books for eight- to twelve-year-olds, the character is more complex, reacting strongly to his or her world, self, problems, and the people around him or her. He must have a number of character traits, a definite personality. Your reader should feel that if he or she met your character on the street, the reader would recognize him or her. Many a fan letter to the author of a convincing character in this age bracket asks for an address, "so I can visit or write him/ her."

In the teenage book, the characters are as fully developed as in adult writing. The only difference between the adult and the quality young adult book now is the kinds of problems the main characters face, the situations into which they are plunged, and the ages of the main characters.

Until you learn to handle all the elements of the writer's craft, avoid creating a thoroughly unlikable character—an antihero—in the main role, regardless of the age group for which you are writing. The reader wants to identify with the hero and isn't going to do so with a nasty person. Neither should the main character be a goody-goody; the normal boy or girl is equally unwilling to identify with *too* virtuous a character. No one is perfect, and the reader certainly knows *he* or *she* isn't, having been told so often enough by those around him or her.

SELECTING AND INDIVIDUALIZING YOUR STORY PEOPLE

Use only the number of characters absolutely necessary to carry out your story action, but never limit your list to *one.* It takes two to tangle—and tangles make the most interesting reading.

However few or many characters you have, be sure to vary their personalities. Joan must never be exactly like Kate, even if they are twins. Twins may be mirror-images of each other, but their inner selves must be different. Each character must be an individual, unmistakable person in his or her own right.

FLAT AND ROUNDED CHARACTERS

Your *total character* is the combination of all the qualities or *traits* that distinguish him as an individual. Short story limitations allow only for the *flat* delineation of a type. The character exhibits a single trait or perhaps two, which are distinct and make him different from his story fellows. (He or she might be *timid,* but have *a strong sense of responsibility* that causes him to overcome his fears in the end.)

The *rounded* character is for book lengths. This character

should have a number of traits, and these may even be somewhat inconsistent—as in real life: brave—but not always; loyal—but perhaps a bit envious; honest—most of the time. He or she may be rather relaxed when it comes to causes that excite his or her young friends. Yet when goaded into action (perhaps by injustice) he or she leaps into the fray. If the character is your hero or heroine, he or she can be richly endowed with character traits. But if the role is a minor one, the traits must be trimmed down to bare essentials.

Character traits make possible the variety of personalities and the contrasts that lend color and interest to a story. If one character is careful, make another careless. If one is loud, make another soft-spoken. Lively-sad; cruel-kind; thoughtful-thoughtless; ambitious-lazy; brave-timid; neat-sloppy; wildly imaginative or earthbound-practical.

A copy of *Roget's Thesaurus of Words and Phrases* is an indispensable part of your writing equipment. When you are thinking up characters in contrast to each other, a thesaurus will provide you with a quantity of descriptive words which may serve as character trait leads. And when you have selected the traits, you will also have a vocabulary with which to convey them to the reader.

For the lively character you will find at least a dozen words to convey the impression: joyous, gleeful, light-hearted, merry, carefree. If sad, you will find: sorrowful, downcast, unhappy, low-spirited, moody. Use defining words judiciously, however; to stamp the character on the reader's mind, make his actions prove the point.

There is a latent danger in secondary characters. No matter how necessary he or she is to the plot, never make a minor character so interesting that he or she steals the show away from your main character. It can happen, and the hero ends by standing around watching the minor character perform. *It is an absolute rule that heroes and heroines must be doers, not people watchers.* Should this happen in your story, tone the offending character down at once. If this show-stealer is that interesting, make him or her the lead in your next story.

Although for the best character interpretation the writer should "step into a character's skin," the writer in real life seldom thinks or acts the way his character does in any given circumstance. In the course of writing, you are every character you portray, but every character is not you, as you naturally are. This is an important fact to remember. When dealing with characters and situations not your own, you must shed your personal views and take on those of the time and place in your story.

TAGGING YOUR CHARACTERS

Tags are devices by which a character may be identified each time he or she appears on the scene. A tag might be a gesture, a characteristic mannerism such as tossing the head, shuffling, touching a finger to the side of the nose in thought, or flaring the nostrils in anger. A character might habitually pull down on an ear lobe, crack knuckles, swing a key chain, or chew on a strand of hair. He or she might collect string, or pick threads off himself or others, or brush imaginary specks of dust off (probably irate) friends. Smacking the lips before or after speaking might also be an annoying tag. A character might think that to flick his or her tongue out is cute, unaware that she reminds others of a frog, fly-hunting. Or worse, a snake.

A character might give a little hop when walking, indicating a physical disability. Posture can be used as a characteristic tag. When someone usually portrayed as brisk and erect is shown with slumped shoulders and dragging feet, the reader instantly knows something is wrong. The possibilities for using tags are infinite and anything that *individualizes* your story actor is to the good.

You might want to use a speech tag, such as tone of voice or manner of speaking. Or your character might use some expression repeatedly. A character might sing or whistle one particular song, and this habit, later on, could be used to play a significant part in the plot. Tags are not hung on the characters willy-nilly, but for story purposes. Choose them as carefully as you choose traits and names for your story people.

NAMING YOUR CHARACTERS

Your character becomes more of a person as soon as you name him or her. Names enable you to characterize and individualize your story people. They help you and your readers to visualize your characters. And names also help to contrast characters.

If you find any difficulty in naming your story people, it is probably because they are not yet fully realized in your own mind. When you know your story actors and begin to juggle names in your mind, the right combination will click into place for you.

Characters must be named appropriately. Avoid fancy names that may detract from the effectiveness of your story. Don't be afraid of common names like Janie, Susie, Barbara, Dick, and Bill, but do not overdo simplicity and make all your characters Johns and Marys. Variety adds interest to everything. Do not have two or more names beginning with the same letter, as John, Jean, Jill, Jodie, or the reader will soon be very mixed up. Vary the number of syllables in the names as well.

Even the sound of names must be considered, because readers "hear" as well as see them. The difference in the sound helps characters to stand out and not meld into an undistinguishable mass. Harsh consonants in a name, for example, give the impression of ruggedness.

Incidentally, did you know that in the original version of *Gone with the Wind,* the heroine was called *Pansy* instead of *Scarlett O'Hara?* What a difference the name makes in our mental picture of the heroine! A rose may smell as sweet by any other name—but what euphonious appeal would *Romeo and Teresa* have? All the romantic bell-tones would be reduced to a dull thunk. The names of story characters are important.

And the name of the game is indeed characterization. More stories and novels are rejected because there is weak characterization than for any other single reason. The clues that were offered in this chapter will help you create believable characters. But don't forget your mental image must be fully conceived first. Focus on the inner person, what he or she thinks, feels, believes in so firmly that no confrontation will alter his or her stand. Only when the internal person is ultraclear to you will he or she assume life on the printed page.

Characterization is so important to our fiction that the next chapter will continue our discussion, dealing with the two opposing major characters in a dramatic situation.

6
The Hero . . . the Villain . . . and the Vital Viewpoint

Generally your hero or heroine should be a fairly familiar type, with motives, desires, and traits common to most young people. At the same time, there should be a streak of the unusual in his or her makeup — the potential for whatever hero-action that will be called for later. He must be defined clearly, as an interesting individual to whom things happen — and who *makes* things happen.

To create a main character who promises the reader never a dull moment, *you* must have a clear mental image of him or her. Get inside the character's mind so that you know what he or she thinks, feels, and hopes to achieve in *this* story. Choose one major and two or three minor characterizing traits very carefully, because it is these traits that will determine the course of your story.

If your heroine is to win a singing contest in the end, somewhere among her attributes must be a good voice, or a voice capable of being trained. The other attributes you give her should make her way to success possible — the drive of ambition, the initiative to take a job to pay for expensive lessons. At the same time, these very qualities can make her path more difficult — ambition might make her trample over other people (until she learns better); she might work to the point of exhaustion, endangering her voice. Such complications, the opposition a plot requires, might make for a really gripping story.

If a boy hero must, in a tight spot, be able to throw an object and hit the mark, somewhere along the line you'd better give him some athletic skill — and let the reader see him demonstrate it — so he can then convincingly accomplish the necessary feat.

Your main characters, those who *make* things happen, must have a function and an ability to perform it. Determine what it is they must do, then endow them with the necessary skill. And don't overlook a logical supply of the weapon or tool with which they must perform this action—as in the story of the boy who always overloaded himself on hikes. When he insisted on taking along a coil of rope, his friend said it was a dumb thing to do because they didn't need it. But they did, for the friend fell over a cliff and had to be rescued—and there was the rope, logically at the start of the story.

Now then, *who is your main character? What's the age?* Age is an important means of characterization. Be sure to edge it toward the top of the specific bracket for which you're writing, in order to insure maximum reader interest. Establish the age of your character as soon as possible in the beginning. People at different age levels react differently to given situations and emotional impacts, so determining age at the start will aid you in your plotting.

What does your hero or heroine look like? What sort of person is he or she? What kind of hero or heroine do you *need* to solve the problems or reach the goal through individual effort in the story? The hero or heroine must win out in the end—but only through his or her own actions.

The truly appealing character is not wholly good or wholly bad, but possesses a balance of positive (good) and negative (bad) qualities. In the hero, the good outweighs the bad—but the negative traits, just as the positive ones, must be chosen with care since they, too, should affect the course of the story. Because of these negative traits the character acts or reacts in a certain significant way and thus affects the plot. So the "faults" selected by the author are chosen for this purpose. Faults might be impulsiveness, exaggeration, procrastination—weaknesses which will also make the leading character appear human and likable, because the reader can identify with this sort of "imperfect" person and sympathize with his predicaments.

Especially appealing to young people are lively heroes and heroines who leap before they look, who speak before they think. Overhelpfulness can be a major trait as can a character's overactive imagination.

TO SHOW OR TELL

The worst possible way of characterizing any story actor, major or minor, is to *tell* the reader that he is this or that kind of person; that he is high-spirited, inventive, or scatter-brained, kind, or unkind. This sort of *telling* will have the reader yawning and reaching for the TV switch. To hold the reader's attention and keep him or her reading, you must continually show the story in word pictures.

Don't, for example, say anything as vague and colorless as this: "Tommy came into the house and put his books on the hall table," if the kind of boy Tommy really is in your story would be more likely to provide action like this:

> The door opened with a whoosh and Tommy skidded on the hall rug as he flung his books on the table. *Mathematics for the Fifth Grade* thudded on the floor. Tommy leaped over it and rushed through the house toward the back porch. . . .

Tommy is characterized at once as a lively, none-too-careful youngster. His age is suggested rather than stated. Readers will assume that he's ten or eleven, because of the fifth grade book he dropped. They will also wonder why he is in such a hurry. What's on the porch?

Unless a character description comes alive with detail, it is likely to bog down a story. Consider this example: "Ted's history teacher was an autocratic, old woman, who terrorized students past and present." Well, that's all right—to be used in a pinch. But why skimp when it's better and more fun for a writer to *show* a character rather than to *tell* about him or her?

> The chalk in Miss Sprintner's wrinkled hand pecked at the chalkboard, launching yellow flecks. "Now you will realize how close the thirteen states came to returning under England's rule because they couldn't *cooperate*." She made the word unbearably important. "Imagine. Failure after that long and dreadful war."
>
> Ted wondered if teachers ever realized the long and dreadful war that students fought against drowsiness during class time. Miss Sprintner—and God help the student who called her *Ms.* Sprintner—was a legend of two generations of Rocky Cove graduates. Physically, she seemed unable to combat the lusty demands of twenty-five juniors. Thin, snow-white hair capped an ascetic face that truly seemed a hundred years old. Her short stature lifted her pink scalp to Ted's Adam's apple. She used a dark, rubber-tipped cane to support her expeditions through the crowded cor-

ridors. Yet, Anna Sprintner had been known to cut the most bellig-erent guy into splinters with a few, well-aimed sentences. A human shredding machine! The Little Giant, her nickname, had suitably originated from her fierceness and her American history curriculum.

This was a description of a major secondary character as seen through the main character's eyes. Not only do we learn much about Miss Sprintner, but we also are getting a clear picture of how Ted's mind works, what looms important for him, the sort of person he fears. Therefore, in effect, this character description is telling us about two people: our hero, and an important minor character who appears to be a villain at this point in the story but becomes a positive force in Ted's life.

THE VILLAIN
Even as you think over the word, your eyes narrow and you tense a bit. For "villain" is a base and wicked person, a scoundrel—the one who makes life difficult for your hero or heroine. But what would a story be without difficulties? Without opposition to the straight flight toward the goal? I can tell you: it would be dull reading.

Without a powerful villain you will not have a dramatic, suspenseful plot action. If your villain is a paper tiger there can be no question of your hero's easy success—and easy winnings are no fun to read about. The villain must be strong and cunning—and must on several occasions outwit or even clobber the brave, struggling hero. In fact, the hero should have some healthy qualms about going on with the quest, in the face of this opposition. But, after licking any wounds, and thinking things over, he or she *does* because a hero *must*.

How to characterize your villain? Consider the function. *What does he or she want?* What must he or she *do* to maintain villain status? How must he or she be able to compete with your hero's strength, skill, or cleverness?

When you know this, endow the villain with the necessary character traits so that the conflict between your "good" hero and your "bad" villain will be interesting to watch. The two must appear to be almost equally matched—but the faults and flaws in the character of the villain, and the high purpose, courage, and perseverance on the hero's part are what bring defeat to the one and victory to the other.

Modern villains are not wholly evil, although their negative qualities do outweigh the positive ones. I manage to gray my villains up a bit by allowing them to be kind to animals — or very small children — or old people. But not too often! They must not be allowed to run around doing a whole string of good deeds, or they lose their credibility as the bad eggs of the script.

At the same time, in your efforts to prove that your hero or heroine has some well-rounded human flaws, do not allow him or her to buzz around flaunting them because the character, too, will lose his or her standing and support from the reader. One or two unworthy thoughts or deeds should fill the quota.

In contemporary novels, the mother or father of the main character may be cast as the villain. But there are degrees of villainy. Perhaps the parent merely does not understand the youngster or has not been able to adapt to the change in morality and life styles. Other times either parent may have a psychological problem such as alcoholism or may abuse the youngster physically and emotionally. Even the most realistic novel generally has an ending that features the establishment of new bonds between parents and child; or the main character gains insight into the parent's problem and is able to cope with the difficult adult.

Stepmothers have suffered much defamation since the earliest days of Cinderella, so a wicked one today might be considered a stock character. In modern fiction it is often the well-meaning stepmother who needs the love and understanding of her antagonistic new family.

In naming my villains I exercise a personal idiosyncrasy: I try to avoid giving my "bad people" common names, so that no Bill or Jim or Dick or Janie will pick up one of my books or stories and find himself cast in the role of a major villain.

THE WHY OF VILLAINS

Villains are villains because of their poor characters — not because of the way they look, or the job or profession they may have, or because of their race or religion. They are *individuals* and their villainy never casts aspersions on the group from which they spring. If an artist does something dishonorable, it is not because artists are like that, but because *this* artist has the flaw of envy, avarice, pride, or whatever makes him act ignobly.

A well-drawn villain adds much to the excitement of your story. The character must be interesting, but not so fascinating that the reader starts cheering for the villain instead of for the hero! If you make it clear *why* he or she is such a nasty person, you and the reader may even sympathize with him or her. But don't overdo it. It's very well to understand villains and their villainy, but they still have to be foiled and the hero or heroine must win.

Since villains are part of plot and conflict, they will be further discussed in later chapters.

VIEWPOINT

Some writers have difficulty understanding what is meant by *viewpoint* in a story. This term does not mean *which person* (author, hero, onlooker) tells the story, but through *whose eyes and heart the story is told.* Once you understand this important distinction, selecting and maintaining the proper viewpoint should not be difficult.

A story for young people should be told from the viewpoint of the main character—your hero or heroine—the person with the problem to solve or the goal to reach, and therefore, the most involved emotionally. Everything that happens in the story should be presented through his/her eyes, senses, feelings, and thoughts. This is called the *single viewpoint,* and most successful writers use it.

Here is a scene from Kristi D. Holl's novel, *The Rose Beyond the Wall.* We live this scene through the main character, Rachel, thinking her thoughts, experiencing her physical reactions as she tries to deal with her feelings about Jim. Their once childhood friendship has deepened and matured for Rachel, but this does not appear to be true for Jim. That belief is creating emotional havoc for the teenage girl. Note how everything is presented through Rachel's eyes.

> "Hi, Amy." Rachel forced her frozen lips into a small smile. "I'd better get going. Have a good time." She hurried away, the knife in her chest stabbing deeper with each step.
> *When* was she ever going to learn?
> She shook her head angrily until stringy strands of hair stung

her eyes. Jim had shown her all year that he had outgrown their childhood friendship. As often as he had rejected her lately, it shouldn't hurt so much this time.

But it did.

She clenched her jaw until her teeth ached. She was *not* going to cry. She wouldn't!

As in the above example, be sure that you are telling the story of one person, one central character—who may be surrounded by a number of other people, but it is in this important one that the reader takes the greatest interest. It is with him or her that the reader identifies himself, and it is for him or her that the reader sheds tears or shouts cheers right through to the final outcome of the plot. Begin the story with this person and end it with him or her.

A *skipping viewpoint* can be purely awful—jerking the reader this way and that. I've had stories submitted where everybody's viewpoint was given—even the dog's! Never jump from one character's viewpoint to another, nor from one problem to another. The reader has no idea whose story it is or what the problem is. One cannot get emotionally involved or *care* about any one particular character, identify himself with him or her. This is the main reason for avoiding the use of "everybody's" viewpoint: it's the perfect way to make your story nobody's.

One more viewpoint to avoid is that of "they." This is usually exposed to the reader in characters' thoughts.

"It's a surprise," they thought, when Father entered with the large package.

But one of "them" might have thought: "What a big box!" or "Where did that come from?" or "What is that?" Choral speaking was an acceptable device in ancient Greek drama, but it has no place in modern literature for young people.

In juvenile and teenage fiction, the single viewpoint is a must in the short story field. There are no exceptions. The same rule applies to juvenile books up to and including the ages eight to twelve. Shifting viewpoint can be used in teenage novels, but the changes are done by chapters. One chapter may be seen from the viewpoint of Character A and then the second chapter from Character B's viewpoint. Chapter three returns to Character A's viewpoint.

But even in these YA novels, the single viewpoint is maintained totally for the chapter devoted to that character's view of the story.

Single viewpoint technique is so vital to the author who wishes to write for children or teenagers, the other techniques available to creators of adult fiction will not even be discussed. The most important rule to remember when showing your story through the main character's eyes is easily stated. *You can only show the reader what your main character sees, hears, or knows. No action or dialogue that character cannot see or hear may appear in your story. Picture yourself literally trapped inside the main character's body and stay there for the duration of the story.*

Third Person Viewpoint. The excerpt from *The Rose Beyond the Wall* is third person, subjective. Here, although the main character's name is used, and the pronoun he or she, the single viewpoint makes everything seem to happen to the reader. Here is a second example, again of third person, subjective viewpoint, from George Edward Stanley's nine-to-twelve novel, *The Codebreaker Kids.*

> Dinky gulped. He felt worse. He went upstairs and took a hot shower. Then he put on his pajamas and got into bed. He picked up his English book, then put it down. Why in the world should I study for an English test, he thought, if I'm going to be shot?
>
> Dinky could see it all now. There would be police knocking at the door. He'd be taken away in a paddy wagon with all the neighbors watching. There would be newspaper headlines and the trial and prison and then, in the cold dawn, they'd march him outside, blindfold him, and . . .
>
> BANG! BANG! BANG!
>
> Dinky sat up with a start. Was he already dead? No, his heart was pounding. He couldn't be dead.
>
> BANG! BANG! BANG!
>
> "Dinky? Are you in there?" It was his dad, knocking at the door.

And still another excerpt—from *The Tomorrow Star* by Dorothy B. Francis.

> Lori Coulter pried Pelican Plaque No. 35 from the white picket fence that separated the Coulter yard from the sidewalk and the narrow street. She glanced over her shoulder. Good! Nobody was in sight. Hiding the plaque under her shirt, she turned toward the laurel tree that shaded one side of the house.

Now—why have you been buried in three quotes? Obviously, to cite usage of the single viewpoint as well as the third person, subjective viewpoint. But there was another reason. Although it is considered bad teaching technique to send students back to previously quoted passages, that is exactly what I want you to do. Read all three and study them for the method employed to convey the *thoughts* of the main character.

The method utilized in all three quoted passages is to state the main character's thoughts in the third person and in the past tense. This is much more effective than presenting the reader with the actual words. That is something you only do in special circumstances when you want to emphasize the importance of that thought.

Return for a third time to the Dorothy B. Francis' section of *The Tomorrow Star*. Lori has pried the plaque free and checked over her shoulder. Then she thinks. But we do *not* hear:

> . . . she glanced over her shoulder. "Good," thought Lori. "Nobody saw me. Now I can hide this thing and get it out of here."

The reason the actual words were not stated was that one way to separate the exact words of a thought is by the use of quotation marks. But this can be confusing to a young reader and even to adults. George Edward Stanley used a second method of indicating specific words that occur during a thought. Mr. Stanley simply writes the words without any quotation marks. This is better than those confusing punctuation indicators. Some publishers will italicize the mental wordage of a major character. For instance, see how Stephanie S. Tolan directly states Ty's thoughts in her novel, *A Good Courage*. Within a few sentences, however, Ms. Tolan moves right back into other thoughts written in the third person and past tense.

> "Yahweh, hear us," Brother Daniel said, and his deep voice seemed to reach up through the newly leafed trees on the other side of the creek to the clear blue of the morning sky. "These, thy servants, wish to be admitted to thy holy Kingdom."
>
> *Not exactly true,* Ty thought. Then: *What the heck. One of us does.* He glanced at his mother again. She was smiling that smile she got when she was more than happy, when she was turned on, hooked into something, connected. Ty couldn't help smiling, too.

Times like this he could be sure his mother was okay. Times like this he didn't have to worry at all.

Thoughts of the main character comprise one of the Big Three of Fiction: dialogue, action, thoughts of the view-point character. All the examples provided in this chapter interweave all three. If we rely on only one too long, we risk danger. Dialogue is certainly the best way to reveal character, advance plot action, and add zest to a story. But if characters talk, talk, and *talk* without doing or thinking anything, the reader becomes bored. When Arnold Madison wrote his first novel, *Danger Beats the Drum,* there was an interminable scene where two characters simply talked for a full page. No action. Even worse, no thoughts of the boy who was the leading player. Phyllis A. Whitney criticized this author's manuscript. After fighting her way through a page of Bob's conversation with his friend, Whitney wrote a note in the margin: "Let him shut up and *think*!" Direct, yes, but true. Many new authors have fears that lie in an opposite direction. They hesitate to use dialogue lest they break their single viewpoint. No danger. Remember our definition of single viewpoint: you show only what the main character sees, hears, or knows. Sees = action. Hears = dialogue of other characters. Knows = main character's thoughts.

The First Person Viewpoint. This viewpoint, with "I" as the story teller, is one of the most effective ways to handle viewpoint. The form is so popular that books from the picture book level to the realistic teenage novel feature the first person technique. In addition, many authors find this viewpoint the easiest to write, while the readers feel truly involved with the main character who seems to be speaking directly to them.

Within the last few years, there has been increasing usage of first person-present tense, but only in the teenage novel. Here is an example from the book, *The Kidnapping of Christina Lattimore* by Joan Lowery Nixon.

I don't like the way he's looking at me. It's a kind of creepy look as though the two of us shared some kind of secret, and it's making me uncomfortable.

He's the counterman here at this hamburger place—a tall, stoop-shouldered, skinny guy with dull blond hair that always looks dirty. His beery friends in their sweat-stained shirts, who hunch over the counter talking and laughing in short burps, call him Zack. I don't like the way Zack is staring at me.

For all the power in the first person or first person-present tense viewpoint, there are dangers for the unwary writer. Before attempting first person, get solid control of the third person viewpoint.

One pitfall is that often the first person story is *told* to the reader without the scenes being fully dramatized with description, action, and dialogue. Even worse are the first person stories where the narrator is only an observer, never really involved in the center of the action. If the main character is standing on the sidelines, only reporting what he or she sees, then the reader feels removed and never becomes caught up in the story. Readers want to worry along with a main character who is actively working to solve a problem or attain a goal.

So—approach first person carefully and with respect. In the right hands, the technique is a valuable tool. But those hands are usually the experienced author who has firm control over the third person viewpoint before venturing into the land of the first person.

DESCRIBING THE VIEWPOINT CHARACTER

If you've been studying the examples carefully and heeding the advice in the last few pages, a major question is now uppermost in your mind.

"Wait!" you gasp. "If I can only show what the main character sees, hears, or knows, how in the world am I ever going to describe that character to the reader?"

First, you're right. If Jed is your main character, you cannot say in your story: "Jed pounded the desk, his dark eyes flashing." After all, he can't see his own eyes.

Using only Jed's mahogany-colored eyes as an example, let's see the ways we can slip in the viewpoint character's description.

a. His thoughts: Jed gazed at his father's face, realizing that Dad's eyes were the exact deep shade of brown as his own.
b. Another character's dialogue: Heather sat in the passenger seat, gazing at Jed. "Lord, how I wish my eyes were brown like yours. Think of the colors I could wear."

c. Photographs or reflected images: Your main character can study him/herself in a snapshot from a family get-together, the videotape a friend made of a cross-country ski trip, a reflection in a window or mirror.

> Jed knuckled the sleep from his eyes to see the blurred mirror image more clearly. Not a bad looking guy if he said so himself. Seventeen. A thin face with dark brown eyes and blond hair. Well, okay, so it was only an everyday kind of face. But wasn't that a face that Leslie Henderson might be able to bear gazing at over pizza and Pepsi?

There is a common belief that editors have grown weary of characters seeing their reflections in shiny surfaces. This is only half true. Editors have grown tired of main characters who see their reflection and think about it for no particular reason. The person must want something back from that mirror image. A polished surface reflects reality, but the person sees what he or she wants to or what is hoped another person might see. The motivation for Jed to peer into the mirror was to view his face as Leslie might. Another main character could take a moment to study her reflection in a store window to see how effective her new diet has been. Or still another might glance into his car's rearview mirror entering Hamburger Heaven to apply for a job. Whatever the motivation, a definite incentive to study the reflected image has to cause the action and then the main character's emotional reaction to what he or she sees *is* needed to make this device acceptable to editors.

d. The camera view. At the very beginning of your story, you can stand off and describe the scene or situation through another's eyes rather than that of the main character. True, this is not in the single viewpoint, and that is why you can only do it in the opening sentences. Once your character thinks or feels or speaks, you immediately move into his or her viewpoint—the single viewpoint—and stay there. The following example of the camera view is from Phyllis A. Whitney's novel, *Mystery of the Black Diamonds.*

> There was a sign at the foot of the canyon and Angie Wetheral

stopped to read it. The morning sun of Colorado was already hot upon her bare head. It touched the shiny red of short curls and brightened a sprinkling of freckles across her nose.

The author goes on to describe brother Mark, younger but taller than Angie and dark, like their father (which takes care of him, too). Angie speaks and from then on she carries the viewpoint ball.

In your own writing, remember that you cannot characterize (describe) your story actors once and for all the duration of the book or story, expecting the reader to remember what you said. He won't—and neither will he go back through the pages to find out just who Betty is and what she looks like. You have to re-portray and re-identify your actors as the story progresses, not repeating what you said the first time, but making some reference to an outstanding characteristic. The major traits of your main character must be stressed again and again—his bravery or loyalty or cleverness—so that when the trait is needed to accomplish his purpose or goal, the reader will have been prepared for it. The character will not seem to "come brave all over" all at once, or become suddenly talented in some field.

CHARACTER GROWTH

From the short story or picture book aimed at the younger reader to the novel for teenagers, the main character must experience a degree of character growth. Without this change, your story has no point and will probably be rejected as "slight" by an editor. The character should grow, change, learn something about him-herself, other people, or life through the events of the story.

Life is never static. Its impacts change people—at all social and age levels. All experiences, new friendships, successes, or losses should have an effect on the story characters involved, too. The changes should not be sudden. The reader should see them happening gradually in the course of the story. Gradual character development contributes to the reality of your story illusion.

Part of the fun of writing is creating characters. In creating story people you can be anybody or anything, of any age, time, social condition, or vocation, sampling any life you choose. And when you're plotting a story (while you're working on characters, you *are* plotting), and the characters suddenly spring into life and become "real," you may be sure you'll have no difficulty in getting them down on paper. You'll just have to write faster!

7
Dialogue

Have you ever watched a youngster pick a book from the library shelves? One of the first things he or she looks for is quotation marks, the sign of dialogue. The little symbols mean people, at least two of them, talking about something—maybe planning an adventure or unraveling a mystery. Having discovered the "conversation," the prospective book borrower will read over a few passages. If the conversation is lively, "like real kids talking," and filled with promise of exciting things to come, the child will take the book out.

Dialogue is a means of catching your reader—but to be effective it must sound natural. To sound natural, it must bear out whatever traits you have given your story actors. It is one of the most useful mediums for characterization. Yet in many beginners' stories all the characters sound exactly alike. This weakness can only stem from poor acquaintance with one's story people, along with insufficient skill in effective writing technique.

LISTEN!
As you study people—grownups and children—listen to them speak. Cultivate an ear for dialogue from your reading and from the live models around you.

What your story people say can be every bit as interesting as what they do. *What* they say and *how* they say it not only reveal the kind of people they are, but speech presented convincingly also lends reality to your tale. So, listen, read, study, and learn to adapt spoken words to your own fictional needs.

You've heard people talking all your life, but have you

ever paused to analyze their speech? Have you considered the *tone of voice* used, the *choice of words,* or the *tempo* at which they were spoken? All these affect the characterization of your story people.

Before long your observations will make clear to you that everyone speaks somewhat differently. What is said and how it is said is affected by the speaker's age, emotional state at that moment, family and cultural background, job, profession or occupation—and by whether the speaker is male or female. Even tiny boys have a definitely masculine way of expressing themselves, just as little girls express themselves in a clearly feminine manner.

When you first meet a stranger, you quickly observe his or her physical appearance, and you immediately draw certain conclusions about his or her personality. The moment this person *speaks,* you begin to find out how right or wrong you were. The first thing that jars or charms you is the tone of voice. Is it pleasant, well modulated? Or is it nasal, twangy, similar in sound to a foghorn?

The voice quality you choose for a character must be in keeping with the kind of person that character is. A sweet, motherly woman would not be given a stentorian bellow. Your boy lead would not wheeze and whine; your heroine would not screech every time she opens her mouth.

As for the story actor's vocabulary—my Tommy-in-a-hurry, introduced some pages back—probably would not use impeccable English. A tough character would not speak as a sensitive, carefully reared lad. The boy interested only in sports would lace his speech with terms related to his activities. The budding scientist might also be interested in sports, but not to the degree of the athlete—and his talk should show it. A Puerto Rican girl, new to the United States, would not talk like an American professor's daughter. To write about her, you'd have to *know* how Puerto Ricans talk.

A TOUCH OF FLAVOR— FOREIGN AND DOMESTIC

If you think you'd like to use foreign-born persons in your stories, you might prepare yourself ahead of time by collecting foreign words and phrases which can be immediately understood or explained. I like to use Italian, French, Spanish, German, and Russian characters, with a sprinkling of Orientals, usually as secondary or minor actors. For this reason I have "Talk Cards" in my file with typical sample words and phrases. Even something so small as a *Si,* a *Da,* a *Non, non!* or an *Ach,* can lend flavor to a scene. Foreign dictionaries and phrase books, plus an attentive eye and ear, tell me all I need to know for my story people.

One way of characterizing a foreigner who has learned English is to have the character express himself or herself in stilted phrases, without contractions, idioms, or slang: "Excuse please that I am taking the liberty to write you. I am a Nigerian boy seeking a pen pal friend in the United States. . . . My hobbies are foot-balling and swimming. . . ."

Don't attempt to reproduce foreign dialogue or regional dialect exactly—it will make awkward reading—and never attempt it at all, unless you are truly familiar with it. It is not necessary to drop "g's" or pepper your story with hard-to-read contractions. Instead, depend on the idioms and speech patterns typical of certain regions, races, or countries. This will mean research and study, but it will be well worth it, for the added flavor to your narrative will contribute to its "realness" and authenticity.

Beware of slang, especially in short stories. Magazine editors frown upon it, though in book form a small amount is allowed. The real danger of using slang is that it changes quickly; even while it is current the same expressions do not always mean the same thing in all parts of the country. But most important, your stories are sure to outlive the slang—which will then either "date" your work, destroying its sense of here-and-now immediacy, or make it incomprehensible to the new crop of readers. So confine yourself to such expressions as have become a part of our language, or coin some phrases tailored to your particular character— and use in moderation. Your story actors can speak *in character,* even without the tinsel riches of a slang wardrobe.

WHEN YOUR CHARACTERS SPEAK

Good dialogue, when it captures the reader's attention, becomes so real that the author seems to vanish and the characters to move under their own power. The reader *hears* them and believes in their reality. Dialogue is the breath of life for your story people.

It is good practice to read your dialogue aloud when your scene or story is complete. This is the acid test: *Do the words sound natural on the tongue?* If slow or stilted, the fault will then show up. If you are too close to your creation, perhaps you can ask someone else to read the material to you. It may be easier for you then to be more critical. Often, when I read manuscripts in class, a student's ungrateful brainchild seems to develop a serpent's tooth. I see the author writhe — and draw a step closer to a professional attitude toward his or her work. When you can recognize the flaws, you can learn to correct them.

REAL TALK AND DIALOGUE

Written dialogue only simulates the talk of actual people. Real talk can be vague, or terse. It can wander in and out among clauses, drop into "well's," or grunt and grind along on "er's." It can also last for hours.

Written dialogue not only must be meaningful to the story, but it must be telescoped — condensed — to keep the reader's interest at high pitch. Neither in life nor in a book does anyone (and the young reader especially) want to be talked numb. While story conversations must serve a definite purpose, they do not need to be completed to the last goodbye, as they are in life. You can stop them at any point and finish whatever needs to be finished by some writer's device at your command — perhaps in the main character's thought, or by a bit of physical action, or narration, or a few words of transition that lead the reader smoothly into the next scene.

No character should be allowed to talk too long without a break. Thick paragraphs of monologue are just as unattractive to the reader as blocks of description. If a character must tell about something at length, be sure to have someone break in from time to time with a question, a comment, an exclamation. Or fit in some sort of action — at least a pause, in which the speaker looks around his or her audience, sighs, draws a deep breath, groans, laughs, or does whatever is appropriate. Anything that will alleviate the solid, dull look of the page is to the good—provided it fits smoothly into the story flow.

A word of caution about the use of dialogue: No matter how charming and witty the conversations you've devised may be, unless dialogue advances the plot it has no place in the story.

HOW DIALOGUE CAN MOVE
YOUR STORY FORWARD

Fictional dialogue can serve many purposes and your skillful use of it reflects your ability as a writer. Besides *characterizing the speakers,* it can *inform* the reader of facts that the speakers already know and that the author wishes revealed to the reader. Dialogue can also *further the action of the plot* by having some change like a decision or a quarrel take place during the conversation. In addition, it can *reveal the emotional state* of the speakers or point up conflict and thus build *suspense* as to what will happen next. Dialogue can also *characterize other people* in the story more convincingly than can expository statements.

Read the following examples and note how the above items and more can be accomplished through dialogue. In the opening of *On My Honor,* a Newbery Honor book, author Marion Dane Bauer wished to introduce her main characters, set the scene, and establish their relationship.

> "Climb the Starved Rock Bluffs? You've gotta be kidding!" Joel's spine tingled at the mere thought of trying to scale the sheer river bluffs in the state park. He looked Tony square in the eye. "Somebody got killed last year trying to do that! Don't you remember?"
>
> Tony shrugged, popped a wheelie on his battered BMX, spun in place. "Nobody knows if that guy was really trying to climb the bluffs. He might have fallen off the top . . . or even jumped."
>
> Joel bent over his Schwinn ten-speed and brushed imaginary dust off the fender. "Well, I'm not going to ride out there with you if that's what you're going to do. It's dumb." He tried to sound tough, sure of himself. Maybe, for once, he would be able to talk Tony out of one of his crazy ideas.
>
> "You don't have to climb if you're scared, Bates," Tony said.
>
> "Who's scared?" Joel licked his lips, which seemed to have gone dry. "I'd just rather go swimming, that's all. It's going to be a scorcher today. Or we could work on our tree house. My dad got us some more wood."

"We can do the tree house later," Tony said, "after we get back. And I don't feel like swimming."

"You never feel like swimming," Joel muttered, seeing in his mind the shining blue water of the municipal pool. The truth was, Tony rarely felt like doing anything that Joel wanted to do. Joel wondered, sometimes, why they stayed friends. There had to be something more than their having been born across the street from each other twelve years ago, their birthdays less than a week apart.

Or you can use dialogue to create suspense and foreshadow plot developments, such as in *Terror on Sunset Point* by Arnold Madison. Early in the story, the heroine Janice is preparing to leave for a campout with her high school hiking club. She enters the kitchen, discovering her mother already awake.

"Hey, Mom, it's only six-thirty!"

Mom managed a weak smile. "I couldn't sleep. Lianna left about fifteen minutes ago. Everything ready?"

"Almost. Just a few last things for the day-pack, and I'll be set." Jan pulled a bowl and a box of natural cereal from a cupboard. When Mom had left for work yesterday, she was all together and had really looked neat. But this morning she looked ragged. "Are you feeling okay, Mom?"

"Oh, sure." Mom tried to brighten her smile, failed and two-fingered another cigarette from the green and white pack. The match shook slightly as she held it to the cigarette. "Mr. and Mrs. Veeder meeting you at eight?"

"Yes. I'm walking over to their . . ."

"Janice. . . ." Her mother paused, pushing the dead cigarettes around the ashtray with the burning one. "Janice, why don't you stay home this weekend?"

"What?"

"Maybe go on the next campout."

"I can't."

"They would understand. Lots of other members are staying home to see the senior class play tonight."

"But *I* don't understand." Jan studied Mom, noticing that worry lay deep in her brown eyes. "I already asked for time off from my part time job."

"I had this dream last night. I saw powerful hands coming toward you."

"Powerful hands? Mom, that was Lianna you saw. She has to fight off all those guys and their hands. The only thing that comes my way are heavy discussions about environment and inflation. I'd kind of like to see some powerful hands."

Mom frowned. "Remember the time you fell in phys ed and broke your arm? I was all set to go on duty at the restaurant and didn't know about it. But I *felt* something was wrong and rushed home. No sooner did I step into this house than your school called to tell me."

Jan had heard that story before plus others. She opened the refrigerator, grabbed a milk carton and stood there, pretending to search for something else.

"Look, Mom. I really will be careful. I'll avoid all guys with powerful hands." Jan faced her mother. "I'm not being sarcastic. I *will* be careful."

Skillful use of dialogue, such as in Opal Dean Young's short story "A Real Live Valentine" (from *Wee Wisdom*), can move a story forward as well as accomplish other functions. Read this section and see how much information Ms. Young gives the reader.

"Oh, no! Not Robert!" groaned the class when Robert's name was drawn to pass out the valentines at the Valentine's Day party tomorrow.

"Robert's too shy. He wouldn't call out our names," complained Lisa.

"He never says anything," said Todd.

Mrs. Graves, the teacher, looked at Robert and smiled. "Oh, I wouldn't say that. Robert had plenty to say at the Halloween party."

"That's because he was wearing a cat mask," Scott said with a grin, "and could meow a lot."

Everyone laughed.

Through this conflict scene (Robert vs. the class), we learn much about Robert's relationship with his class and especially about Robert. This is an excellent example of how we can characterize through what other characters say about a person. Young is also building in a sense of anticipation. What is going to happen now? You have a painfully shy boy placed in a situation where he must be outgoing. He is torn between his teacher and his class. His classmates have no faith in him while Mrs. Graves apparently does. All that information, in only six short paragraphs!

SOME DON'T'S AND DO'S

Don't have conversations taking place in empty space. Weave in background details of where the action (dialogue is a form of "action") is taking place. Don't have invisible people talking, either. Let the reader *see* them as they speak—their facial expressions and gestures. And by all means "cue" the speeches to the speakers.

TAG LINES TO CONVERSATIONS

Never have a page of dialogue—even between only two characters—where the person speaking is not identified from time to time. The reader never wants to grope back and start all over again to find out whether it was Andy or Jack who spoke in the sixth paragraph.

To preface or conclude every speech with the word "said" is dull, but vary with care. An overzealous beginner with a thesaurus syndrome might achieve a hair-raising effect like this: asked, inquired, rejoined, asserted, retorted, remarked, insinuated, mumbled, muttered, grumbled, bawled, shrieked, whispered, thundered, cried, howled, yelled, hissed—and maybe ululated, for good measure. While this assortment in a single tale might have a horrid fascination for the reader, it will never get by a sober editor.

Notice how in the preceding three examples the dialogue was tagged with "said" and a few synonyms and how sometimes it was leavened by a bit of action, placed before or after a speech, to change the pattern of the page and to relieve the reader's eye and mental ear.

Here are some tags to avoid because they create an incongruous effect which may distract the reader from the flow of your story. Time and again I've stopped in reading student manuscripts in which a character performs like this: " 'I don't know,' he *shrugged*"—or, " 'Never!' she *seethed*"—or " 'Don't do it,' she *hissed*." You can't possibly *hiss* that last word without sibilants—"s" sounds. And, if you wish to have a smile or a shrug accompany a line of dialogue, put a decent little period at the end of the speech, and then say: "He smiled." Or—without the period—"he said, smiling."

Beware of characters who are so happy or so good-natured that they "beam" their remarks. Quite an impossible feat, you know. Instead of writing, " 'Oh, thank you,' Sally beamed," say " 'Oh, thank you.' (Period) Sally beamed."

If your character "laughs" a remark, first be sure it is something to laugh about. Quite often, in beginners' stories, it is not. And even if it is, take care to use the word smoothly. " 'How funny,' Joan said, and laughed" reads better than "laughed Joan." Pay attention to small details, and the results will be better writing and less risk of jolting the reader out of the illusion of your story—possibly for keeps.

To involve readers in their story, some writers prefer to set the stage, bring on the story actors, give them something to do to catch the reader's attention, *and then have their people speak*. However, a catchy opening can be created with dialogue too, if the very first speech indicates that there is an interesting problem or situation confronting the characters. In a short story a dialogue opening can save a lot of words and plunge the reader right into the heart of the matter.

However you do it, master dialogue you must, for dialogue is one of the most useful techniques of fiction because it can perform so many story-telling tasks. Study, read, observe. Work on your characters until they come alive—then let *them* do the talking!

8
The Story Problem . . . Motivation . . . and Significance

If a character has no problem to solve, there is no point in writing about him or her. It is the urgent problem confronting your main character and how he or she goes about solving it—against stalwart opposition, of course—that gives the character appeal and involves the reader in your tale.

What does your main character want? *What vitally important thing must he or she have that cannot easily be obtained?* This you must decide early in your story planning, because the *want* or *need* will not only indicate the kind of main character he or she will be, but also what other people will do to support or oppose him or her.

In writing for juniors, the conflict must interest the children of the age for which you are writing. The teenage girl will be much more interested in problems involving the social success of the storybook heroine, in her romances or career ambitions, than she will be in getting the heroine's maiden aunt married. The ten-year-old will be more intrigued by a book dealing with a "Horse for Keeps," than in getting great-uncle Henry a fancy chess set. The easy-to-read-age lad will be more interested in a story of how the neighborhood's kids got themselves a clubhouse than in how somebody's big sister got herself a prom date with the football captain. Tailor your problems to your potential audience: make them the kind that children of that age can conceivably solve.

THREE TYPES OF PROBLEMS
YOU MIGHT USE
1. *Purpose problem.* The character has a goal and knows what he or she wants. It might be a career, a place on the

team, the lead in a play, or a chance to take ballet lessons. It might be a dog or a horse, perhaps a bicycle or a car (for a special worthy purpose). Whatever it is, it must be something he or she will be willing to fight for with tremendous drive and force.

2. *Situation problem.* The main character wants to change the existing situation, or a situation brought about at the beginning of the story. This is done with a great deal of discouraging struggle and effort.

The situation might be caused by moving into a new neighborhood, going away to school, losing one's parents, having a parent remarry, or suffering a serious accident which destroys the young person's original goal in life.

3. *Decision problems.* Here the main character must decide which way to go, right or left, up or down. Often a moral decision is involved in this kind of conflict — personal integrity or the effect such a decision will have on others. It should be similar to a tug-of-war, and for greatest reader interest and suspense, the pulls should be equal, so that the final decision will be very hard to make — and is made, in the end, only because of the strengths with which you have endowed your hero or heroine.

Beware of letting your characters have cheap or trivial goals. The boy who merely wants to humiliate someone is not worthy of being a hero. The new girl who longs to be liked by her classmates can be made a sympathetic heroine — and all the more if she is awkward in her attempts; but the vain girl who sets out to steal boy friends from other girls is cheap and petty and does not deserve to be made the heroine of a story. (But she might make good opposition, and the reader can dislike her heartily.)

Why must the main character get whatever it is he or she is after? What would happen if he or she failed? The consequences of failure should be serious, as the reader (and the character) should be well aware. Thus the problem should be a vital one to your hero or heroine. (*Vital* comes from the Latin word *vitalis,* meaning "life." Therefore the problem in your story should be — relatively — one of "life and death" importance.) Upon its solution should depend the main character's happiness; and then you should involve your reader so thoroughly that he or she will cheer for, fear for, and support the hero to the last period in your manuscript.

MOTIVATION — THE WHY
BEHIND THE WHAT

If a boy wants a dog because everybody else on the block has one, or if a girl wants a fancy poodle only because she thinks they're "cute," the action of the story will be weakly motivated. The reader will not care if these characters get what they want, and certainly it will make no real difference in the lives of either one.

On the other hand, if a boy wants a dog because he is a lonely orphan being reared as a "duty" by a cold, strict aunt or uncle, his motivation becomes more meaningful. The dog would fill the boy's need for a playmate and a friend. The motives for this boy's efforts would be strong, and the reader would be entirely in sympathy with him.

One of the basic truths of which the experienced writer and editor are aware is that *strong motives make for strong, convincing stories and weak motives make for weak and unconvincing tales.* Your main character's problem, want, or need must not only be something worth fighting for, but it must also be the sort of thing *this* particular character might *logically* need and want and fight for. The conviction that lies behind the logic is backed up by motivation—*the reason that prompts your character to take action to get what he wants.*

Motives are urges, conscious or subconscious, that lie behind everything we do. These urges stem from our personalities which, psychologically speaking, are the sum of all our physical, mental, emotional, and social characteristics. Some of these urges are instinctive, some emotional, and some are fostered by cold logic and design. All of them can furnish motives for the problems and upheavals created in fictional lives.

THREE POWERFUL URGES —
FOR ALL AGES

The *life urge,* the drive for self-preservation or survival, heads the list. The struggle to maintain life might be a problem, and certainly a powerful motivation, in a hair-raising adventure tale or a mystery.

Love in all its forms, among children as well as adults, is strong motivation for many actions. This *includes* loyalty as well as pity. Youthful romance can present many problems and poignant heartaches and can be a painful experience.

The *power urge* can be used both positively and negatively in stories. Your hero might long for a certain high office because of a genuine desire to serve. The antagonist or villain fights for the same office, but this motivation is a desire to dominate, to use the office to further selfish ends.

There are many other urgent motivating factors, but these are enough to give you an idea of how they can be used. In the course of the story, the writer must let the reader know the motives or forces driving the characters. Then the reader will be able to recognize the *significance* of the various actions in the working out of the story problem.

To understand what makes certain people want certain things, you need to know something about human psychology—but not so much that you wind up writing psychological treatises and fictional case histories instead of stories.

Your own life experience and common sense can be a reliable guide for your writing, but it is also reassuring to have the backing of experts for your own beliefs and conclusions. Be alert, always, to new books and articles by children's specialists, and to radio and TV discussions. Browse through the child guidance shelves of your community library and your local bookstore. And remember, no matter what you know, you can demonstrate it to your readers only by means of a story. So, become aware, but not bogged down with knowledge.

SIGNIFICANCE—HAVING SOMETHING TO SAY

In order to have something to say, it is no more necessary to have traveled the whole world—physically—or to have undergone unusual experiences and the gamut of emotions—personally—than it is necessary to commit murder in order to write a murder mystery. You need only to live in a world of people, with all our senses tuned, and to observe everyone and everything about you with sensitivity and compassion. The cool and detached attitude is not for the writer—and woe to you if it creeps into your writing. Instead of significance, your writing will then reflect indifference, even callousness, which will chill your reader.

Having "something to say" does not mean you must have some earthshaking revelation. It means, simply, that you have a very strong interest in your subject and are sufficiently informed about it—and skilled in your craft—to write about it meaningfully for the reader.

THEME AND VARIATIONS

Story significance, besides reflecting basic human needs, also involves a lesson in living, in human attitudes; it might point up a "moral"—the kind found in Aesop, and in books or proverbs or epigrams—*but never, stated in words.* Your theme must come through the action and reaction of your story characters.

These themes—proverbs, maxims, epigrams, wise-saws—are a crystallization of widespread human experience. That is precisely what makes them interesting and understandable to the reader. The common experience they summarize makes it possible for him to identify with the story characters. So, here is another addition to that helpful file of yours, a section labeled "Themes." From now on, distill the stories you read to their basic themes and jot them down. When you're casting about for story material, one of these may prove a springboard to a sparkling, fresh idea.

In one of my short stories with a Korean background, "Donkey Cough" (the Korean term for whooping cough), I used the theme that *understanding and helpfulness overcome suspicion and distrust and lead to friendship.* If you break down this thought, you'll see that it contains the capsule synopsis of a story. *Understanding and helpfulness* suggests the characters; *suspicion and distrust* suggests the problem; *overcome,* the conflict and the outcome; and *lead to friendship,* the resolution and happy ending.

Although I wrote of an American missionary family and an influential Korean family, and practical medicine as opposed to superstition to illustrate my theme, that same theme can be used again and again with variations. All that is necessary is a change of location, people, and the specific problem. The end result would be the same, and yet it would be an entirely different story.

This is where the value of a theme you can state to yourself lies: when you break it down so that it suggests characters, problems, action, and a solution, all you need to do is create the characters to carry it out, or *prove* the statement. To be useful to you in this way, the basic theme should be stated in such a way that it suggests action-conflict. *Honesty is the best policy* may be true, but it does not suggest a definite course of story action. Stated as *Honesty can triumph over dishonesty,* you immediately have an honest and dishonest character to work with. *Triumph* suggests conflict as well as the outcome for the honest character.

You don't need to strain for a meaningful theme before you write your story; if you have strong ethical convictions, they will come through in your writing. If you believe that a small boy should not be tormented by a bully, you will create a story in which the little fellow will somehow get the best of the big meany. (Theme: Through wit and courage, the small and weak *can* overcome the big and bad.) David and Goliath, along with any number of old fairy tales, illustrates this popular theme. Basic story themes are not original—only the variations on the theme are.

Theme is your melody, the motive, the dominant *idea* you develop through your story. This is what the story is *about.* At the same time, in the larger, universal sense, theme is the nugget of human wisdom illuminated by your story. It can be expressed through a familiar proverb or paraphrased to mean the same thing—if you are required to define it. This is what is meant when you are asked to *tell what your story is about in a single sentence.* Editors are always on the alert for stories that deftly handle meaningful universal themes because these are the plus features which make stories worthwhile.

A writer must believe in what his or her story is about. Otherwise the writing will be thin, not convincing, as rejection slips will be quick to confirm. Significant factors cannot be tacked on to make a story "worthwhile."

THE BASIC NEEDS
Children's fundamental needs are no different from yours and mine—or from the concerns of the teenage boy or girl.

1. *The need to love and be loved.* Everyone, in all times and places, has the need to be loved and to love in return. No one ever outgrows the need for love. Children deprived of love do not develop into well-balanced human beings. Whether this basic emotional need is fulfilled or not affects our relationships and attitudes toward others. Stories of deep and moving significance can be woven around this subject.

2. *The need to belong.* First to be accepted by one's family, then by one's peers, is often desperately desired by children of all ages. Trying to fulfill this need can lead youngsters to all sorts of extremes in conduct such as showing off, joining a street gang, or becoming whatever happens to be the *in* thing when you're *out* and deeply hurt and resentful. However, positive acts as well as negative ones can result from rejection.

3. *The need to achieve.* To *do* or *be* something, which not only gives one a feeling of personal satisfaction and worth, but also elicits respect from others, is a built-in hunger in many people. Sometimes rejection by one's peers becomes ambition's spur and the victim strives to excel in some field in order to prove himself or herself before others.

Overcoming physical handicaps can also provide important fiction themes, especially if the character has to learn to live with them, and not feel self-pity. It is also important for the whole in body not to show pity for the handicapped.

4. *The need for security—material, emotional, spiritual.* To be secure means to be free from anxieties and fears—a utopian dream on a par with the lip-happy formula for contentment: to have a million dollars. No one is completely free of anxieties or fears. *How* these are faced, or not faced, provides innumerable story themes for the writer.

Youngsters can be caught in the middle of adult strivings for *material* wealth—or even bare existence—and suffer from the attendant anxiety and fear, resentment, envy, and frustration. The youthful character can be badly warped by such tensions, or tempered and strengthened by adversity—depending on the influences he or she comes under. Children can thrive under the most adverse physical and social conditions if the home atmosphere is happy—and the writer can demonstrate this truth.

And, since today's stories for children do not shrink away

from realism, the opposite picture can be drawn of the result of a lack of family unity.

Emotional security involves and depends on all the other needs.

Spiritual security. A sense of values and moral purpose often comes from religious faith, but in fiction, moral and spiritual considerations are best illustrated within the framework of family life and through character action and reaction. Such stories can serve as guideposts for courses of action contemplated or taken by young readers.

5. *The need to know* has filled our bookshelves with tomes on every conceivable subject. Even quiz books, those fascinating grab bags of interesting facts, fall into this important category. Small children show their curiosity when they lie on their stomachs and inspect blades of grass and study insect life most adults walk over unheeding. People from time immemorial have sought to know the *how* and *why* of things. This need is responsible for inventions and discoveries and flight into space—*and it is your reason for reading this book!*

If you use any of the fundamental needs of all people everywhere, no matter what their age or station in life, you have a powerful magnet for holding the reader's interest, because the basic needs you dramatize are his needs also. But have a care. As Emerson put it, "The universal does not attract us until housed by an individual." Ralph Bunche distilled the thought further, by saying, "If you want to put an idea across, wrap it up in a man." Significance and emotion are tied together so closely that one springs from the other. If you want the reader to have a strong emotional reaction to your story, you must have something to say. But evoking emotion also depends upon the quality of your writing. The techniques you can use to obtain that emotional response I shall take up in the next chapter.

9
**Making the Reader Feel
Emotion . . . Mood . . . Atmosphere**

To be moved—to "get a feeling" or an *emotional experience*—is the reader's chief goal in reading fiction; though he or she may not realize it, *you* must! Any book or story that leaves the reader unmoved is not likely to be a success.

It is the magic of fiction that allows the young reader to "escape" from ordinary day-to-day doings and to live more fully in a heightened, highlighted version of life, with adventure possible at every turn of the page. The reader's emotional involvement in a story effects this escape because to feel it is to experience. Your job is to *make the reader feel*, but not in a free-fall tumble into any emotion. The readers must feel *what* you want them to feel, *where* you want them to feel it, and *when.* Their emotions must be under your control, and that control is exercised by the choice of words you use. This choice, in turn, is governed by what you know about human emotion, and what you know of your craft.

As a writer you are not concerned with the clinical aspects of emotion. You do not analyze it for the reader, you dramatize it. What you need is a practical understanding of children and grownups, an awareness of how they are apt to feel and appear under the stress of varying circumstances. For this understanding you have the best possible source of observation: *yourself.*

THE BASIC EMOTIONS
In the course of your life you have felt many emotions, major and minor, and observed them in others. No one is a stranger to love, anger, fear, hope, despair, grief, joy. These are fundamental and universal. And so are the minor ones, which include jealousy, envy, loneliness, self-pity, vanity,

ambition, greed, humility, stubbornness, courage, timidity, boredom, amusement, pride, suspicion, shame, guilt, gratitude. In some degree everyone, even the small child, has experienced these.

Remember the classics mentioned earlier? What makes these books live on and on? It is their appeal to human emotions, their genuine portrayal of people and their feelings. In every era people differ greatly in their thoughts and particular wants — the things they believe indispensable to their happiness, the gods they worship, and the customs they follow. But *basic emotions are universal, and physical sensations are common to everyone, regardless of age or the time in which he or she lives.* You can always count on reaching your reader through the primary emotions.

Yet it isn't all that simple. You know what these emotions are. But to *know* is not enough for the writer. *You must be able to express the emotion in words,* for it is only through words that you can transmit the feeling to your reader. And these must not be glib clichés ("She was bursting with happiness," "The air was charged with anger"), but carefully chosen words which make the emotion poignant, understandable, "seeable" and "feelable" to your young audience.

To see how a writer can stir the emotions and physical feelings of a reader, study this short selection from Jeffie Ross Gordon's novel, *A Touch of Genius.*

> Cass wasn't sure getting to school early to get seats for the election assembly was such a good idea. A million little balls were playing Ping-Pong inside her stomach; her forehead was sweaty, and chills shivered from her neck down her spine. "Paulie," she whispered, "I feel like I'm going to throw up."

EMOTIONS — FROM EXPERIENCE

Emotion never stops touching our lives. It springs from many causes, and we are affected by it every waking moment. Train yourself to observe the signs of emotion in people of all ages, small children at play or in fights or frights or temper tantrums; expressions you catch on the faces of friends, neighbors, strangers in a crowd. How do they *look?*

What exactly do they *do*? *say*? What is the look of anger, tenderness, compassion, tension?

How did *you* feel when you were waiting for someone very dear to you and the hours dragged by and the person did not come? Or the telephone did not ring? Did you make up waiting games to occupy your mind, or did you pace about, wringing your hands?

Analyzing your own past experiences—when you're sufficiently distant from the happening to see it outside yourself as well as from the inside—will help you understand how other people might feel under similar circumstances, and help you tell the reader, so he too will understand. Everything is grist for that writing mill of ours—the remembrance of the report card we hated to show Dad, the loss of a pet, that very first invitation to a dance, even a car smashup you might have been in. I adapted my vivid recollection of an auto accident for a novel and readers have told me how *real* it seemed. It was!

In your reading of published material, note how the authors create their effects, how they catch at your feelings and involve you to the point where you're living the story right along with the main character—*empathizing* with this person.

SYMPATHY AND EMPATHY

The sympathetic rapport between the writer and his or her character should be so great that to all intents and purposes the writer becomes that character—thinking, feeling, seeing, smelling, touching, *and reacting* to everything that affects that character as if it were all happening to the writer. This kind of entering into another's being is called *empathy:* feeling *as* the subject, or character, feels. *Sympathy*, however, is a different degree of emotional response. If you sympathize with someone, you feel *for* that person, but the twinges are not nearly so strong.

FACTS AND FEELINGS

If the story has a vital problem, the emotion will grow out of the dramatic situation—out of your story people—and how they feel about what is happening. A story is composed of *facts*—the happenings—and *feelings*—the emotional effect these happenings have on the story actors involved.

This is where the author takes control of the reader through technique — the know-how of his or her craft.

As you list the characters in planning your story, write down opposite the name of each character the specific emotion you want the reader to feel toward this person. This will help you be consistent in your characterization, too.

How the story people feel toward others depends on the course of the plot. Feelings can create all sorts of clashes that result in story drama. In Arnold Madison's story, "Terror on Sunset Point," Janice envies her younger sister, Lianna, because the girl is attractive and boys gravitate toward her. Lianna is jealous of Janice because the older girl is so intelligent. The characters clash in the story, but at the end, they have learned more about themselves as well as having established a deeper bond between them. The dominant traits with which you endow your story actors affect not only the action, but also the emotional tone of the story. And you must devise incidents and situations that will allow these character traits, and their corresponding emotions, full scope for expression.

You cannot merely name an emotion and have the reader see and feel it. The reader must be *shown* the emotion in action and reaction before he or she can "experience" it through reading. Your reader will see it if you give John's outward signs of anger to look at, and will *feel* with the character as you tell how John feels inside and what he does as a result.

> John stared up into Al Haskins' sneering face and his stomach tightened. His legs began to shake. His hands curled into fists, the nails biting into the flesh. The blood began to pound in his head and his chest felt so tight, he could scarcely breathe. He saw the towering big bully through a kind of red haze. And then, without thinking of the consequences he lunged at Al, both arms flailing . . .

That's *anger.* You know it and the reader knows it. And even with this economy of words you know that John is small because Al "towers" over him, and yet anger — which ignores logic — makes the smaller boy "lunge" at the "big bully."

Whenever I read this passage in class someone always

asks, "What happened? Did John get the best of the bully?"

I don't know. This is not from a story. It's just a made-up passage to illustrate a point. But the question proves that it has enough *feeling* in it to generate interest.

Learn to know the visible and audible signs of different emotions, the physical way in which they are expressed, and use these correctly. If you were to say: "Susie jumped up and down *hopelessly*" your reader would recognize it at once as nonsense. People jump for joy, in impatience. But without hope, the whole body droops and there's no impulse to jump.

"Her eyes *flashed* indifference, . . ." is from a student manuscript. But *flash* indicates a lively emotion—anger, suspicion, interest perhaps, rather than "indifference," which has a lackluster quality.

In an angry quarrel you do not say, "Kindly close that wide-open orifice from which all that nasty language is coming." You say instead, "SHUT UP!" Could anything be clearer? The choice of words is governed by emotion also. If you know and *feel* the emotion yourself while you are writing, the chances are you'll use the right words.

To demonstrate emotion in your story characters you can use dialogue; thoughts—of the viewpoint character, of course—and descriptive action. You can heighten the whole effect through the *mood* you create.

YOUR STORY'S MOOD AND ATMOSPHERE

Some pages back I said that your story's theme might be called its "melody." Following this analogy, we might then call your story's *mood* its "key"—high, low; major, minor. The mood or "key" sets your story's tone. Is it cheerful, comic, fantastic, sharp with strife, or somber with painful social problems? A story should have an overall mood: romantic, mysterious, serious, adventurous, humorous—and although the action and emotion in different scenes may vary greatly, the story as a whole must never lose its pervading dominant air. Whatever setting, description, dialogue, or characterization is used, it should be unified with the mood you want to create and with the emotion you want to rouse in your reader.

In life chance and coincidence are often present; all sorts of things happen without logic. But a story is an *illusion* of real life, and therefore it must be a unified, artistic presentation, with nothing left to the vagaries of chance, not even the weather. *All story effects must be preplanned for that overall effect you want.* Knowing how to plan and what to plan and why makes all the difference between a professional and an amateur literary performance.

10
Sensory Details
and What They Do to Feelings

All that we know about our world, whatever our age, has been learned through our five senses: sight, hearing, touch, taste, smell—and the "sixth sense"—our reaction to what the other five have told us. Wherever we go, we take our senses—and the reactions which affect our feelings—with us.

How often have you said, "I can't help how I feel, can I?" We are all apt to see things through the filter of our emotional state at a given moment, and this personal mood can color our attitude toward everything around us. *Moods can—and should—color your characters' thinking and responses, too.*

Children react strongly to the color, size, shape, sound, smell, and *feel* of things. And, as Ursula Nordstrom, former editor of Harper and Row, said, "We must remember that children are *new,* and the whole world is new to them." Therefore writers must learn to see the world with young eyes and through the filter of young moods, in order to present youthful adventures through the viewpoint of young story people.

A flash of light—sudden darkness; heat—cold; something rough to the touch—something soft or smooth; sweet—sour—bitter; pleasing scents—disagreeable odors; a loud noise—a tinkle of melody. What are these sensory impressions *like* to young people?

Too often beginning writers assume that they *know,* until the moment of truth when they must put their "knowledge" down in words. Then they suddenly find their minds cluttered with stereotypes and blocked to original thought. To exercise your word-picture-making imagination, gather sensory impressions and practice writing them down in colorful, fresh phrases and figures of speech. File them for easy reference, and they'll be there, ready for tailoring to a particular story and its characters. Use words which will create images in the minds of readers for whom your writing is intended. Flat, colorless statements won't do it. To a grownup, a leg may be asleep, but to a child "it feels like ginger ale, all tingly." Study the following passage for sensory detail and appeal:

> We stepped out on the front porch in the midst of a bright, quiet dawn. There wasn't any wind, but we could see the results of the blizzard. On the distant fields, great drifts of snow had swirled up into high-pointed peaks, while right beside them the ground was nearly bare. The snow seemed to be rising and falling like waves in a stormy lake.
>
> "Wow!" Larry heaved a big breath and it hung visible in the cold air. "You can't even see where the road is."
>
> He was right. Flat, unmarred, white emptiness stretched out in all directions. The trees and their branches were covered with snow; there wasn't a bird in sight. I shaded my eyes and tried to see my house in the distance — or at least see a sign of smoke from the chimney, but there was only more whiteness. "We could have never made it home last night," I whispered.
>
> We clomped down the rickety porch stairs. The snow squeaked when we walked on it, and all our footprints from the night before were buried. Tiny crystals of snow sparkled on the surface like diamonds. The sunlight was getting brighter and stronger. I filled my lungs with the cold air, and it felt good.

Notice the sensory details Carol Farley has provided in this selection from her novel *Mystery of the Melted Diamonds.* Visual images, sounds (or lack of), the sense of feel. And most important, her main character reacts emotionally to the setting. That's the clincher.

WHEN YOU CAN DO SOMETHING ABOUT THE WEATHER

Everybody talks about the weather — but writers can *do* something about it. They can make their own. Story weather can play an important role by helping to set an emotional mood or even providing a climax for your tale. Notice how often mystery and suspense stories utilize the terrors of nature, uncontrollable by man, with all the stops out and all the sound effects turned up full blast.

When you use weather in a story, your imagination will come to your aid *if* you give it experience to feed upon. An English proverb states: "Seeing is believing, but feeling is the naked truth." To get at that "naked truth," *you* must look, listen, touch, sniff, taste, then strip the sensory perception down to the "naked truth," and tell the reader about it in such precise and colorful terms that he or she will experience the same feeling also.

Study the elements. Rain, snow, wind, fog—all these obligingly repeat themselves. Next time it storms, get yourself a writing sample. See how a storm blows up, how it breaks, how it blows away. What is it like seen from outdoors? From shelter inside the house? How might a child, a teenage boy, an old woman feel about a blizzard or a hurricane? How do you react to being caught in the rain? Though I'm not suggesting you go out and catch pneumonia, if you should, pay attention! Remember what it was *like*—reconstruct it as soon as you can after you're on the mend—and jot it down, just in case one of your characters ever has to have it in the course of your story plot.

A CALENDAR OF WEATHER AND OTHER USEFUL FACTS

Much of the material mentioned in this chapter came from a loose-leaf notebook bristling with index tabs that I've kept over the years as a catchall for random observations. Once, riding through a hilly countryside, I saw the contour-plowed fields as "rivers of chocolate," to the delight of a small sweet-toothed companion. Another time, looking out the windows of my mother's apartment in New York, on a foggy afternoon in March, I had "a strange feeling of being suspended in fog over the city—and the top of the Empire State Building floating toward me out of the haze. . . ."

Summer . . . fall . . . winter . . . spring . . . What are they *like?* The whole round of the seasons—at home, abroad, in the country, city, at the seashore or the mountains, or the desert has over the years found its way into my notebook. The words help me recapture the feelings I need: the searing heat of sun on bare skin—on a freezing midwinter day—

or the dry crunching squeak of snow under boots — in June!

The mere act of setting down impressions fixes them more firmly in the mind. It is the sort of knowledge that helps to put sureness and speed into a writer's fingers as they fly over the typewriter keys, building a bridge of words to the reader's mind and heart.

BACKGROUND — A SENSE OF PLACE

To have reality for the reader, your story must happen somewhere on the globe — in a certain country, in a particular city, village, farm, or wilderness. This is your *place.* The more you can narrow the place down to a particular spot, the better, because always it is the particular, not the general, that transmits a sense of here and now reality to your reader.

This particular place, then, must have a definite *background setting,* against which the action will be visualized. And it must be complete with all the things of life likely to surround your characters: a house, or castle, or hovel, or tent; appropriate scenery, flora and fauna; particular views from different windows; furniture and bric-a-brac; pots and pans and strings and things — the objects which tie the story people to life as it is lived in their time, place, and social atmosphere.

Social environment means a manner of life as well as the background setting in your story. In writing for young people, you will usually have some sort of family life. Is the family rich, poor, middle class? Are they city people, small-town folk, farm dwellers, seafarers, mountain people, ranchers, migrant workers?

THE WHERE OF IT

Wherever and however you choose to locate your story, make the setting vivid. But avoid piling on too many details. The modern reader is not pleased by lengthy passages of "scenery" which slow down the story. His or her reaction in such instances is to skip — and if the reader skips too much, the person may skip right out of your story and turn on the TV. Hold the reader's attention by building descriptive detail into the action of your story people.

If the location you've selected is an actual place, read up on it (see the chapters on research in Part II). This information will be a plus feature. Many a book has been firmly entrenched on important buying lists because of such extra background research.

No one can doubt the authority of a descriptive setting like this one from *Mystery at Fire Island* by Hope Campbell, or miss the atmosphere it exudes.

> Monday, the Fourth of July, arrived in the weirdest way. Early in the morning the island was blanketed by a low mist. By noon it had become a thick fog. By late afternoon everything was black as night, and hidden in what one usually thought of as a London pea-souper, only worse. Yesterday's wind still prevailed and was blowing in hard from the sea, while along the beach, people were setting off firecrackers. They flew back inland, snatched and carried by the wind. Streaks of red sailed through the fog, landing on dune grass, boardwalks, the wooden decks and roofs of ocean-front houses.

TIME — THE WHEN OF IT

Unless the reader is told almost at once when the story is taking place, he or she will assume that it is the present. So if on page eleven the reader suddenly discovers that the year is 1820, he or she will become understandably confused. The mental images made will disintegrate, and with them, quite possibly, all interest in the story.

Properly handled, your story's time helps to establish the atmosphere. It can affect the story's mood and its emotional tone; certainly the kind of characters you use and how you characterize them (as present day or period people or historical characters); and the background against which the action takes place and all the "things of life" with which you fill it. Authors, realizing the importance of establishing the time especially when it is not the present, occasionally state it in their very first sentence.

WHEN TOO MUCH IS TOO BAD

Sensory, emotion-producing material must be kept under control. No matter how moving the scene you're writing, you must develop the ability to be both *inside*, in a state of complete empathy, and at the same time *outside,* looking on and describing. If your tendency is to overwrite, to spill over with emotion and cry right into your typewriter, be prepared to cut copiously when you revise.

The most important emotion the writer must aim for in his story as a whole is the reader's complete satisfaction with the way it all turned out. Sometimes this response is a wistful sigh because the story did end, and the reader has had to say goodbye to all those delightful story people. Then you're likely to get letters asking you to continue their adventures.

But beware of stirring feelings too deeply. The reader's purpose in reading is to "escape" the everyday world, to live more excitingly—but not to wallow in grief, or experience too much unhappiness or pain. Be sparing in your details of accidents, bereavements, operations, and amputations.

Some tenderhearted children will not read animal stories, "because something terrible always happens to them"; and even though reading experience has shown that usually "everything turns out all right in the end," for some, this assurance is not reason enough for the agony in between. Even I, a veteran book reviewer, sometimes find I have to "escape" from an animal tale because it's just too, too much.

"Escape" for the reader is a revolving door. Readers are perfectly willing to go book-adventuring, because they know that they can always "save" themselves if things get too rough. By the simple expedient of closing the book they can escape right back into their safe everyday world. Consider this fact also in your writing.

11
Conflict, Opposition, Suspense — How to Keep the Reader Reading

Writers of fiction might well follow the example of Shakespeare's redoubtable witches in *Macbeth* when cooking up conflicts and calamities for their story characters. "Double, double toil and trouble," is a reliable recipe for holding the reader's interest.

Life without adversities may be pleasant to contemplate, but it makes dull reading. It's not the kind of "living" a reader looks for in a story. *The course of fictional life must never run smoothly.* This advice has come to us from the oldest story tellers. "There is nothing better fitted to delight the reader than changes of circumstances and varieties of fortune," said the Roman philosopher Cicero, sometime between 106 and 43 B.C. — and the rule was ancient then.

No trouble — no story. Without problems, conflicts, opposition, there is no suspense; and without suspense a reader won't keep reading. It is this important element that you must build into a story once you have created a leading character so interesting and appealing that the reader *cares* what happens to this person.

Conflict is the struggle of your leading character against opposition. The outcome of this struggle should never seem to be a "sure thing." Despite the reader's assurance from previous experiences that the hero usually wins in the end, there must be a lack of absolute certainty to keep the reader turning the pages.

HOW TO BUILD SUSPENSE
You must rouse *curiosity*. The reader must wonder: What is going to happen next? You must also rouse the reader's anxiety. He or she *must worry* about your main character:

How in the world will the character get out of this predicament?

To reduce this phase of writing technique to a formula: *Character plus anxiety equals suspense.* Your reader should bristle with anxious questions about the welfare of your main character—with whom he or she now identifies—but he or she should not be able to guess the outcome.

If you feel that the outcome of your story may perhaps be obvious, rework it. You may have given away too much information or been too generous with clues foreshadowing the conclusion. You may have made the opposition too weak, the path to attainment all too easy for your character. Develop a receptive ear to the voice of your own built-in critic. All too often it gives sound advice which the writer refuses to hear—because it means more work! But professional writing success requires hard work, a fact you might as well face. There is no future for the lazy.

Realize also that the brilliant, easy ideas for conflict and complications that first flash into your mind are apt to glitter with fool's gold. Screen those ''instant inspirations'' carefully. With additional thought you may come up with something more effective for harassment of your story people. Always reverse the Golden Rule when it comes to making trouble for them; you do *not* do unto them as you would be done to!

Your success as a writer depends on your ability to think up problems, harrowing complications, and satisfying solutions for your story actors.

OBSTACLES AND OPPOSITIONS

The obstacles and oppositions that cause your main character's struggle must not be teacup tempests or flimsy misunderstandings which a few words of explanation at any point would clear up. The struggle must not be simply delayed action for a measured number of scenes. (''He/she doesn't succeed, he/she doesn't succeed, he's/she's beginning to succeed, he/she succeeds.'') That's too obvious and dull a pattern even for the youngest child. Today's young people are knowledgeable readers with no scarcity of books from which to choose. They will read your story only if you offer them something fresh, entertaining, and exciting.

Your story problem must be a real one and important for the main character to solve. The goal must be worthwhile and troublesome to reach. The struggles and conflicts must appear to be difficult ones, not merely postponements to the final triumph.

Money-raising stories are likely to fall into the postponement-of-success category. The idea has been used just too often to be convincing or suspenseful. The reader knows the necessary amount will be raised in the end—unless you can think up some fresh twist to the whole situation.

CONFLICT
Opposition means conflict. Your main character can be in conflict with the environment, with others, or with himself or herself. Having given your character some desire or dissatisfaction with things as they are, you can heighten suspense by making it necessary for him or her to accomplish his or her purpose within a certain length of time.

Although trouble is of utmost importance, remember that in a child's story you can't pour it on as in a soap opera; and it can't be the kind of trouble a child or young adult is unable to face or surmount realistically. So temper the afflictions of your characters, but also avoid stories awash in sweetness and light.

THREE TYPES OF CONFLICT
Generally speaking, there are three types of conflict that can be used singly or in combination.

1. *Person against nature.* This kind of conflict involves any natural phenomenon as the "enemy" or opposition: a blizzard, a hurricane, a fire, a flood, a wild beast. A story character might be trapped on a mountain, lost in the woods, or adrift and helpless on the ocean. He or she might be caught at the bottom of the sea with fouled diving gear, or might be whirling in space, out of control.

Any of these situations can be very exciting but also difficult to write about, especially at length. A short story might be built around a young boy left in charge of the family farm, for example, with an unexpected blizzard or flood cutting him off completely from help. How he copes with the situation is the story. But it is not easy to keep a reader interested in the doings of a single character, even in a short tale. If your story involves a conflict with nature, plan to use at least two, and preferably more characters for contrast of personalities, reactions, and additional conflict and suspense.

2. *Person against him/herself.* This type of conflict is bound to have psychological overtones, the struggle arising from the strengths and weaknesses and the war between good and evil within the character. Such a story will inevitably include a great deal of "think stuff" which is slow-paced and generally uninteresting to the young reader, who prefers *action* and lots of it!

3. *Person against person.* This is usually the most absorbing form of conflict because the greatest interest of most readers is what happens to other people — especially if they can identify with them — regardless of the time or place of the story.

The most successful stories and novels employ at least two of these types of conflict and if possible all three. For example, in Harry Mazer's *Snow Bound,* a teenage boy and girl are trapped in a snowstorm. Not only do they have to face the danger of the storm, but their personalities conflict and each is besieged by doubts and guilt. The combination of conflicts produces a novel that keeps the reader turning the pages to learn the story's outcome.

VARY THE OBSTACLE COURSE

Be sure that the obstacles or difficulties that prevent your character from getting what he or she wants are not all of one type. To maintain the highest peak of interest, your hero or heroine must not always nearly drown in the same ocean, or flounder through one desert after another, or be clobbered continually by the same opponent. That would be about as gripping as having one flat tire after another.

Conflict and adversity test the mettle of your story people and show them for what they really are. How they meet disaster, grapple with it, deal with an opponent, and overcome the obstacles in their way *must* be a part of your story planning. Things must never "just happen" to your main character—or to anyone else in your tale.

THE RIGHT PROPORTION

Conflict, opposition, and suspense must be used in the right proportion; too much of any of these, like too much seasoning in a stew, spoil the effect. Any prolonged periods of action or tension should be broken with rest periods for your reader, so that he or she can take up the story action again with renewed zest and interest. "Think stuff" slows the pace—so here is the place to use it. Let your character mull over his situation—which will, in effect, recap for the reader what has been gained or lost, reminding him of what the story is all about. A brief, quiet scene is all you need.

So far I have dealt with the ingredients that go into a story and with some of the mechanics of the writing craft. Now let's see how these can be put together most effectively.

12
Plot and Plotting

A well-constructed story is never written "off the top of the head" with a happy-go-lucky trust that "everything will come out right," that it will jell and sell; ninety-nine times out of a hundred it won't. Anybody can have an idea, but an idea that has not been executed with professional competence might as well have never been born. That is why *plot* and *plotting* are so important.

WHAT IS PLOT?
Often the word strikes terror in a writer's heart and numbs his or her mind. Don't let *plot* discombobulate you! Everything that you have been reading in this book has been preparing you to plot. What you read now will tell you how to go about it in an organized manner. Commit the following definition to memory and never allow yourself to forget it: *Plot is a plan of action devised to achieve a definite and much desired end—through cause and effect.*

In a plotted story, *cause* sets your main character off to take certain action to solve a problem, get out of a situation, or reach a certain goal. The *effect* is what happens to this person as a *result* of the action taken. The character must struggle to get what he or she wants and must be opposed vigorously, either by someone who wants the same thing, or by circumstances that stand in the way of the goal.

The odds must grow against your hero or heroine so that the goal appears more and more attainable, no matter how he or she struggles toward it, until he or she reaches a black moment where all seems lost. That's when the hero or heroine makes one more super-human effort, and emerges victorious.

You have seen this plot demonstrated again and again on your TV screen. Every Western, every spy drama, every adventure yarn uses this tried-and-true method for achieving drama, for holding the viewer's interest through the final scene—and every suspenseful, interest-gripping book and story uses it, though you may not recognize it so readily in print.

Plotting means planning. All planning, regardless of what it is for—a route for a six-week motor journey or a picnic supper in your backyard—has to begin with a solid period of thinking. Just so, in plotting a story you need thinking time to *devise* a course of events that leads to a resounding climax; events which happen *because* of something that occurred before. In other words, yours must be a *cause and effect* sort of thinking.

"This happens and this happens and this happens" is not a plot. It is a string of unconnected incidents, even if they do happen to the same person. But when you have *this happen* because *that happened,* you have plot. Cause and effect is in operation.

THE INSEPARABLES—PLOT AND CHARACTER

There is no single component of a story that is more important than another component, unless it is *character.* But even character, given nothing to do, might as well be a heap of sand. So another important part is *action.* But action which is not devised to further the plot to a planned conclusion might as equally well be a heap of sand—with the wind blowing it in all directions.

Character plus meaningful, directed action toward a previously planned desired end—that is the meaning and purpose of plot.

The desired end is what the character wants.

Writers go about plotting in different ways. How I start depends on the kind of story I'm planning to write. But there is one rule which I feel a writer should remember when developing a plot:

If you take a character from one area or situation where he or she is content and place this person in another area or situation where he or she is not, problems are bound to

be generated. Immediately there is a state of unrest, conflict, all kinds of story stuff—especially if your character decides to do something to improve his or her lot, attain a
goal, or be assertive in some way.

THE "WHAT IF . . . ?" FORMULA

Before you can begin to plot you must have an idea that sets
your creative wheels in motion. Your idea file, suggested
earlier, may provide one, or you may prefer to cast about
for ideas. In the latter case you can bait your hook with the
"What If . . . ?" formula. It spurs creative thinking through
many writing problems.

What if a girl wanted to become an architect? What if a
promising ballerina were suddenly crippled and could
never dance again? What if a boy and his grandmother suddenly inherited a trained ostrich? What if a modern family
lived in a castle—in New Jersey—and the children found an
ancient, left-over dragon in one of the towers . . . a girl
dragon . . . named Amelia? What if two children received a
baby chick and a baby duck for Easter—and unlike the usual
fate of such pets—they survived . . . in a city apartment . . .
and grew . . . and grew . . . and then the kids added other
pets . . . a talking parrot from a white elephant sale . . . a
baby pig, won at a country fair . . . ?

At various times, every one of these *what if's* has started
a successful short story or a book for me.

The thing to do is narrow down your thinking to the one
idea that intrigues you most. *Never undertake to write
about something that interests you only mildly*—especially
if you are contemplating a book. The subject will certainly
not interest the reader if you, yourself, are not excited about
it.

TWELVE POINT RECIPE FOR PLOTTING

Having settled on the idea, consider the "what if . . . ?"
possibilities that apply directly to it—and soon your story
will begin to emerge. Characters, situations, backgrounds,
conflicts will spring into your mind. These are the *makings*
of a plot, and when you organize the action into its most

effective order, you will have a story. But first you must ask yourself some pertinent questions—*and answer them on paper.* These will form your *Twelve Point Recipe for Plotting:*

1. Who is the main character?
2. Who (or what) is the antagonist?
3. Who are the other people in the story?
4. What does the main character want? Why? What is his or her problem, goal, situation, greatest need? (This *need* or *want* will govern the kind of person the main character must be in your story. It must be suitable to his or her age and attainable—but only through considerable effort.
5. How important is it for the individual to get what he or she wants? (It should be vital. A great deal should be at stake, with serious consequences if failure occurs.)
6. How does the antagonist prevent the main character from getting what he or she wants? (This is the conflict, the opposition.)
7. What does the main character *do* about this obstacle? (Our heroes, big and little, male and female, must be *doers,* not people-watchers. They must win through their own power, not through luck or coincidence. *It is their doing something about the situation* that starts the story action.)
8. What are the results of his or her initial action? (Here complications should set in—new difficulties that make the main character's situation worse than before, intensifying the struggles.)
9. What do these struggles lead to? (This is the crisis, the crucial point for the main character. Things just can't get any worse; here consider the possible Black Moment.)
10. What is the climax? (This is the moment of decision, the point of no return, where intensity and interest in the story have reached their highest pitch. The main character must decide which way to go *because of the kind of person you have made him or her.* The person's action now governs the answer to the next question.)
11. Does the main character accomplish his or her purpose or abandon it in favor of something else? (This is the

story outcome, the resolution or *denouement.*)

12. What is the theme? What basic truth have you illustrated through your character's action and reaction?

All the foregoing chapters will help you answer these important questions, and the ones that follow will show you how to carry your story through to the end.

BEFORE YOU WRITE, OUTLINE! — AND WHY

The answers to the preceding twelve points in plotting will provide you with a basic outline for your story. Beginning writers often rebel at the thought of outlining, for it seems such drudgery. But what they really mind is the discipline. The purpose of an outline is to clarify your thinking, guide you through an orderly sequence of events and keep you from wandering off at tangents the moment something new streaks into your mind.

A complete outline gives you something else; your story's ending. In the various courses I have given, I've had many students tell me that they have dozens of unfinished manuscripts stashed away in their desks or attics, unfinished because they did not know how to end them! They wasted time and effort because they embarked on the heady crest of a newborn idea without thinking it through in orderly outline form. *Never begin writing a story before you know how it will end.* And never fail to outline your story, however sketchily, before you begin to write it!

THE SHORT STORY SYNOPSIS

With the twelve point outline before you, your characters, situations, and ending clear in mind, write out a *brief*, note-style synopsis of your story. Put down a general account of *what happens* from the opening scene through to the end, making the main problem clear as early as possible in the ideas you will develop into opening paragraphs. *Write in the present tense* so that this preliminary sketch of your story will feel distinctly different from your actual writing. The synopsis might go something like this:

The Sparta High School basketball team is in the last moments of its game. The winning point is scored, and the team is only one game away from winning the tournament. But player Al Gorman does not share the happiness of his team.

In the locker room, Gorman is again asked by the team captain to play dirty the next day. The leading player on the opposing team gets riled easily. Al can't give the captain an answer yet; but he knows the team is depending on him because it's the first time a Sparta team has been so close to a trophy.

Al walks through the snow to his girlfriend's house, thinking back over the years and on how basketball and sportsmanship and clean playing have been such an important part of his life. Should he abandon those beliefs and engage in dirty playing to help his team?

At Lori's house, Al meets Mr. Daniels, the leader of his church youth group. Mr. Daniels tells Al that the whole town will be out for tomorrow's game. People living in small towns often view their local sports with greater interest than they display in professional sports played in a distant city. Another burden has been placed on Al.

The following afternoon, Al is in the locker room, suiting up, when the team captain comes to him for an answer.

Although the above is a partial synopsis, you will go on to plan the entire story. Once the synopsis is written, you will need to study it. A good time to begin revision of a story is *before* you write the piece. So, check the synopsis to save work later on. Your beginning should dramatically introduce the main character and the problem faced by that individual. The middle or body of the story should show the problem intensifying. Static problems — those that never worsen — will cause reader interest to slowly drop. Has your main character facilitated the resolution through his or her own actions? Don't let an accident or coincidence or someone else step in and solve everything.

When satisfied that these larger sections are in the best possible shape, read through the synopsis again. Does each scene kick off the next scene? Are you letting two scenes do the job one can? Are there any characters you can eliminate because their role is unimportant and can be assumed by that of another character? Give yourself plenty of time to consider the story plan from all angles. You will be anxious to begin the actual writing, but time spent on the synopsis will prevent much time being spent rewriting.

The synopsis is not engraved in marble. Change it if you get better ideas for the story line. Once you are completely satisfied, go ahead and write. With your story so thoroughly planned, you should be able to get it down fast.

NINE AND SIXTY WAYS

Writing is an intensely personal form of communication. That is what gives it variety, freshness, interest, and surprise. No single method can be proclaimed *the* one to use. No writer should be forced to use another's method, no matter how successful that method is for that writer. Even the way a story is initially considered varies from writer to writer.

Do you like to talk your stories over beforehand? Do they seem to jell better if you discuss them first? If so, talk away. But many writers cannot discuss their stories and then write them. Other people's criticism smothers the project or exhausts the need for communication with the reader—and that's the end of that tale. Analyze yourself on this score, and if you must be a clam, *be* a clam. It may also be that you have an extraordinarily logical mind and retentive memory. You may be able to think every detail through entirely in your head—well and good. The proof of the pudding is your success in selling stories. If the percentage is impressive, then don't change your method. But if your stories fail to sell, do try the plot plan I suggest.

13
How to Organize a Book

No matter how brilliant your mental faculties, you cannot carry in your mind the multitude of details that go into the writing of a full-length book.

You have a larger cast of characters whose main problem is more complex. There are secondary themes involving additional people who are involved with the main problem. And there are more scenes — and more word space for you to move around in, which is part of the fun of writing a book. You don't feel cramped by the number of words in which to tell your tale.

At the same time, the sheer quantity of the words you are allowed can prove awesome to someone who has written only short stories. I grew up to full-length books by writing three-, four-, and five-part serials. Learning how to think these through, outline and synopsize them helped me to develop an organized book plan.

IS YOUR IDEA BOOKWORTHY?
Before embarking on a book project test your idea for its worth. *Is it big enough for a book?*

It would be difficult to stretch a girl's concern with "a date for the junior prom" into a full-length book, but with a fresh twist the idea might make a fine short story. On the other hand, the story of a girl who comes to New York to make a career in fashion could scarcely be covered in 3,000 words. It *requires* book-length treatment.

HOW TO THINK BOOK
Full-length junior books usually run from 20,000 to 60,000 words, depending on the age level you're aiming for. But

don't let the number of words terrify you. Don't even think of the number of pages you must produce if such thoughts bother you. Instead, consider the ten to twelve pages you have been accustomed to write for a short story. That's about the length of a chapter: 2,500 to 3,000 words. *Think of your book a chapter at a time.* Even if you plan twenty chapters, by writing one chapter a week you will have a book in twenty weeks. Viewed in this way the whole prospect becomes less frightening.

YOUR CURRENT PROJECT FOLDER

Once you have chosen your book project, label a file folder with the working title of your project. Into this folder put all the odds and ends pertaining to it—newspaper clippings, articles, pictures, brochures, and notes that you don't know what to do with—yet. Collect any books, magazines, or other reference material that you'll need close to your working area. A small bookcase on wheels or a serving table with two or three tiers is handy for this purpose.

YOUR WORKBOOK

Select a loose-leaf notebook of a convenient size, with large rings so that you can put lots of paper into it. My favorite takes 6-by-9½-inch fillers. Use linen tabs that you can cut yourself, or notebook dividers that come in different colors to index the various departments.

Below is a description of how I divide my workbook, but you may decide to label and organize the sections differently. Every professional writer eventually develops his or her own system for ordering work.

Tab I. Title—I use a page to list titles as they come to mind, even when I begin with one; along the way something better may present itself.

Then I use a page for a variety of pertinent data:

a. Deadline: the date when I hope to have the manuscript completed. (Since I usually work under contract now, my target date is a positive one; however, under any circumstances, it is psychologically advisable to establish a deadline for yourself. Like a professional, you work toward a definite goal.)

b. Length: Skipping a couple of lines, I set down the number of words this book should have 20, 30, 40,000. This is to plant the figure in my subconscious, but not to brood upon. Some of my editors like short books, others long ones.

c. Theme: Again skipping a few lines. I leave a space to write in theme — when it is clear to me. (See Chapter 8 for guidance on this point.)

d. Chapters: The number of chapters I expect to have — usually I aim for twenty, but the result may be as few as ten or as many as twenty-two.

e. Date when actual writing is begun:

f. Date when first draft is finished: (As a matter of statistics, it is interesting to have a record of how long it has taken you to write your various books. Besides, after you are published, people will ask you.)

If you are very methodical, you may want a separate page for a work log, a record of your day-by-day output. This may be simply a date and the number of words written on that day, with a total for the week.

What should be your quota? That depends on you — your creativity, your experience — not to mention your typing skill. Usually I can do better than 2,000 words a day, and once I wrote a 40,000-word book in ten days, but that was a kind of miracle! (In nonfiction I work much more slowly. And Elizabeth George Speare, two-time winner of the Newbery Award, told me that she considers herself lucky if she gets 500 words done in a day. Each of us must work at his or her own pace.)

How many hours should you spend writing? That again depends on your personal makeup and circumstances. Many literary successes in the juvenile and adult fields actually write only three hours a day. But as Somerset Maugham once commented:

> . . . the author does not only write when he is at his desk; he writes all day long, when he is thinking, when he is reading, when he is experiencing; everything he sees and feels is significant to his purpose and, consciously or unconsciously, he is forever storing his impressions.

Tab 2. Plot — the story plan. When this is clear to me, I

type it in here in synopsis form. To me, the synopsis is what the preliminary sketch is to an artist. I set down only the essential features of my story in a brief, general account. But long before I write a trial synopsis, I start working in the other sections of my workbook.

Tab 3. Situation—The several pages included in this section usually get written first, for here I put down the things that happen before my story actually takes off. These are the circumstances that *cause* my main character to take action: the difficulties that set up a pattern of discontent, the desire or challenge to accomplish some aim. These are the bits and pieces from which my beginning will spring.

And here lies a *difference between the short story and the book:* In the short story the problem is stated at once and the main character goes to work on it immediately. But in the full-length book the reasons which lead up to the problem are usually built up first; then the problem is stated, and the main character proceeds to solve it.

Tab 4. Problem(s)—Here I detail the main problem of my main character—the thing the story is about—the thing he or she must solve through personal effort and against almost overwhelming odds. Please notice the *almost.* No matter how serious the problem, or how close to life-or-death the struggle, the problem should be one the main character *can* do something about. In stories for young people, our characters are not usually allowed to beat their heads against the granite walls of impossible odds. There should be a chink in the wall of opposition which the main character can find and widen for the triumphant leap to victory.*

Into this section I also put all sorts of incidents and other problems and complications and developments that might be used in the course of the story; not chronologically, but just as they occur to me. Some of these will be used, some

---

*Since all rules seem to have exceptions, I must add that some current "realistic" books and stories do not observe the rule for happy endings, or even the one for ending on a note of hope. Unhappy endings are acceptable, if the emotional impact is sufficient to warrant them. And sometimes, when the subject matter and writing are exceptional, a story ends without a rounded-out plot, usually because it has none, but is rather a spinning out of any episode—long or short—in the life of a character. It's like a slice of life—a wedge cut out from a whole, not a story which moves full circle from a problem or goal to a satisfying solution.

discarded, but all are useful in getting me wound up in my story. These are the items I refer to constantly as I begin to develop my story. I take the pages out of the loose-leaf binder, shuffle them about, and whenever I use an item, I cross it out, thus reducing the bulk of notes.

Tab 5. Chapters—In this section I write down the numerals from one through twenty (or whatever number of chapters I think I'll have), with a few lines between on the page and a two-inch margin at the left. (The margin is for a specific purpose so keep it in mind.) Next to the numerals I shall eventually put either a chapter heading or a working title to serve as a clue to what the chapter is about, should I need to look up some point in the manuscript.

Then I allow a page for each individual chapter, where I can put down what might happen. But until my plot is set these ideas are very tentative, subject to change or discard. Once the plot is set, I become more positive about the chapter happenings—but not inflexible! Characters have a way of taking over the story, once you breathe life into them. They can work out their own destinies, a phenomenon of which the author should take advantage.

I do not include any dialogue unless it is something especially witty that I don't want to forget.

While setting down chapter incidents, I try to think in terms of drama, scene interest, setting, action, emotion. I write in detail about a third or even half of the chapters before beginning to write the story. The last half can be outlined later, based on how the book evolves. But of course, before I ever get to this writing stage, I must know the ending and the probable climax scene. Otherwise there cannot be a complete plot outline to work from.

Although chapter titles are almost always used in books for young children, they are not necessary for teenagers. Whenever you do use them, don't give away the story through chapter headings which are too revealing, such as "Kip Finds the Treasure," or "Judy Wins the Prize."

Even the youngest child is annoyed when suspense is ruined in this way.

Time—In your planning, decide on the length of time your story will cover. Make this as short as possible, because a short period (or a time limit to accomplish what must be done) intensifies interest and drama. It also automatically affects the pace at which you write. A brisk pace conveys the sense of immediacy, of urgency, and is always preferable to the slow, leisurely one.

Books for young people should not have long time lapses covering years in the main character's life. A month, a year, one summer, even a period of a few days is far more likely to hold the reader's interest. The exception applies to career books, where the main character's success must be kept within the realm of plausibility. Too rapid a success for your hero will make your story unbelievable. (See Chapter 16 for a discussion of how to handle time transitions in novels that cover several years in time.)

Be sure to establish the historical period in which your story takes place—past, present, or future (as in a fantasy); and the chronological time that will be involved, as "from May to December." Jot down the time covered in every chapter; the season, the month, the day of the week, even the hour(s), if pertinent. *Making the reader aware of the passage of time adds to the reality of your story.*

For a quick check of the time involved at any point, note it in the wide margin to the left of your numerical chapter listing, or use an extra workbook page to list the time sequences as your story develops. In that case make an extra tab and put this just before the chapter tab so you can find it easily. The important thing is not to slip into Friday if your action is taking place on Tuesday, or into May if your action is still taking place in April.

Historicals—If yours is a story about a period in history, you must be especially careful of the chronology. (See the chapters on research in Part II.) In this case, put in a tab labeled *Historical Chronology* and consult it frequently during the planning and writing.

Tab 6. Characters—As my characters evolve, I make a list of them in order of their importance, choosing their names with the greatest of care and juggling these until I feel they are exactly right for the people in *this* story. (See the section on names in Chapter 5.)

Then I assemble them into family groups on another page, for easy reference.

Next I allow a page or more for each important character's delineation. Half a page may do for minor story actors. At the top of each character's page, I tabulate pertinent data such as age, coloring, eyes, hair, build, physical characteristics—so that I can find them quickly if I should forget what someone on page seventy-five looks like when I want to insert a bit of description to refresh the reader's memory.

Then I jot down chronology of birth, and anything important that might have happened to the story actors to color their personalities, create their social attitudes, establish their goals, in short, make them what they are at the opening of the story. (Refer to Chapters 5, 6, 7.)

Finally I write the individual character sketches which I hope will change my "types" into flesh-and-blood people, with problems, goals, emotions, and reactions to all the other characters around them. It is important to know exactly what each character thinks and feels about every other character in the story. In each character sketch I immerse myself in that particular person and view the world through his or her eyes.

Working with the characters in this way can be most fruitful plot-wise. Each one can make a spontaneous contribution—and with the *Problem(s)* and *Situations* sections in the workbook, none of these ideas will be lost.

Tab 7. Background—Here I note down everything that I'll need for the setting of my story in general, and for the individual chapters and scenes. This may include layout sketches of grounds, streets, towns, topography of the land, houseplans—the arrangement and furnishing of rooms— the things of life. (See Chapter 10 for details on this topic.)

Tab 8. Research—The importance of this section cannot be over-emphasized. It is what makes your story "authentic," whether the setting is in the immediate present or the very distant past. Usually, I prefer to use a separate notebook (as suggested in the chapters on research in Part II). However, if comparatively few notes are required for a project, the research can go directly into the workbook, along with a page for bibliography and one for authorities, listing all the books and people I may have consulted while preparing to write.

Tab 9. Check—Even the most careful research can leave a trail of question marks in the actual writing. Rather than stop the creative flow to look anything up or recheck a fact that I've put down somewhere, I make a note in this section and find the answer at a more convenient time. Once I write the question down, it no longer nags and I can go on with the work I should be doing.

Tab 10. Inserts—This is for additional useful information that I think of after I have started the actual writing. Background details, some bit of character business, anything at all that I may want to put already written into the story is safe here until I'm ready to use it.

Tab 11. Words and Phrases—This, too, is a "safe deposit" section—for anything that might add sparkle to my writing: figures of speech, which do not always occur to the writer at the moment he needs them; bits of dialogue that can make the characters sound more witty; quotations; etc.

. . . AND ONE TO GROW ON!

There is one more section—at the *back* of my workbook. It is a duplicate set of the front tabs, for the capture of any ideas I may get for my *next* project while working on *this* one. As a professional writer, I always have plans for at least one book beyond the one in work. Whenever I finish the current project, I simply move the back section into the front, and make ready another set of tabs for the project to follow!

The workbook is not only a more efficient project organizer, but it is also an idea generator. By providing yourself with definite sections to work in, you always have a place to put down whatever comes into your mind. As you write in the different sections you can *see* and *feel* your story grow and develop and quicken with life. The characters clamor to be released to their adventuring, and at last you are ready and eager to let them—and *write!*

14
The Actual Writing—
the Good Days and the Bad

With the organization work finished, you can recapture your original excitement as you merge yourself with your characters and their lives. Now is the time to stop thinking of the "rules" and allow your imagination to take wing. If you have grounded yourself thoroughly in the writing of short stories, you have absorbed the necessary pointers on technique—and you have your book plan to guide you.

Allow no doubts of your ability to enter your mind at this stage. Creative people thrive on a positive attitude. If any signs point to a flagging self-confidence, here is a quote from that many-sided genius, Goethe, to elevate your spirits and (I hope) galvanize you into action:

> Are you in earnest?
> Seize this very minute!
> What you can do, or dream you can, begin it!
> Boldness has genius, power and magic in it.
> *Only engage, and then the mind grows heated.*
> BEGIN, and then the work will be completed.

Consider the wisdom of these lines. They state a psychological principle: *Interest follows action.* You begin to work—*to write*—to engage the gears of your mind. Interest awakens, your imagination is freed, ideas begin to flow. This does not happen the other way around. If you sit and stew and wait for "inspiration" it may never come! Such pressure is more likely to block off creative thought.

SOME DON'TS AND DO'S
Do not attempt to analyze or perfect your words while you are getting them down in the first draft. Write as fast as you

are able, letting spontaneity take over. The time to criticize and take apart comes later — when the work is inescapably on paper.

No matter how engrossed you are in your project, do not work at it every day until you're limp. More is involved in this kind of creation than the physical act of pounding the typewriter. "Living" through every scene you write can be exhausting, and so, too, is the intense concentration you give your work. You can drive yourself just so far, and if you overdo repeatedly, your subconscious will build up such a resistance that you won't want to go back to your desk.

Be sensible about your work. Along with a set time for writing, decide on the number of pages you should do each day and *do* them, but don't push too much beyond that limit. In fact, it is often best to stop in the middle of some interesting scene. Jot down the next action in the middle of a paragraph or sentence. Leave your desk and do something else. When your next writing session rolls around, it will be easy to recapture the mood and plunge into the story with freshness and vigor.

There is sound psychology behind this advice. Finished business can be forgotten, but something left undone will linger in your mind — and your subconscious will helpfully churn away at it. Yet there's no need for *you* to be restless, because the act of writing a note on what's to happen next frees your conscious mind of the problem until you're ready to return to it.

Catching the emotional mood of your story is hardest during the first half hour or so of your writing session. I frequently begin my new day's work with a "wastebasket exercise" — retyping the last page or two written the day before. In this way I wind myself into the mood of the story quickly and am ready to go on with the new action and developments.

You can also catch the mood by reading over what you have written. However, do not read any more than the previous day's output, and only enough of that to enable you to go on from where you left off.

With my book plan completed, I usually embark on the writing of four to six chapters, and this brings the whole thing to life; the book takes a definite shape and direction. When these chapters are done, I go back, reread and revise them until I am satisfied with this beginning. Sometimes this "trial flight" suggests significant changes in character and plot, as it shows me the book in a different light. In that case, *I make the changes, both in the synopsis and the outline, to avoid possible confusion later.* However, such changes should be made only after serious consideration.

Chapter lengths are not arbitrary, either. When a chapter runs too long you can divide it into two chapters. Sometimes you may find that chapter events can be condensed for a better effect and story pace; two chapters may need to become one. This letting out or tucking in is to be done later, however—in revision—when the technical tests should be applied to what you have written.

Don't let worry over sentence length, construction or vocabulary hamper the writing of your first draft. Just write naturally. Incidentally, use smooth, sixteen-pound paper for typing your first draft. You'll be able to work on it with pen or pencil during revision, scratching out or erasing without having the paper disintegrate under pressure. Double space, and allow wide margins for corrections and interpolations.

With one chapter finished, read over the outline of the next and think about it with quiet confidence. Read over the character sketches, the background notes, the various situations as you've jotted them down. Don't forget these aids in the organized sections of your workbook.

Do not attempt to polish your writing while you're creating the story. This is wasteful, and every interruption will make it harder to plunge ahead with your original zeal. Enthusiasm must last a long time for a book! And yet you can't expect it to remain at the same high pitch all through the writing.

Action scenes are less apt to give you trouble. Often they seem to write themselves out of your own absorption and excitement in what is happening. But "think stuff," descriptions, and transition scenes frequently must be labored over and hauled and tugged out on paper.

OVERCOMING WRITER'S BLOCKS

You must be prepared to work on the bad days, when nothing seems to come right, as well as the good, productive ones. At such times, your professional attitude must see you through—with some help from your workbook.

If you hit a block, it often means that you have not given enough thought to that particular part of the story. Don't fret and stew—unproductively. Instead, consult your workbook and *think constructively,* confident that the solution will come to you. Check over the outline, the characters and their problems, the opposition, the complications. Use the "What if . . ." method until the right answer comes to you— and then the words will flow again.

15
The Beginning – Getting Your Story
Off to a Running Start

How you begin depends on the kind of story you want to tell.

If it is to be an *action* tale – an adventure – think up an arresting incident with which to start it off. If you are going to rely heavily on the *mood,* then play up the interesting or exotic setting. Should yours be a *character* story, present the main character in a fresh, exciting way. Make this person sound like someone around whom things happen.

The beginning is your chance to catch the interest of the reader, at a moment when there is the most curiosity about what you have to offer. At the same time, your reader is not yet involved with your story people, or what happens to them. Before the reader's attention strays to something else, you must seize and hold it.

No matter what exciting things *you* know are going to happen on page five or ten or fifty, your readers (and your first reader is that important someone in the editor's office) will not stay with you that long unless you snag them on page one and lure them into reading on.

WHAT YOU MUST
ACCOMPLISH IN YOUR
STORY OPENING

1. *Catch the interest of your reader.* The most important consideration in working out your opening is the audience for whom your story is intended. With this in mind, present characters in whom your particular reader is likely to be interested, doing something which is likely to be of interest. If your opening action concerns characters who are much older or much younger than the reader, he or she will reach for another book on the shelf.

2. *Introduce the characters.* Since the reader has been preconditioned to assume the first character to be introduced is the main character, be sure to open immediately with that character on stage and show the story through his or her viewpoint. It is seldom possible or necessary to introduce or even to mention all the characters in the beginning, but the existence of each one should be indicated in some way as soon as practical.

So get the main character in. Introduce him or her by name — *all of it.* Indicate personality or background quality. The first glimpse of your hero should put the reader in sympathy with the person. Show him or her as a likable person, with some human weaknesses and troubles, but willing to fight.

If you must open your story with just one character on the scene, be sure to show him or her *doing* something interesting before you allow the character to think about anything. You can simplify the job of characterization by having an animal, a creature he or she can talk to or pet. (See Chapters 5, 6 and 7, dealing with the creation of characters. Take special note of the "camera view" for describing your viewpoint character, in Chapter 6.)

3. *Set the stage.* The reader must know what the setting is: the time, place, and social atmosphere. You must let him or her know at once if you are dealing with the present or if this is a period piece, a space opera, or some other kind of fantasy. (See Chapter 10.)

4. *Introduce the problem* or the situation that will bring on the problem — the sooner the better in a book; right away in a short story.

5. *Set the mood.* Letting the reader know what kind of emotional tone will dominate your story is one of the best means to catch his or her interest. (See Chapter 9.) Indicate quickly whether one may expect to laugh or cry, feel romantic, brave with adventure, or all shivery over a mystery. You can do this with some typical dialogue, a characterization, or your description of the setting.

6. *Suggest the complication.* Begin to reveal the story gradually by hinting at the various things to come — not necessarily the main problem, for it may take time to develop

and reveal it (in a book), but indicate some difficulties that
beset your hero or heroine.

7. *Hint at the solution.* Even in the beginning, the final
solution of your hero's or heroine's dilemma must be prepared for, so that when it comes, it will be convincing.

One way to make fiction believable is to *show* the readers
how things happen and *prepare* them for things that *might*
happen. Such preparation beforehand consists of two literary devices called *plants* and *pointers.*

When an author *plants* something, he or she lets the
reader know that certain conditions exist. The author might
plant the knowledge of certain skills the character has, or
equip him or her with special characteristics — courage,
stubborn perseverance, or a lively curiosity — which will
then lead the character into or out of certain situations.
(See Chapter 6.)

Your beginning should be full of *plants* that unobtru-
sively inform the reader and make everything that happens
in your story later sound plausible to him.

To *point* or *foreshadow* is to indicate that a certain thing
might, could, or will happen later on in the story. This device differs from the *plant* in that it suggests an *event* that
will follow.

The seven points of the opening, as I have outlined them
for you, must be covered quickly and effectively, in an interesting manner. They need not be used in the order in which
I have given them, but until they are covered, your beginning is not complete.

HOW TO WRITE
YOUR OPENING

There are various ways to write your story beginning. Narrative exposition is the poorest, because it just tells and explains, without *showing* the characters in action or allowing
them to say a word. A much sounder way to begin a story
is to show your main character in an interesting setting,
doing something of interest to the reader, and talking with
at least one other story actor. Be sure to mix thought, action, and dialogue — and never use any of these unless they
move the story forward.

Incidentally, when you begin with action, don't throw a

terrific slam-bang scene at the reader before he or she knows who is fighting whom for what and with which! The reader should never stand on the sidelines and wonder which side to cheer. Your reader should always cheer for the hero or heroine — so let him know as quickly as possible who the hero or heroine is and what worthy cause he or she is fighting for.

The best place to begin your story is where the flow of events leads directly into the action your main character must take in order to get what he or she wants. Whatever the story, the beginning should have lots of dramatic potentials, and then a turning point for contrast — anticipation of one thing and getting something else, for example.

THE WAY TO DO IT

Now let's take a look at the beginnings from two short stories. Remember the basic rule about an opening. In your first sentence, your main character must be doing or saying something. *Never* begin with a paragraph where you the author tell the reader the background of the main character. Action and dialogue are the key words when planning a story opening that will immediately seize the reader's interest. And the action or dialogue lead the reader not only into the story but also to the problem facing the main character.

Action Beginning: Here is the opening from Sam Zotian's short story, "The Mysterious Power."

> As she slowly kicked a crumpled brown bag across the school playground, Karen wondered why she had never noticed that particular light fixture before today.
>
> "I guess there isn't anything *that* unusual about it — except for the flashing!"
>
> The vision of that bare bulb flickering on and off under its battered green shade gave her goose bumps. It was only an outdoor light fixed to the concrete side of the school building. But every time she saw those flashes, Karen got the feeling that some mystical force was present. And that light wasn't the only mystery that had puzzled her since her arrival at Harris Hill School.
>
> The main thing she couldn't figure out was how to get accepted by the other fifth-grade girls. No one had really been unfriendly to her. But she was a newcomer — an outsider.

A minor point to note. Earlier, the way of writing thoughts was shown. In this opening segment, Sam Zotian gave us the actual words that entered Karen's mind. There was a definite reason. Basically, the opening is composed of several paragraphs of action and thoughts. To give us the *feeling* of dialogue before any actually appears, Mr. Zotian wrote Karen's thoughts as an internal dialogue.

Dialogue Beginning: Through the opening dialogue between Wade and his doctor in Arnold Madison's short story, "My Best Shot," we are moved right into the story as well as being offered clues about characterization, background, and Wade's desperate situation.

> I stared at Dr. Nemachek. "You're warning me that the operation might not work."
>
> "Wade, we need everything going for us we can get."
>
> "What else can I do? I feel good about your skill. And I accept there's only a sixty-forty chance the operation will succeed. Now it's up to you and science."
>
> "Maybe not."
>
> Dr. Nemachek wiped a palm across his chin. He was a top neurosurgeon flown in from Houston just for my operation. And he'd been honest with me. Yes, the operation *might* restore feeling to my legs which had been paralyzed since the drunk driver smashed into me. How I hated that kid who had done this to me.
>
> Sighing, Dr. Nemachek said, "I understand they're bringing in a roommate for you today. Perhaps company will change your attitude."
>
> "Attitude?"
>
> "Time is running out, Wade. I can't operate until the conditions are right. And I do have other operations scheduled in Houston."

Notice that although we label these two openings as either action or dialogue, they are not exclusively that. The action beginning contains the other two of the Big Three: dialogue (of a sort) and the thought of the main character. On the other hand, the dialogue opening also provides action and the leading player's thoughts. Always keep the Big Three of fiction in mind: action, dialogue, thoughts of the main character. New authors tend to neglect one or two of these in story beginnings.

The beginning extends to the point where the problem confronting your main character is clear to the reader.

Now the main character should decide to *do* something about his or her problem or goal, or should be precipitated into doing something about it by some outside influence or force.

This is the real takeoff point for your story: *the day that is different,* the day your hero or heroine is no longer content to put up with the situation. And this brings *you* into the problem of your story's middle.

16
And Then . . . ? Problems of Your Story's Middle

Now you must begin to fulfill the interesting promises of your story opening as you clarify the *why* (motivation) of your main character and reveal *how* he or she copes with his situations.

The moment the character leaves the safety island of "things as they are" he or she must be confronted by a barrier of opposition. Each obstacle, whatever its form, presents a problem to be solved, a disaster to be averted, or an opponent to be overcome. But such is the nature of successful storytelling that the solving of one problem must immediately bring on more difficulties. The hero or heroine must leap from the frying pan into the fire.

In your story middle you must have a course of ups and downs—of "furtherances" toward the character's ultimate goal, and of "hindrances" that thwart and frustrate attempts to succeed in his or her purpose. These must occur at irregular intervals, so that the reader will not be able to anticipate success or failure on your character's part and lose the excitement of suspense and curiosity as to how it will all come out. He or she will never stop reading as long as there is an incompleted situation presented.

One simple device that will keep him or her reading from chapter to chapter is never to end a chapter on a completed incident. Break it off at a crucial, suspenseful moment, and pick it up again in the next chapter.

YOUR STORY— SCENE BY SCENE
Scenes expand your story synopsis or outline into dramatized units of action. A story should be divided into different

scenes to give the reader action as well as a change of setting.

In a short story you must be wary of skipping around and
thereby creating a jerky effect. But in a book you have far
greater freedom. A chapter might require three, four, or
more scenes to complete its purpose. But in either story
form, once your main character has set about solving his or
her problem, *every subsequent scene should reveal some
sort of struggle or conflict, or the solving of a problem, with
a carry-over of interest which makes one scene flow into
another with unbroken continuity.*

Make a practice of thinking your story through in
scenes—like segments of your main character's life, each
against its own definite background.

Each scene must move your story forward. Its action
must be an outgrowth of what went before, and in itself,
support and *cause* or *affect* the action that will follow. This
is the test of a scene's importance to the story: *If it is really
vital to the plot, it cannot be cut out without damaging
the story.* The removal of a *necessary* scene would leave a
gaping hole in your story tapestry, as jarring to the eye as
the leaving out of a bar of music from a familiar melody
would be to the ear.

TRANSITIONS

Characters and readers must often be moved from place to
place, from one time to another, and from one emotion to
another mood. The device for such changes is called the
transition. It may consist of only a few words, but sometimes a paragraph or a longer passage may be involved
when several of these objectives must be accomplished, or
when some thinking needs to be done by a character after
a period of particularly lively action. The reader cannot sus-
tain the same high pitch of interest indefinitely. Like your
main actor, the reader needs a rest scene now and then.
This is where the transition can take the form of a "think-
over," a recapitulation of events that went before, and perhaps a reaffirmation of the goal ahead.

Lazy or inexperienced writers sometimes avoid the transition and plunge the reader from one event or time to another by the easy device of leaving three or four lines of
blank space between paragraphs. *Don't!* The abrupt change

of thought or scene is bound to jolt the reader out of your story's life. As the reader "comes to" and notices the white space and maybe looks at the clock, he or she may also say, "Here's a good place to put the book (or story) down." For keeps! And no author wants to put such a notion into the reader's head. On the contrary, you want your readers to feel that they can't possibly put your story down — not until they have finished it and know how it all came out.

Smooth, easy transitions make scenes dovetail and continuity remain unbroken, even though one sentence can move the story forward a day, an hour, or a year. For clarity, it is best to put transition words first; use very little detail; summarize quickly and get on with the story. In time transitions it is permissible to use the simplest phrases: "that night," "the next day," "two weeks later." But do avoid tired clichés and florid phrases: "time passed," "winter came at last," "the day dawned bright and clear."

There are many ways to word a transition. Add the search for samples to your study of published material. And remember, *the object of the transition is the same as that of a shortcut; to get from here to there — fast.*

FLASHBACKS

When it is necessary to retell some background event or experience that *now* motivates the character's actions or clarifies his or her present attitude toward something, the device used is called a *flashback.* It must be used skillfully, or it will bring the present action of the story to a grinding halt. The young reader is far more interested in what is happening *now* and in what is going to happen *next* than in what occurred last summer, or last year, or ten years ago. The necessary flashback must be worked into the story line imperceptibly, so that the reader is in and out of it — and properly informed — without being aware of the literary maneuver.

Sometimes bits of what went before can be woven into the story, as in the following example. In "The Case of the Disappearing D. J." by Arnold Madison, a flashback is needed to show why the seventeen-year-old heroine is having recurring nightmares.

With a start, Kristy Martin was awake. She lay still a moment, the sheets damp from her perspiration. Again. That dream. The nightmare that was real. The reality that had become a nightmare.

She dragged the pillow upright behind her, sitting and hugging her knees under the covers. The action stilled the shivers pulsing through her body.

A month and a half had passed since the accident. Why couldn't she remember? All that ever came back was the image of Dad walking toward her. Then, the headlights — growing larger until everything ended in an exploding flash. . . .

The hit-and-run killer was free. She was the only witness to her father's death, and her mind refused to yield the memory.

Something a character sees can trigger a mental flash-back. Any object can become a symbol that jogs the memory and sends us into another type of flashback: the fully drama-tized variety. In this kind of flashback, the scene is fully written as if it was happening like any other scene in the story.

In another story, seventeen-year-old Pete, his memories stirred by a kitchen ornament, is remembering his girlfriend of the previous summer.

Dad talked to the agent about a motel in Stag's Leap that was teetering on bankruptcy, so Pete sat, gazing around the kitchen. Above the sink, copper gelatin salad molds lined the wall: once functional, now ornamental. A raised flower design. A cluster of bulbous grapes. A sea horse. The last, the curved creature, ignited a memory.

Jones Beach. Long Island. Last summer. Jan had carried her baby sister, Debbie, as they had walked along the concrete espla-nade by the West Bathhouse. The heated air had been tinged with the odor of iodine from the ocean ahead of them; the white sand blindingly bright. As usual, Pete had left his sneakers and socks in the car, figuring there would be less to carry back and forth to the beach, and, as usual, he had regretted the action.

"Yeow!" The hot surface underfoot made him think of those Asians who trod on burning coals. "Walk faster."

Jan increased her pace, but smiled wickedly.

The last thing he needed, Pete decided, was a girlfriend who knew how to smile evilly. He danced about, trying to find a cooler spot on the sun-bleached concrete.

"Jesus Christ! This stuff is hot."

Four-year-old Debbie laughed. "Why's Pete walking so funny?"

"Pete's walking funny," Jan said, "because he's trying to be macho."

"Aw, shit!" Pete leaped from side to side, trying to move forward at the same time. "Does this look macho to you? I feel like a fool."

Jan's straw sandals slip-slapped along the gritty walkway that was coated with windblown sand. "Why don't you wrap our towels around your feet?"

"Very funny. I'd look like the homeless in Africa."

A hop to the right and one to the front. The beach appeared miles away rather than the actual few hundred feet. He skipped along the concrete, landing on a sea horse, a mosiac of large shapes of colored concrete, set in the fiercely hot, white surface. For some reason, the tinted pattern was cool. Well, not cool, but certainly *cooler.*

"Why the hell didn't they color the entire walk?" he asked, pain clouding his logic.

The reply came. But the voice wasn't from a Jones Beach July but an upstate New York March. Pete glissaded from concrete sea horse to copper sea horse to Mom who smiled at him, waiting. She had the expression of someone who had posed a question, fully expecting a positive answer.

"Don't you think it would be nice?" she asked, probably repeating herself.

The real test for the need of a flashback is whether or not it clarifies or intensifies what is happening now. The flashback we just saw of Pete and his girlfriend offers us a view of the girl he once dated as opposed to a character in the story—a girl that he is dating now, whom we'll meet in the novel's next chapter.

If the flashback does not *add* anything to the main story you do not need it. In fact, you should not use it because it is then merely padding that interrupts the flow of your story. But if it does contribute something to the reader's knowledge, then flashback quickly. Dramatize it as much as necessary, and then get back into current flow of the story.

And that "flow" is now carrying us to the story climax and conclusion.

17
Climax Scene and Ending

Every scene in your story should lead up to the dramatic final climax. Your main character's path should become increasingly difficult—with the main problem or goal still out of reach—when he or she arrives at the point where a decision must be made. Depending on what your story is about, the decision might be to fight or flee; to abandon a goal or press on. Under certain circumstances it might even involve the sacrifice of some hard-won prize.

The necessity to make a fateful decision should bring on a crisis in the main character's affairs—"life or death" for all his or her desires. The person is plunged into the blackest of black moments. Success or failure hangs in the balance, and only the leading player can take the decisive step. What will he or she do?

Here must come the most intense struggle for the main character—and the highest point of interest in the story— the *climax*. The reader should want the hero to succeed, to make the right decision. Sometimes the reader knows what that should be. But will the hero know? The eagerness to find out should make the reader take a firmer grip on the book. A good climax will not allow him or her to let go and do something else. How often have you delayed some task because you just *had* to finish a story you were reading? That's the sort of climax you should try to write!

THE MUSTS OF A
SUCCESSFUL CLIMAX
Exploit every possibility for a smashing emotional outburst among your story actors. And above all, don't get lazy and

skip the big explosion altogether! I have seen this done not only in student manuscripts but also in some that I have read for publishers — and rejected. Some writers bring their leading character to the brink of disaster — then blithely skip a few lines and show the main character being congratulated for solving the problem.

"Afterwards he couldn't tell exactly how it had happened, but there he was, safely at the bottom of the cliff" simply will not do. Readers always want to know *how* it happened. Not only that, they want to *see* it happen — and even *be there* vicariously when it does.

PLAY FAIR WITH THE READER

Never cheat your reader by dabbling in plots that deliberately set out to deceive, such as harrowing adventure tales or mysteries chopped off at the climax with the revelation that it's all been a dream. Editors do not look kindly on such shenanigans. The same holds true for "surprise twists" too surprising to be believed and stories where the author leaves the ending up to the reader.

The reader should be left with a sense of completeness, a sense of rightness, instead of with restless questions in his mind. It is the author's job to finish a story, not the reader's.

The story problem that is finally solved must not be a mistake or a misunderstanding that could have been cleared up anywhere along the line by a sensible main character. Such pseudoproblems can be made to come off in short stories, but it would be difficult, if not impossible, to hold the reader's interest with much ado about nothing for the length of a book. A humorous story can revolve around a comedy of errors caused by misunderstanding, but a more serious piece can only suffer from it.

CLIMAX AND CHARACTER

Since the solving of the main problem is of greatest importance to your main character, he or she is the one most affected by the climax. Thus, you must never show a minor character taking the lead at this point, for that would not only diminish your hero or heroine, but it would also de-

stroy the unity of purpose in your story by shifting the spotlight to the wrong person.

Concentration on *the* problem, by constantly "spotting"
the main character's goal, brings the character and the other
story people into focus, and makes all the action meaningful. It gives your story or book a definite beginning, a middle, a climax, and an end.

The main characters must get what they deserve, and they
must get it in a rousing, dramatic fashion. At this stage, that
very necessary ingredient, suspense, arises from the balanced struggle between the hero or heroine and the circumstances he must overcome, whether these be physical
or mental. Suspense is sustained by the reader's uncertainty
as to what the hero or heroine will do in the critical climax.
It is heightened by the conflict of emotions in the hero's or
heroine's heart and mind that keeps this person and the
reader sticking to the problem and fighting it out together.

In the climax of "Terror on Sunset Point" by Arnold Madison, the heroine Janice is trapped in a cave with a potential
murderer. All through the story, there had been a rivalry
between Jan and her prettier sister, Lianna, as well as the
need for Jan to sort out her feelings about Chip, the leader
of the hiking club. The climax of the story must clear up the
external plot of the suspense story, and also resolve the
problems of the sisters' emotions, and those of Chip and
Janice. Another quality of the climax and ending is that
these jobs be done dramatically and succinctly as possible.

> Stones rattled near the entrance. Greg swung the flashlight, but
> kept close watch on Jan. Lianna, calm and bright-eyed, walked
> into Greg's light.
> "Only me," she said.
> Lianna must have known Greg's plan. In fact, she would proba-
> bly have got help for him when the group returned to L.A. Lianna
> smiled at Jan.
> "You have all the brains in the family. But I'm going to have all
> the money. Greg's father will get us out of the country, and we're
> going to get married." Lianna walked a few steps closer, coming
> to Greg's side. "He's all a girl could ever want."
> The trap was sealed. Lianna stood by the rock and Greg on the
> ledge by the water. No route existed for escape.
> "Some guys have it all," Greg said. "Looks, personality, and—
> ooof!"
> Lianna shoved Greg's chest so he fell backward, arms flailing,

into the water. His lighted flashlight spiraled down into the black sea water.

"Quick, Jan. Hurry!" Lianna dragged her toward the entrance.

The two girls stumbled and tripped as they followed the bouncing beam of Lianna's flashlight. Ahead, the mouth gaped. Freedom!

As Jan stepped outside, two strong arms wrapped around her. A scream was cut off by a powerful hand.

"It's all right. It's me—Chip," he whispered. "We want to get Greg."

The hand left her mouth, and Jan made out shadowy figures in the mist. Lianna had clicked off the light. Everyone was frozen: fog-wreathed statues on both sides of the cave mouth. A minute passed, three. Had Greg drowned? Five minutes. Footsteps crunched in the cave. Greg muttered a curse and took several more noisy steps. A deeper shadow separated from the black cave mouth.

Flashlights exploded into life. A soggy, dripping Greg stood confused in the circle of light. Pete Valdez stepped forward, his wallet opened in one hand and a silvery revolver in the other.

"Los Angeles Police. You're under arrest." A police badge in the wallet flashed as Pete slipped it into his back pocket and told Greg his rights.

Pete and Coach Veeder tied Greg's hands behind his back. With Greg safely bound, Pete handed the gun back to the coach.

"Thanks. That came in handy."

Coach Veeder's moustache flapped as he chuckled. "And I thought I'd only get a little target practice in."

As Pete and the coach led Greg away, Lianna came to Jan and wrapped her arms around her. "Oh, Jan. I was such an idiot. When we got here, Greg got me alone and told me his plan. He purposely made everyone angry with him so they'd think it was murder. I was supposed to get them thinking that way. The money sounded so wonderful."

Jan hugged Lianna. "The only one dumb enough to think that way was me. And I did it without your help."

"But tonight," Lianna said, "when you talked about Mom and us, I realized what a dummy I had been. I didn't know what to do."

Chip laughed. "So she ran up and down the hall, screaming for us to get up and save you. And—here we are—together again."

As Jan, Chip, and Lianna walked toward the stone ramp, Chip's arm slipped around Jan's waist and his other hand held hers. She felt encircled by strength and security.

"Together," he whispered huskily. "That's what you are lady. A together person, and I like that."

The trio walked through the wet sand, heavy whiteness floating around them. Jan remembered this morning. Yes, Mom had again been right. Powerful hands had come toward her all right. But a girl had to pick and choose when it came to powerful hands. And she wanted the ones that held her right now.

THE COME-TO-REALIZE ENDING

But all climax situations are not like that. Often, in stories for young people, there is a *come-to-realize climax and ending.*

This must be handled with special care. It will be weak and unconvincing if the main character *comes-to-realize* whatever it is he or she should do or avoid doing *alone* — by thinking things out and making a decision, for example, or by reading a letter. A climax will also be weak if someone tells the main character to change his or her ways, and he or she does. Real people simply don't behave that way and every young reader knows it.

The best method for resolving this kind of an ending is to have something happen to your main character to *make* him or her "come-to-realize." It should be some powerful personal experience that shocks, rocks, or even floors him or her. Whatever it is, it must have a terrific impact. A scene with these elements is bound to produce action and drama and an emotional involvement for the reader. Then you should have a quiet scene, for the change in the main character must in no way resemble instant magic. The hero should think over what has happened and realize the impact and implications, and resolve to change course or mend his or her ways. Readers will not lose interest because now they will have another question in their minds: *Does the person mean it?*

Next comes the clincher for this kind of ending: you must devise a scene in which the hero or heroine can *prove* that he or she has indeed changed. This is absolutely essential. Worked out this way, the "come-to-realize" ending is effective and satisfying.

CONCLUSION

Stop when your story ends! Once the hero has surmounted all difficulties and solved the problems, your story is over.

The original situation has changed considerably, and so has the character—and it was all brought about by the events in the story. If you handled the writing technique properly, your readers *saw* it happen; they even *lived* through it. So don't rehash everything over again in a compulsive summation. The readers are no longer in your grip, once the suspense element of "how it will all come out" is gone. Let them go with a graceful parting.

Your story really ends with the climax, you know, but because the readers don't want to leave the delightful people in your book, they stay around for the *resolution,* the final disentanglement and outcome of the character's affairs. So tie up the little ends, and close the story *inside* the main character, in his or her thoughts, which reveal his or her true feelings.

Never end the story with a scene between minor characters. All secondary plot threads should be tied up before the big climax. In the conclusion, be brisk, be brief, and be gone.

18
How to Revise . . . and Polish

No story or book should ever go to a publisher hot off the typewriter. What may seem flawless to you in the heat of creation can turn out to be anything but—in the cool of reason a month or so later. Never send out anything that is not your absolute best. It may not be perfect—even the work of our most distinguished writers isn't always that—but *it must be the best of which you are capable at that moment in your writing career.*

It's not writing but *rewriting* that makes a smooth-flowing tale. And although many writers groan over revision, it is easier than creation. You have something to work *on*; you are not pulling a story out of imagination's skein. And you are not working in marble, but on paper. Words can be easily changed.

Your just-completed short story (a book is another matter) must be put away to cool in a file folder, and you should get *busy immediately on your next project.* When that is finished, proceed with the next one, and perhaps the one after that, so you have two or more stories "on ice" and something in work before you attempt to read and revise the first one. Your subconscious may continue to flash out ideas for all sorts of changes and interpolations in the completed stories. Jot these down, slip them into the proper story folders for consideration later, *and go on with whatever you're currently writing.*

This enforced cooling-off period will sharpen your critical faculties. If you read your first draft immediately on completion, you may become enchanted with the sheer beauty of your words, the splendid delineation of your characters, the remarkable ramifications of your plot, and the terrific climax, to say nothing of the "Monumental Significance" of the whole opus!

On the other hand, you may go to the opposite extreme and decide that the manuscript is worthless — and tear it up. Every now and then a student admits to such an act of waste and foolishness. Never, never allow yourself to destroy an irreplaceable draft in a fit of hypercritical melancholy, caused by a lack of proper perspective.

The mind works faster than the hand; that's why the brilliant passages we compose in our heads are often disappointing when we view them on paper. Something gets lost in the transcription to type — but in revision we have a second chance to recapture the magic of the original concept, and improve upon it.

With a long book, however, there's no need to wait. By the time the project is finished, you should be able to read it from the beginning with a fairly level head.

COMMON FAULTS
OF FIRST DRAFTS

Book or short story, most first drafts are wordy and can be improved by cutting and pruning. Sentences are likely to be long and involved. These should be untangled and simplified. For very easy reading, experts recommend sentences of eight to ten words, or less. Relatively easy reading calls for sentences of no more than eleven to fourteen words. The standard length for sixth, seventh, and eighth grades is seventeen to twenty words, while anything over that falls into the "difficult" category. This does not mean that you can't have an occasional extra long sentence.

Difficult words that can be understood in the context of the sentence may be used here and there, but too many will prove stumbling blocks to the reader. Nothing should interfere with the flow of your story. Check such words and find easier substitutes for them.

The healthiest attitude you can cultivate toward your work is one that admits that nothing you've set down on paper is sacred or unchangeable. Such an attitude is one of the marked differences between the professional and the amateur. The "pro" willingly discards pages, even chapters, shifts scenes for the best effects, and rewords "finished" writing again and again.

Skillful revision can make the difference between salable and unsalable material, so it is very much to your advantage to master every step of this process. The best preparation for revision is familiarity with effective writing techniques and the components of story structure. These have been progressively detailed in every chapter of this text.

FOUR-STEP PLAN FOR REVISION

I revise and rewrite to some extent all through the first draft of a book. Whenever I reread the previous day's output, I inevitably find some things I want to change. With the book finished, I'm ready for the "Four-Step Plan," which can also be adapted for revising short stories:

1. *A quick, silent reading, for an overall impression* — and I try to be as beady-eyed and objective as possible. Whenever I come to a passage that jars me even slightly, I make a marginal check next to it. I do not stop to analyze and correct then and there. Continuity and pace are the most important factors in this reading.

2. *Next I analyze my reactions.* Does the main character stand out as an interesting individual? Is it possible to identify with him? Do all the story actors who surround him appear to be real people? Is the main character's problem or goal important and worth struggling for? Is it a problem that is suitable for a young person of his age? Will it concern the young readers for whom this story is intended?

What about conflict? Is the opposition strong? Are there enough complications thwarting the main character's struggles to solve his or her problem or reach his or her goal? Or are there so many that the story sounds like soap opera? How about background details, atmosphere, a sense of movement? Will the reader feel enough suspense to keep turning the pages to the very end to see how it all comes out?

Descriptions get a thorough scrutiny. Are they interwoven with characterization, dialogue, action? Are the five senses utilized to heighten the reality of the details? Has the *effect* of the sensation on the characters been described instead of dull, declarative statements given that make the reader yawn?

If questions like these raise doubts in your mind about *your* story, jot them on a work sheet, and then track down the technique for handling them in the various chapters of this text.

3. *In step three I concentrate on the structural components* of my story: the beginning, middle, climax, and end. Is each part of my story (or book) handled in the most effective way possible?

Have I begun at the right point? Have I begun as close as possible to the "day that is different"? Have I covered the seven points of the story opening as outlined in Chapter 15?

When you come to this point in revising your material, make a check list based on the contents of Chapters 15, 16, and 17 and consider your story accordingly. Questions raised in your mind now may lead you further back into the text, to the chapters on plotting, sensory details, or dialogue.

Now you should read parts of the manuscript *aloud* to yourself, with a minimum of "expression" which might deflect your attention from flaws in the writing. You can catch many problems by ear such as poor, awkward phrasing, unrealistic dialogue, or slow-paced action.

Do not work on more than two or three chapters a day. You must be fresh and alert to do your best. If you stay too long at revision, you'll tire. As your mind grows less clear, you'll become permissive and allow all kinds of rough spots to get by.

If your work requires a great deal of rewriting, limit yourself to no more than two hours at a stretch. At the end of a set work period, leave your desk and occupy yourself with something entirely different for half an hour or so — some physical action, a household task, or perhaps a short brisk walk. You'll return refreshed, and your manuscript will benefit from it.

4. *With this step we come to the final processing of the manuscript* — the polishing: word-editing, the grace notes, the literary embellishments which give professional tone, sparkle, and *style* to your writing.

YOU AND YOUR STYLE

Next to plot, *style* rates as the number two mystery word for many writers. What is it? How can you acquire it?

A writer's style is indicated by his or her selection and arrangement of words. It depends on personality, outlook on life, the quality of his imagination; environment, family and social background (past and present); education (which continues to the end of his days through life experiences if nothing else); beliefs, ethics, ambitions, and frustrations; and subject matter.

Your writing style is you, modified by the type of expression your subject calls for. If you write on a variety of subjects, or about different kinds of people in many fields and circumstances, your *style,* your choice of words and their arrangement, are bound to vary with each story.

Never strain for "style." Never imitate the writing of some author you admire. Your style will emerge when you learn your craft and write with natural ease, a ready vocabulary, and an apt turn of phrase. With each piece you write strive to be clear, unself-conscious.

THE INDISPENSABLE WORD FINDERS

Now, as you polish, is the time to use a good dictionary and your *Roget's Thesaurus,* a word finder most writers rely on. It is available in paperback, but the book gets such a workout that a hardbound edition is more practical.

THE FINE-TOOTH COMB

Make sure you have used the right word in the right place for maximum effect. Check the meaning of the words if you have any doubts as to their accuracy.

Do your words help to create the mood required by the different scenes in your story? Dreamy, romantic, adventurous, terrifying, elated, despairing—your words can, and must, convey what you want the reader to feel.

Clarity is achieved through the use of the familiar word in preference to the unfamiliar, as *hero,* instead of *protagonist, thin,* instead of *attenuated.* Short words are preferable to long, erudite words, which merely seem labored and affected. Always use the concrete word instead of a general term: *shot-gun,* rather than *weapon,* which might be anything from a club to a stiletto.

The single word is preferable to a phrase as a rule: instead of "Jill *ran quickly* across the courtyard," say "Jill *raced. . . .*" It even sounds faster.

Take out the extra words in sentences which only clutter, not clarify what you are trying to say. Delete excessive adverbs and beloved adjectives (which Clifton Fadiman calls the "banana peels" of our language). Instead of weak modifiers, use strong, colorful action verbs which will make for tighter, more vigorous writing. Analyze the action you want and then find the verb to convey the proper image to the reader's mind. If you mean that "Tony *limped* into the room," don't say, "Tony walked in slowly."

Beware of flat-wheeled, nondescriptive verbs such as *came, ran, walked.* There are dozens of substitutes for this imageless collection; all you need to know is the exact *action* of your character. What did he or she do? Stride, strut, trudge, clump, thump, stagger, drag, fumble, stalk, hurtle, fly, thunder, float, dance, dart, creep, sweep, hobble, whirl? There are many more, and certainly the right one for your need.

As Mark Twain put it: *The difference between the right word and the almost right word is the difference between lightning and the lightning bug.*

Words that evoke no image in the mind of the reader are useless to the writer. Words that bring up the wrong images can destroy the story. Your story is an illusion—an imagined experience for the reader. Never jolt him or her out of the illusion by the use of the wrong word or phrase. If you find the illusion broken at any point get rid of that sentence, that word, that phrase.

SOME DO'S AND DON'T'S FOR THE INVISIBLE STORYTELLER

At all times remain the invisible storyteller, for therein lies your most powerful magic. Never break into the story flow with: "Now what do you suppose happened next?" Bringing the reader out of the story like that isn't fair. To *whom* is he or she to answer? You are not supposed to be there while your reader is reading!

Do not inject your opinions. If you feel strongly about something, wrap your ideas around the characters and let them voice the opinions and show them in action, but only if both the ideas and the action *belong* in the story.

Avoid redundancy — the use of needless words to express an idea, as "a blonde girl with light yellow hair." Snow is usually white, so there's no more need to say "white snow" than there is to say "green grass." If trees or mountains seem to reach the sky, the reader will assume they're tall. A four-foot man *is* short and a six-footer tall, so if you give the footage of either one, there is no need to say "short" or "tall" as well.

Watch out for silly actions that stop the reader cold. I once edited a manuscript in which a character "put on her glasses in order to hear better" — only this was long before they built hearing aids into the ear pieces. Here are some other gems that were caught in revision — and some, alas, that got by and were published:

> Betty took her head out of the locker and grinned.

> And he had a big sister who wore lipstick, a big bouncy dog, and a big piano. . . .

The published classic of them all is probably this one:

> Lincoln crossed his right leg over his left knee, and planted both feet solidly on the ground.

Eyes are sometimes required to perform strange feats also:

> The nurse looked at him with calm, horror-stricken eyes . . .

> The girl ran down to the water's edge and *cast her eyes* out to sea. . . .

> Wendy watched them, fascinated, *her eyes jumping back and forth* with the conversation, like a tennis ball in a match.

I reviewed a British book in which "Jill had to *screw up her eyes* to read. . . ." but then, eyes often are subjected to painful maneuvers. They pop, fall, rivet, swivel, drop, follow, cling — all seemingly independent of the character they belong to. Watch those eyes! Let them gaze occasionally, as well as look. And don't overwork them with stares.

WORD WEEDING
Among the words you'll want to weed out are the following; too many of them will mark you as an amateur:

very	but
then (and then)	looked
so	little
look	oh (or, OH!)
tiny	and
suddenly	just

There may be others on your personal string, like *well, clearly,* or *problem.* Be wary of any favorites you're apt to overwork.

Cut hesitant, noncommittal wording: "she *probably* knew," "he *seemed* to think," "he *obviously* felt." As the author you know if he did or didn't. Make such statements definite.

In the "what else" category are sentences like these:

> Mike *nodded his head.* [What else could he possibly nod but his head!]

Catch also the overloaded, earthbound phrases which sound very much like, "About to commence to start to begin," and streamline them.

THE GRACE NOTES
Figures of speech are the grace notes in your writing. Your ability to compose word images is a measure of your skill. Figures of speech sharpen the picture, spotlight a character or a scene so that it becomes more vivid and real. They make the reader *feel* much more intensely, heightening his or her emotional reaction to your story. They serve another purpose by eliminating the dozens of less colorful words it takes to get the same idea across.

Using figurative language involves the ability to see similarities between one thing and another. A thin, tall boy; an excitable girl; a tiny, nervous woman; a big, roaring bully of a man—*what does each resemble?* Sometimes comparisons flash into your mind by happy accident, but as a rule such image-making is a cultivated skill. Whenever figures of speech come to you, jot them down on file cards or in your notebook, then pull them out as you need them to strengthen passages you are polishing. Never stop the flow of creative thought to search for apt figurative language.

You have already been introduced to this process in Chapter 10, dealing with sensory details. The important thing is not to succumb to clichés, those deft phrases which have become trite through overuse.

For examples in tune with today's world, read fiction in the popular magazines. Poetry is full of imagery which can sensitize your mind. Browse through a good anthology now and then and see what it can do to enrich the color of your phrasing.

As an aid to developing this power-plus in your imagination, here is a brief listing of the most used figures of picturesque speech:

A *simile* is a comparison of one thing with another, linked by the words "like" or "as."

> Mr. Ormsby was as pale as a mushroom.

> The crowd closed around her like a wall.

The *metaphor* omits "like" and "as," and states boldly that one thing *is* another, which literally, it is not. This of course puts the matter in stronger terms and the effect is more dramatic. The metaphor may be used to characterize major and minor characters by emphasizing some personal trait:

> Oliver was a sheep. [Lacking in leadership qualities]

> A brown, shaggy bear of a man . . . [Suggests ruggedness]

Metaphor by itself, or combined with a simile, makes for effective descriptions:

> The revolving doors made Babs think of huge spools winding long strings of people in and out of the store.

Enthusiasm for figurative language sometimes produces a Frankenstein, the *mixed* metaphor. Two or more figures are incongruously combined, resulting in a confusing or even ludicrous image. Here is a classic example:

> Let's get our ship on its feet, men. Let us put our shoulders to the wheel and iron out all the bottlenecks.

Personification gives human characteristics to inanimate objects and things in nature. The device can be used to lend color and excitement to a narrative; to set a mood; to heighten suspense or a sense of danger:

> The cloud-hung mountain glowered at the two girls laboring up its steep side. With the next crash of thunder it sent a threatening rockslide of disapproval across their path, as if warning them to come no closer to the secret buried near its jagged peak.

In an entirely different mood:

> Snuggled inside the friendly arms of the wing chair, Ellin listened as the warm summer rain whispered and chuckled in the eaves.

Whatever figure of speech is used, it must fit the mood, period, setting, and characters of your story. The comparisons must be within the range of experience of the age for which you are writing. A seacoast story should not have figures of speech that compare anything there to life on a desert, a dairy farm, or a lumber camp. Somebody's Aunt Hetty might scream like a gull—at the seashore—and gabble like a turkey on an inland farm.

Anachronisms must be avoided in figures of speech, similes, metaphors, and onomatopoeia. A seventeenth-century sound should not be compared to the whine of a twentieth-century jet; the swish of nylon does not belong in a Victorian England setting.

Any number of effective word pictures can be worked out with the basic group of grace note patterns given here. A dictionary of literary terms or a book on rhetoric will detail others for you, but remember: A story top-heavy with "images" is as badly crafted as one full of clichés. Moreover, you are primarily a storyteller, not a phrase-monger. This should be a comfort to those of you who simply do not see things figuratively—or at least, not without a great deal of labored thought. The grace notes, while desirable, are not indispensable, and their absence is less likely to be noticed unfavorably than an extravagant bedecking of your prose.

The more you learn about the craft of writing, the more critical you will become of your own output. However, like all good craftspersons, you must realize that there is a point beyond which tinkering will do more harm than good. By all means revise, and by all means polish, but within reason. When you've done your best, *stop*.

Your next step is to retype your manuscript for professional submission.

19
How to Prepare Your Manuscript for Submission

A professional-looking manuscript suggests professional competence in the writer; make the most of this psychological advantage!

Your manuscript must be typed. Either pica or the smaller elite type may be used, but be consistent throughout. Otherwise it will be difficult to estimate the length of your work. Do not use fancy type that writes everything in italics, or Old English, or capital letters. And if you use a computer, do not submit a manuscript printed with an inexpensive matrix printer. Many have styles that are difficult to read.

Use a good grade of white bond paper with some rag content, for it will stand up better than the sulphite papers, on which erasures can make holes as well as ugly blurs. My own preference is an 8½-by-11-inch, sixteen-pound bond for original copies. (Twenty-pound costs more to buy and mail, and anything lighter will wear-and-tear too easily.)

Although erasable papers have some advantages, I've given in to plaintive cries from my editors and no longer use them. Penciled editorial corrections smudge, and the whole lines that should stand are too easily erased.

For carbon copies I like the inexpensive, sixteen-pound, smooth finished bond (no rag content) because it is durable, takes a clear imprint, and does not smudge as readily as the soft finishes. In making multiple copies I use colored sheets to make collating simpler (yellow, green, pink). The pink copy I usually keep for my own files.

Standard weight carbon, suitable for making as many as five copies at a time, is satisfactory. Thinner carbon curls annoyingly.

Always make at least one carbon copy of any work submitted for publication, preferably two or even three. One copy *must* go into your file; the others (especially in the case of a book) may be required for the artist, for book club consideration, or for submission for foreign rights.

PEN NAMES

If you decide to use a *nom de plume,* select it with care; once you have started to build a new name for yourself, you won't want to change your mind and begin all over again.

You may choose to adopt a pen name for various reasons. You might have a name that is difficult to pronounce and therefore remember; you may simply want a more euphonious name than the one you have. Editors have no objection to pen names, provided the writer does not hop from one to another (your "name" is important to your publisher too).

The legal aspects of adopting a pen name can be easily arranged. See an official at your bank to make a proper record of your professional name. Clear proof that you are *you* under two names should eliminate any problem in opening an account (or changing one) in your new name or in paying taxes on savings bank interest. A checking account in your pen name only, however, may cause trouble later for your heirs. Thus, as an extra precaution, let your lawyer know your pen name and have it duly recorded in your will.

Notify the Post Office. There you don't have to explain anything to have mail duly delivered to your new name at the same address. Before long the mailman will come to realize that you're a writer! And he'll sigh when he brings in those fat envelopes with rejected manuscripts and grin broadly when the thin (check) envelopes arrive.

THE FORMAT

A book manuscript should have a title or cover page. Short material does not require this, but it's a good idea to have it anyway because it helps to keep the script looking fresh through several submissions.

Do not decorate the cover page in any way even if you are an accomplished artist. The only things that belong on this page are your name and address in the upper left hand corner (an inch or so from the top); the approximate number of words in your manuscript on a line at the right; and halfway down the page, centered neatly, the title of your story. Two or three lines below this, center the word "by," and two or three lines below that, type your name — or pseudonym — *exactly as you want it to appear in print.* (If a pseudonym is used in your byline, type it in parentheses under your legal name in the heading of this page so your editor won't think your real name is the name of your agent.)

If your manuscript is book length, there will usually be a table of contents and sometimes a preface or some introductory material. This is known as "front matter" and should be typed on separate sheets and numbered in the upper right corner in small Roman numerals. A dedication (also typed on a separate page) may be included or supplied after the book is accepted.

Your first page of text should also have your name and address (single spaced) on the left, about one-half inch from the top of the page. (This repetition is a must in case the title page should somehow be lost.) Type in the approximate number of words at top right, as shown in the sample format opposite.

Under this some people indicate the "rights" they are offering for sale. On a book manuscript, *don't.* These rights should be negotiated after the book is accepted and the editor invites you to talk over your contract. (See the chapter on markets and marketing.)

On a short story, leave out such beginner's trademarks as "For Sale," or "Usual Rights — Usual Rates." The editor knows that script is for sale, and rates are set by company policy.

The stipulation of "First Serial Rights Only" (which means the right to publish first, and once only in that particular magazine for the fee paid you), is acceptable to some magazines but not to others, whose policy is to buy all rights. In that case the editor may prefer to return the story to you unread rather than argue with you. In any event, such notices on the manuscript afford scant legal protection. *The rights specified on the check or voucher in pay-*

Your Legal Name
(Pen Name)
Street Address
City, State, Zip Code   About _____ words

CENTER YOUR TITLE IN CAPS
by
Your Name

Begin your story three or four spaces below your name. Indent
paragraphs three to five spaces. <u>Always double space your copy,
and type only on one side of the paper</u>. Double space between
paragraphs.

    Letters, telegrams, etc. used within the text should also be
double spaced and be given an extra identation.

    <u>For pica type</u>, margins should be 1-½″ at the top and left and
about one inch on the right and bottom. <u>For elite type</u>, use 1-¼″
on all four sides.

    Beginning with page two, type your last name or a key word
from the title in the upper

your name   2

left-hand corner in small letters and number the pages consecutively in the upper right-hand corner.

Each chapter should begin on a new page. Number these
pages consecutively, never as separate units. Do not write
"More" or any other directions at the bottom of the page.

At the end of your story you may go down five spaces, center
the page, and tap the underlining bar a few times. But do not
write "The End," "Finis," etc. You may type your name and
address at bottom left on the last page.

Twenty-six lines per page is a good compromise between over-
crowding and too much white space. With the margins suggested, each line (in pica type) will have about 10 words. Twenty-six lines per page will average about 250 words. This makes
it simple to estimate the number of words in your manuscript.
The estimate is always approximate: to the nearest 25 or 50
words in a short story and to the nearest 100 in a book. Never
count every word.

Some typewriters can adjust to a one-and-a-half line space.
Do not use this capability. Editors hate it.

Remember that even the appearance of your typed page must
come under your scrutiny. Be sure paragraphs are of different
lengths so that the page does not have a dull, "measured off
with a ruler" appearance. Also, do not have a line of "He's" or
"She's" or "Susie's" beginning each paragraph all down the
page. It can happen and it looks terrible.

ment for your work, which you are required to sign, consti- tute the legal agreement between you and the publishing company. Rights need not be a matter of great concern, however. I have found that most magazines in the juvenile field are generous in returning unused rights after first pub- lication, and as a rule, book rights to the story are automati- cally retained by you. (More detail on the subject in the next two chapters.)

Your title should be dropped about one-third of the way down the page.

It is wise, by the way, to make two or three extra copies of the first page of your manuscript, and two or three of the last page. If the story is not immediately accepted, wear and tear on these pages is inevitable even with a cover sheet, and a travelworn appearance might prejudice an editor. After a number of submissions you can insert fresh copies, with type color to match the rest of the manuscript, and no one but you will be the wiser.

Consistency is important, so it is always wise to have your own "style sheet" handy. Some names can be spelled in several ways. On the style sheet mark down the variation you have used to avoid having *Edith, Edyth,* and *Edythe,* or *Terrie, Terry,* and *Terri* all in one story. Words like *blonde* and *blond* may be a problem. Hyphenation is optional in some cases. Consistency will endear you both to your editor and copy editor.

PUNCTUATION
AND GRAMMAR

In dialogue *a new paragraph is required with each change of speaker.* Any gesture, action, or thought of the speaker belongs in the same paragraph as his or her speech:

> Migsy thought hard. "I simply can't do it," she said at last. She pulled back her hair with both hands and suddenly started to run.

Words spoken in dialogue must be enclosed in double quotation marks. Anything quoted within a speech is then enclosed in single quotes:

> "Did you hear what she said? 'I won't go and you can't make me!' Did you hear that?" Miss Price quivered with indignation.

Too many commas in a sentence suggest that it might be

better to break it up and reword it. An exclamatory sentence should reveal itself to the reader through your choice of words. Resist the urge to use the exclamation mark for emphasis too often.

If you want a word, a sentence, or dialogue to have special emphasis, underline it. This means that you want it set up in italics. *Like this.* Foreign words and phrases are usually italicized. In fiction be sparing of both—the foreign words and the italics.

The possessive form of pronouns often nettles even experienced writers. *Hers, its, theirs, yours,* and *oneself* take no apostrophe before the "s." But for emphasis, it is permissible to write *one's self.*

Do not pepper your manuscript with dots (ellipses). Properly used in a story, three . . . indicate the trailing off of a speech (closed with quotation marks) or an incompleted thought or statement. If used in the body of a narrative, the dots indicate a scene shifting or a time jump. When a sentence is completed, the period is followed by three dots:

> He crawled to the edge of the cliff, utterly spent. . . . When he opened his eyes again, the sun was directly overhead.

The *hyphen* is used to join words, like *ten-year-olds,* or to divide a word which comes at the end of a typed line and must be carried over to the next line. Such words should be divided according to their syllables. If you're uncertain of this division, consult your dictionary.

The *dash* is used to indicate a break in thought or an insertion of another thought within the body of a sentence:

> Now that we're all here—except for Roger—let's get down to business.

In typewritten material a dash may be indicated with one stroke of the hyphen key, but then there must be one space before and after it. However, if you strike the hyphen key twice to indicate a dash in your work, no space is necessary. Whichever way you do it, be consistent throughout. A note on your personal style sheet will insure this. Be sparing in your use of dashes.

If you need more help with grammar and punctuation, consult a dictionary of English usage, or such books as *The*

Art of Readable Writing, by Rudolf Flesch or *The Elements of Style,* by Strunk and White.

PROOFREADING THE MANUSCRIPT

Your finished typescript must be proofread carefully. A blotter slid under the lines will slow down your pace and help you to spot errors more readily. Do not proofread for more than an hour at a time without a short "eye-break" or you'll begin to miss transposed letters and words inadvertently left out.

Corrections may be made in pencil, ink, or type. If a word, line, or lines should be omitted, simply draw a line through this material. A page with more than three conspicuous corrections must be retyped.

All corrections must be made on carbon copies also. The professional writer knows how important carbon copies are. Besides protecting him from a total loss of a manuscript (which does happen, though rarely), sometimes a page vanishes from material being readied for the printer. With a carbon on file, a new page can be produced easily and quickly.

HOW TO SEND YOUR MANUSCRIPT

Do not bind a manuscript in any way, or staple the pages; as they are turned for reading, creases inevitably will be made at the staple points. *Never* pin the pages together. Think of that rich editorial blood spilling over them and marking them forever, not to mention the editorial ire aroused by such an injury. Confine your page fastening of short works to the safe and efficient paper clip.

A manuscript of no more than four or five pages may be folded in thirds, like a business letter, and sent in a large business-size envelope (with another stamped, self-addressed envelope folded inside it for return of the material should it not be accepted).

Manuscripts of twelve to fifteen pages may be sent folded in half, in a 7-by-10 inch manila envelope with a 6½-by-9½-inch stamped return envelope fitted inside.

Manuscripts of more than fifteen pages must be sent flat.

You may put them in a plain protective folder which has been trimmed to slip easily into a 9-by-12-inch envelope. Do not fasten the pages in any way. Send the manuscript in a 10-by-13-inch envelope, using the 9-by-12 for return. Cardboard, cut to fit the smaller envelope, will prevent mishandling in transit much more effectively than stamping "Do not bend" on the mailing piece.

Never use decorated folders for your manuscripts, either the short stories or book lengths. The effect will not be pleasing, and will scream "raw beginner" to everyone in the publishing office.

A book manuscript travels best in a box—the kind your rag bond typing paper comes in, or one bought from a writers' supplies house. Make sure that the kind you choose is easy for an editor to open and close—some of the more elaborate boxes feature interlocking tabs and slots that make removing the manuscript a five-to-ten-minute operation! Check ads on this type of service in the writers' magazines. For a sturdy outside wrap for the box, use a cut-open brown paper grocery bag, secured with package sealing tape. Many authors prefer buying a jiffy bag sold in most stationery stores and mailing a book manuscript inside that padded envelope. They feel the minor expense is well compensated for by not having to cut paper bags, wrap boxes, and seal them with tape.

Do not turn any pages upside down to determine whether your manuscript is read. This, a favorite trick among beginners, raises editorial hackles. *All* manuscripts are read because the business of editors is to find publishable stories. However, it is no more necessary for the editor to read an entire story to know that it isn't for that house, than it is to eat a whole pot of stew to discover it has too little meat.

Although it is possible to copyright unpublished manuscripts, to do so is a waste of time and embarrassingly amateurish. Placing the word *copyrighted* or a large *C* on the first page alerts the editor that the writer is a rank beginner.

Do not worry about piracy. Unpublished material is quite safe with any reputable house. (New authors sometimes go to extraordinary lengths to prevent "piracy." One editor told me of a woman who submitted only every other page of her story to make sure *her* brainchild would not be stolen!) Actually you have an automatic, common-law copyright protection on your manuscript. You can validate your claim through the carbon copy of your work in your files, along with some dated material like notes, letters, or a submission record.

LETTERS TO THE EDITOR

Editors who spend many hours *reading* prefer not to read anything they don't have to—like superfluous letters from authors. Don't write to explain the story. Your manuscript must speak for itself. The editor also knows you've sent it because you hope to sell it, so don't include a letter stating something as obvious as that.

A letter is useful only if you have something pertinent to say about the story or yourself. If, for example, you're an expert in the field with which your story is concerned, say so. If some unusual fact is used in the plot, "document" it for authenticity. Many juvenile books are used in the classroom, so the editor must be sure that your statements are true, should a teacher or fact-happy youngster challenge them. In nonfiction and historical writing, documentation is very important, and all the references you have used should be listed at the front or back of your manuscript. This list may be mentioned in a letter to the editor.

By all means write a letter if a well-known author or critic has suggested that you send your story to a particular editor—but make this "introduction" a simple statement. Don't say the person is wild about your tale and thinks it exactly right for that particular publisher. Editors prefer to make up their own minds—and being human, they just might resent being pressured.

If your occupation has a bearing on your material, *do* mention it—briefly. Since you are writing for young people, the fact that you are (or have been) a teacher or librarian would be of interest to the editor. Should you be in any writing field, as with an advertising agency, mention it to suggest that you'd be willing to revise without tantrums, having been already conditioned by your job.

If you have sold or published anything anywhere, even if only a filler, mention that in your letter, listing the magazines, newspapers, or book publishers. But if you have no sales to your credit, don't worry about it. Editors are eager to discover talented newcomers.

Your own printed business stationery for correspondence with editors is a good investment to help promote your "solid citizen" image. Keep it simple—your name, address, and telephone number (including the area code) are all that is needed on your letterhead. Phrases like "Author," "Freelance Writer and Photographer," or "Specialist in Children's Literature" will mark you as an amateur.

FOR YOUR PEACE OF MIND

When you send the manuscript, include a stamped, self-addressed postal card, with the title of your story and the name of the publisher typed on the message side. Whoever handles the arriving manuscripts in the publisher's office will then fill in the blank spaces and drop the card into the outgoing mail, and you'll know that your material has arrived safely. (Some publishers do send company cards or letters acknowledging arrival of material, but some do not. This simple expedient will insure your knowing in either case.)

Your first submission to a magazine or book publishing house should be addressed to the editor by name. If your story is returned with a signed note of any kind by some other person in the editorial department, then address your next submission there to the person who wrote you. Most editorial departments keep an eye on promising people, and the individual who wrote you will be your "contact editor" at the office.

THE WAITING GAME

Magazines, on the average, take from three weeks to two months to report on a story. Book publishers take three months or more—much more, sometimes. No matter how impatient you are to *know*, do not inquire about your manuscript until two months have passed. Then expedite matters with a tracer letter to the editor. Be polite and brief:

Dear Mr./Miss/Mrs./Ms. (Name of Editor):
Would you please let me know the status of my story, (fill in title), submitted to you on (fill in date)?

I am enclosing a stamped, self-addressed postal card for your convenience.

> Sincerely,
> (Sign your name)
> Type your name

Leave the message side blank for the editor to fill in.

There is absolutely no reason not to trust the Postal Service to deliver your precious manuscript, especially if you back your faith with a carbon copy of your work safely filed at home. Postal rates and regulations constantly change so check with your post office to see what is the best way for *you* to mail a particular manuscript. The less expensive postage means slower delivery while speed means higher costs. You will have to decide what fits your situation best.

Do not deliver your manuscript in person. No editor is going to drop whatever she is doing to chat with you, or read your story while you wait. You'll only have to leave your package at the reception desk anyway. It's pointless to make a special trip to the publishing office unless you have other business in the area. Even so, it's a bit chilling to see the receptionist accept your package as if there were nothing special about it. Save yourself the ordeal and *send* your masterpiece.

But *where*?

The next chapter will give you practical guidance on markets and marketing.

PLACE
STAMP
HERE

YOUR NAME
Street Address
City, State, Zip Code

TITLE OF YOUR STORY _____

Date sent _____

To: NAME OF PUBLISHER

Received by _____

Date _____

Postcard Acknowledging Receipt of Manuscript

20
Markets and Marketing . . .
the Business Side of Writing

Every writer must continually study and update the market possibilities for his material. Editors and editorial needs change; new magazines and book publishers appear; some merge with other houses or suspend publication. The only way to keep up with such day-to-day trade news is to read the magazines published for writers. The two I would not be without are *Writer's Digest* and *The Writer.*

Writer's Market, a bound, thick book published by Writer's Digest Books, lists over four thousand markets for freelance writers, divided into categories, with each entry helpfully annotated. The book is revised annually and is always packed with timely tips and other helpful advice for the freelancer.

As you investigate the possibilities, *evolve your own market list — one that fits your particular kind of material.* Use a 3-by-5 card file to record pertinent data: name of publication, its address, name of the juvenile editor, preferred story subjects, word length, rate of pay. Note the ones that allow simultaneous submissions (submitting the same story at one time to several low-paying, denominational markets which do not have overlapping circulations). In each case, when making a simultaneous submission, the writer must so inform the editor. Note also the publications which will not consider simultaneous submissions, magazines which pay good rates and expect the exclusive use of material.

There are some magazines which will buy "second rights" to stories. They reprint published material, on which the writer has sold "first rights" — rights for a one-time appearance in a publication. Make a note of these markets also.

Analyze the types of stories used in the sample issues you collect. One of the chief editorial complaints is that authors do not bother to study specific markets but send stories out haphazardly. Here is what Adelaide Field, a former editor of *Child Life,* had to say on this subject:

> . . . millions of dollars of postage and countless man hours are wasted annually, sending the right horse to the wrong stable. The author, who will spend weeks writing a story, will not spend a few days studying markets. Yet every magazine strives to create a hallmark, a quality peculiarly its own. . . . A little study would keep the breezy story away from the moralizing magazine, the four-installment serial away from the publication that limits itself to two chapters! And that is why editors endorse market-magazines so heartily, not only for the impetus they provide to their readers, and for their specific up-to-date information on current requirements, but also because this information, well applied, will lighten the editor's load. . . .

THE JUNIOR BOOK FIELD

Here too you must know what is being published. Waste no time in becoming a regular, card-carrying visitor of the children's and young adult rooms of your public library. You should also read the junior book reviews in the major newspapers published in your area. Some of these run special sections of reviews and articles in the spring, and also in the fall—to commemorate Children's Book Week. These sections you should keep for reference.

The Horn Book Magazine is a standard reference for librarians, teachers, and parents—and it should be yours. The American Library Association publishes *Booklist,* a review bulletin considered very important by editors.

There is also the *School Library Journal.* Ask your librarian about it. She may also have the *Bulletin of the Center for Children's Books,* published by the University of Chicago Graduate Library School. In these the reviewers are librarians who evaluate books from their professional point of view. Since librarians buy about 80 percent of our output, their views are of tremendous value to the writer who must live by his words.

You should also write for publishers' catalogues and

study them. You'll discover that some houses publish nothing for younger readers, but feature only teenage books. Others lean heavily toward factual material. But there's nothing static about your markets and you must be alert to all changes: they can spell *sales*!

Basing your choice on what you have learned, and revising it as new information filters down to you, make your own selected book market list on 3-by-5 cards, with all the details you can gather on each publisher. Arrange alphabetically and keep this sheaf of cards separate from the ones you made for magazine publishers.

THE ITINERARY

With your manuscript (book or short story) ready for mailing, decide on an appropriate itinerary for it. *List at least five places where you'd like to send it — now, before the manuscript leaves your hands.* This itinerary will serve a double purpose: first as a traveling guide for your brainchild; second, as a morale booster if the manuscript comes back. You won't feel that the rejection spells the end of the road for it, because you'll have another publishing house already picked out — where it might fare better.

Matching your itinerary to editorial tastes is important. In a featured article, a New York agent once told *Writer's Digest* readers what subjects certain editors especially liked, what types of stories especially appealed to them. This is the kind of information you must constantly glean for yourself from the market news, wherever you come upon it, so that you can market your own material intelligently.

I recall the story of a professional client who was referred to me after having suffered considerable discouragement over her book for younger readers. She accepted my stern and lengthy criticism eagerly and creatively (she did not slavishly follow every suggestion; what I said stimulated her own creative thinking and gave freshness, zing — and the right direction — to her tale).

After I saw the revised book, I suggested a handpicked editor to her. The book was accepted enthusiastically in two weeks' time, even though the market was generally thought "very difficult," "slow," "poor," and "dismal" at the time. As long as any publishing is being done, a good story will find a home. But it must be good, it must be written with professional skill, because at all times—good and bad—the competition is fierce.

Reserve a file folder for each story and book in which to keep all kinds of records and letters pertaining to that particular manuscript. The short story carbon should be kept in this folder. Since the full-length book carbon is not likely to fit into a folder, stack it safely away in a box. Keep the records and correspondence folders for your books in your file cabinet.

On the next page you will find a copy of the folder notes an author made for his short story. Folders for books are made out in the same way. This kind of record keeps you from unintentionally sending a story twice to the same editor.

Notice the story did not languish in his files between submissions. And note another important point: he had a carbon of it in his file. Stories seldom get lost, but mishaps do occur. Having a carbon is like taking out insurance on your story's continued life.

Once a story is published, I file away a complete issue of the magazine. But I also keep tearsheets from another issue in my itinerary folder, making for a complete and permanent history.

Note that your magazine stories may have a future value—considerably over and above the initial fee paid you—as picture books or reprints in anthologies. *Notify your publisher of any changes in your address,* identifying yourself by story and date of publication, if you are not a regular contributor. This will prevent frantic—and sometimes futile—hunts for you in years to come, because the Postal Service keeps track of your reported moves for only a limited time.

DON'T'S AND DO'S
ON SUBMISSIONS

To query or not? In fiction it is usually best to submit your completed project, especially if you're a newcomer to the trade. An editor can't possibly judge your writing skill otherwise. "Four chapters and an outline of the rest" isn't much good either. Some people can write fine beginnings and fall flat on the middles—regardless of the exciting promise in

CHART
A HEART FOR TWO

9-12 Story 1,400 Words

ITINERARY	DATE SENT	DATE RETURNED	COMMENTS
Clubhouse	3/16/85	7/15/85	Rejected
Junior Trails	7/16/85		No response in three months
Letter: Editor of *J.T.*	11/1/85		Status of MS?
Letter: From Editor		11/28/85	Manuscript Lost
RETYPED FROM CARBON			
Junior Trails	12/1/85		Purchased! 2/13/86 $42.00 Published 1/18/87 New Title: "Have a Heart"
Letter: Editor of *J.T.*	8/1/87		Request for return of 2nd rights to the author
Letter: From Editor		9/19/87	Request Granted

outline or synopsis. Contracts on such incomplete ventures are rarely given to beginners. Moreover, having your "trial submission" coldly turned down can discourage you from finishing the book. Wait to query until you are established; then you'll probably work from contract with an advance, given to you on a page or two of synopsis because your ability and sales appeal is well-known.

Never submit a manuscript to more than one publisher at a time regardless of the weeks and months involved in the making of an editorial decision. Multiple submissions of stories (unless covered by special editorial dispensation) and books are considered unethical, at least by publishers. Should you take a chance and do so anyway, think how embarrassing it would be for two publishers to accept your story simultaneously! You'd have some explaining to do, and certainly one of the editors, and quite possibly both, would be furious with you—permanently. Don't take that chance.

Never send a carbon of a book to an editor, because his or her first thought will be that you have made multiple submissions—and back will come your manuscript, probably unread. What's more, a big question mark will be added to your name in the editor's mind—and editors have long memories, refreshed by notations on file cards. Publishing is an orderly business, and once you submit to a house, records are kept of your dealings with it.

Some editors will allow you to submit a clear photocopy of your manuscript—one that can be written on easily with a ball point pen—if you indicate on your first page or in a covering letter that it is *not* a simultaneous submission. Others, of course, regard photocopies with the same suspicion they reserve for carbons. Even the editors who accept photocopies may fail to return them, if they become accidentally separated from their return postage.

Never send an editor (even your favorite) two manuscripts at the same time. Editors seldom make a simultaneous purchase of two stories, so in effect you are giving your editor a choice. One story is bound to come back, while on separate submissions you might sell both.

Seasonal material must be submitted five to eight months ahead of schedule, and even ten months is none too soon. Magazine content is planned far in advance, and sometimes material is scheduled ahead several years.

Although editorial decisions often are agonizingly slow in coming, be patient. Most editors are conscientious, but they work with small staffs. The whole department may have only four people to run it — with hundreds of stories to read, besides a myriad of other editorial chores that must be done on schedule. Editor's jobs are not nine-to-five affairs. Most of them take manuscripts home to read at night and on weekends. In the bedroom of one of my editors I once saw a market basket, loaded with manuscripts, hanging from the knob of her night table! This sight strengthened my patience with editors considerably.

Stay away from editors' offices unless you're invited to visit. Don't bother an editor with needless correspondence. If he or she is interested in your material, he or she will call you.

MAGAZINE PAYMENT METHODS

Short story payment is made on acceptance or on publication. First class magazines should pay on acceptance. However, there is a group (with individual magazine circulations of over two hundred thousand) that I formerly considered in the top echelon, which now pay on publication. Since the author is not even told, at the time of acceptance, *when* that publication may come, the arrangement seems to me grossly unfair to the author. Of course no one forces authors to submit to these houses, but I say again: *writers should know their markets* and the consequences of having their work accepted by some of them. The markets which pay the most and *on acceptance* should go on the preferred list for your submissions. It is only sensible and businesslike.

When promise is made to "pay on acceptance" it means that you will get your check as soon as the accounting department can process it. Before you endorse the check, remember that the "rights" you're selling are sometimes printed on the back of the check, above the place intended for your signature.

Some magazines send a short contract form for you to sign. Read it carefully and don't be afraid to question anything you don't understand. Other magazines make the purchase without stating either in letter or contract that they are buying *all* rights to a work, including the right to copyright. If they *do* make such a statement, don't panic. Their reason is that many copyright experts believe a valid copyright cannot be secured for magazine material unless all rights are purchased. If you don't know what rights are being bought, *ask before you cash the check*.

VANITY PUBLISHERS

The *Bookman's Glossary* (R.R. Bowker) defines a "vanity publisher" in this way:

> A trade designation for publishing concerns that specialize in publishing books at the author's risk and expense. They sign publishing contracts with inexperienced authors by appealing to their vanity or natural desire to see their writings in print at whatsoever the cost. They seldom have a sales staff.

Success of a bona fide publishing venture depends (for both the publisher and the author) on how many copies of a book are sold. The publisher who has invested hard cash in a financial advance to the author, in the considerable expense of preparing a manuscript for publication, and in distributing it by means of a large staff of salesmen, is interested in getting the invested money back — and in making a profit. The vanity publisher, who has not invested anything, has no such interests at stake and therefore no incentive to sell the books published. Expenses and profit are included in the sums paid by the author.

Sometimes such publishers offer a fantastic royalty return (in the contract) to the gullible author — something like 40 percent. Some go all out and make it a straight 100 percent. In other words, they are *printers*; the author owns the books and can do with them — all five hundred or two thousand copies — what he pleases. It isn't long before the author discovers some hard and painful facts about *distribution*.

If your writing has commercial merit (and it must have to be accepted by a commercial publishing firm), you will be paid for the privilege given that firm to publish your book. You do not have to pay *them* to publish it. The reputable publishing house assumes all the expense and the risks and responsibility for distributing your book while you sit at home working on your next project.

Don't be discouraged by those first rejections. Keep submitting your book; and if at last you feel that you cannot sell it, then retire it in the hope that you'll have better luck with your next venture. But don't sink into fuzzy thinking on the subject. If commercial houses with well-organized sales staffs felt they could not market your book, how can a vanity press do any better for you? *Do not invest your own money for the publication of your book. Your chances of financial success in such a venture are about three hundred to one — against you.*

The only exception to getting involved in such a project might be if you can easily afford the expense of a private printing (which is what it amounts to, you know). Seeing your book in print may salve your bruised feelings. Or it might be you have written a family or personal history that would not interest thousands of readers, but will interest your family and friends. If you can afford to have it printed (at about thirty-five dollars per page), fine. Have it done, and present copies to your family and friends.

In any case, know what you are about and what is involved. The general feeling (well founded on fact) is that vanity press books are badly written; if illustrated, the illustrations are of poor quality. No one wants to review them. As a reviewer I've had pathetic letters from authors who discovered they were stuck with the selling end of their publications. There was nothing I could do for them. There is no point in wasting review space on such printings because the book stores will not stock them (except possibly on a local level) and the libraries will not buy them. The author's money has been wasted, and such publication hasn't done a thing for his or her reputation. Everyone in the trade knows which houses require "cooperative" subsidization for publication, so if anything, the writer's reputation will suffer.

Sell your books the hard way. It pays!

THE BUSINESS SIDE OF WRITING

If writing is your business and not a sometime hobby, and you can prove it, your business expenses are deductible on your income tax returns — just as your income from writing (a self-employed occupation) is taxable. Here's where those rejection slips may come in handy, so don't throw them away! They're your proof that what you've been writing has been done with the sincere *intention* of selling your material. The fact that you have not sold anything yet does not alter the situation. Many a new business starts off in the red before any profits are shown. Like postage regulations and rates, tax laws always seem to be undergoing change. The best advice I can give you is to check with a tax expert. Just be certain it's one who knows about tax laws related to authors. Not all do.

LOOKING AHEAD—YOU AND POSTERITY

More and more universities and libraries, as well as local historical societies, are showing an interest in collecting memorabilia from writers. It might behoove *you*, as a serious writer, to start saving the work drafts of your books and stories and any outlines, summaries, research notes, sketches, dummies, diaries, journals, as well as letters, and book talks — in fact anything of interest related to you and your work that might be of value to such collections.

If anyone in your family has had the foresight to save your childhood writing efforts, you might take steps to recover such items. These and work drafts of early books are especially hard to come by, what with the general shortage of storage space and the natural urge to clean house periodically. Next time such an urge comes over you, consider twice what you throw away — it may be your claim to immortality *and a deductible tax item,* for such gifts to institutions are tax deductible, under whatever current tax regulations are in effect. Better check that wastebasket right now.

21
When You Sell a Book—
Contracts and Other Matters

Most books are bought on a royalty basis, by contract.

The mass-market cheap editions (low in price, but not necessarily in the quality of the writing) are usually bought outright, with one lump sum paid for *all* rights. Payment for full-length books ranges from five hundred dollars to fifteen hundred dollars, while the popular little full-color books bring from one hundred thirty dollars to five hundred dollars, unless the author has a "name" and can dicker for better terms. Publishers claim that these low-priced items are very expensive to produce (especially those in color) and to distribute, and therefore they cannot do any better for the authors. But these little books often sell for years, so it might be to your advantage to try to place that kind of manuscript with a royalty-paying house before submitting it to the mass-market publishers.

The fly in that honey is that *picture book royalties are split on a fifty-fifty basis with the artist;* and sometimes, when the pictures are considered more important than the text, the division may be on a seventy-five/twenty-five basis in favor of the artist. Still, you do retain an interest in your literary property rights (you and the artist, jointly), and those just might pay off handsomely.

YOUR LITERARY RIGHTS
AND YOUR BOOK
CONTRACT

Rights to a book-length literary property include the following items: prepublication serial (first serial rights); book publication, including book club rights; magazine, second serial rights; newspaper second serial; book reprint; dramatization; motion picture; television; radio; mechanical reproduction; condensation and abridgement; anthology; quotation; translation; syndication; commercial, etc.

When a book publisher offers you a contract, these are the rights that you are required to turn over in whole or in part. You are not expected to sign the contract on the spot. It is a long document, full of awesome-sounding clauses — some based on contingencies never likely to arise in the juvenile trade market. The contract is usually mailed to you for study — and study it you must so that none of the clauses will come as a nasty surprise to you later.

For the publisher's own part, the agreement is to have your manuscript printed and manufactured as a book; to put the book on sale throughout the United States and Canada, and to distribute it through bookstores *entirely at the company's expense.* The publisher also agrees to pay you a sum of money as an advance against future royalties. And for the various rights mentioned, the publisher agrees to pay you a percentage of the money collected. Some of these rights and percentages can be negotiated.

First serial rights, sold *before* the material appears in book form, belong to the author. You can have that specified in your contract. (Some contracts state that they must be sold before the contract is signed.)

If your material is resold for magazine or newspaper publication *after* the book appears (second serial rights), then your earnings must be divided fifty-fifty with the publisher of your book. Incidentally, "serial" refers to the appearance of your material in a periodical — a magazine or newspaper — in one or more parts.

BOOK CLUBS

There are more than two dozen juvenile book clubs featuring hard cover trade books as well as paperback editions. The Junior Literary Guild is the oldest; Scholastic Book Services is the biggest, and their paperback distributions often reach astronomical figures. The clubs handle books for all ages, and it is possible to have one book distributed by several clubs, if nonexclusive rights were sold by your publisher. In that case, each club, or paperback distributor, leases the distribution rights for a specified length of time.

Authors, as a rule, are delighted by this plus sale — but they can do little to promote it. The whole transaction is handled through the publisher and all money received is usually divided on a fifty-fifty basis. (If yours is a heavily illustrated book, you may have to divide your share with the artist.)

PAPERBACK BOOKS
AND REPRINTS
The tremendous demand for paperbacks has given authors another outlet to tap. (Originals may be submitted directly to interested publishers; follow your market listing on these.) Reprint rights, however, are handled through the publishers. Always.

MOVIE RIGHTS
I'm sorry to say that as a rule juvenile stories do not sell to movies. Hollywood script editors won't even read them, and along with a lot of other people in the trade, I feel they miss a great deal of good material that could be adapted to the screen. Miracles do happen occasionally, so it's something to dream about. However, educational companies do make films, records, and tapes of unpublished material, so that is an attainable developing market.

TELEVISION RIGHTS
The tremendous appetite of television for material has improved our chances for sales in that line. Animal and family stories have been filmed successfully, but submissions usually must be made by the special agents of the publishers, or an author's agent. Although *published books* will sometimes be read, *manuscripts* submitted by hopeful authors are invariably returned unopened, to avoid nuisance suits for plagiarism and piracy.

FOREIGN SALES
On books for juniors, this market is better for the ego than the pocketbook. After commissions paid to the publishers' foreign representative or agent, there isn't much cash left to divide between the publisher and the author. There is, however, an immense sense of satisfaction in having your work considered good enough to merit translation or re-

publishing in a country other than your own.

COMMERCIAL RIGHTS
These protect your (and your publisher's) interests in any commercial enterprises that make use of your story characters — dolls, toys, gadgets. Nice — but rare.

ROYALTIES
Royalties on junior books are usually 10 percent of the retail price, which means that on a twelve-dollar book, the author would get one dollar and twenty cents per copy. This is by no means standard. Different percentages are offered, and sometimes these are based on the net price, which is the retail price minus all the trade discounts. In effect, this can mean a return of only 6 percent per copy, based on the list price.

But even with a so-called "straight 10 percent" there are numerous "whittle" clauses in your contract which may reduce your royalty by as much as 50 percent. There isn't much you can do about them (the Author's League is working to improve the situation), but at least you should know these clauses are *there* and what they mean.

There might be a stipulation to reduce royalties after a book has been in print a certain length of time and the sales begin to taper off. Or if a small printing (of one or two thousand copies) is made after the book has been out two years. Small printings are expensive, but it's better to take the reduction than to see your book go out of print.

When the unbound sheets of your book are sold (for reinforced bindings needed for libraries), there is a substantial reduction in your royalty rate.

An expense to watch for concerns galley proof corrections. Most contracts have a clause that reads something like this: *"The cost of alterations in the galley proof or page proof required by the author, other than corrections of printer's errors, in excess of 10 percent of the original cost of composition shall be charged against the author's royalties. . . ."*

This should effectively discourage you from starting to rewrite your book after it is set in galleys, because even the change of one short word for a long one or the addition of a phrase may require the resetting of a whole paragraph. At that rate your 10 percent leeway will be used up in no time and you'll receive a horrendous bill.

You are, of course, responsible for everything that is in the book, whether it's fact or fiction. Should you quote directly any material written by another person, you are expected to procure (at your own expense) written permission to reprint such passages, and present this to your publisher along with the manuscript.

OPTIONS

Option clauses are included in most contracts. Usually you must agree to submit your next book to the same publisher. Sometimes this clause will read: "the next two books"— but then, the refusal of the first (of these two) negates the obligation on the second. *Make certain that this is clearly stated.* If it is not, you may discover that you have agreed to give that publisher a straight option on the next two books. That is, even if the publisher refuses the one, you still must submit another for consideration, with no assurance that it will be taken. Meanwhile, the one refused becomes a kind of albatross. If your submit it to another publisher and that publisher decides to take it, the company will want an option—one that you can't give! As someone has said so aptly: A contract is a legal and binding document—and it can bite the hand that signs it. *Yours* if you don't read what you are signing.

Once a decision is made to accept your book for publication, you may be sure that all its pros and cons have been thoroughly considered. They *want* it! If you have any questions about the contract terms, ask to have them explained. The most beautifully printed contracts can be altered.

You must learn to protect your interests. Your editor will only respect you the more for managing your affairs in a calm, sensible manner. "Authors will accept anything instead of trying to negotiate better terms," an editor once told me. Your editor may not be able to agree to everything you want changed, but it will be a step in the right direction. As you learn to write better, become better known, and as your sales figures improve, *you* will become a more valuable property, and you'll be able to negotiate more favorable contract terms.

THE ADVANCE

On signing the contract, you will usually get an advance payment. If the manuscript is complete and ready for final editing, a full advance of one or two thousand dollars or more may be paid to you. The sum depends on many factors—your reputation as a writer or an authority on the subject, the projected sales on your book, the house policy on advances, and so on.

Some companies pay as little as one hundred fifty dollars as an advance, with a like amount on publication. I understand there are others paying no advance at all. I'm happy to say none of them are among the ones I write for. *Writer's Market* makes every effort to find out such details and print them. Be sure to check these listings when making up your manuscript itinerary. You don't want to be unpleasantly surprised on acceptance.

If extensive changes need to be made on a book, or it still needs to be completed, the author may get only half the advance on signing, with the rest paid on delivery of an acceptable manuscript. That certainly is fair. Whatever sums you do get, remember they are made against future royalties. If you take a big advance, it may take quite a while to make it up in copies sold and to start collecting royalties after publication. But since you keep the advance even if your book never sells enough copies to pay it off against royalties, a large advance can be to your advantage, too.

Most houses make royalty settlements twice a year—which is a long time between paychecks. But if you're a real producer, you'll have a few advances on new works in between; and perhaps you'll turn out a few short stories. Being a freelance writer is not the easiest of occupations, and most writers have another job while they're building up a royalty-paying backlog of books. It's a long haul to become self-supporting at writing—so don't give up a steady job the moment you get your first short story check or sign that first contract!

WHEN YOUR BOOK IS ACCEPTED

With the prospect of actual publication, every author wants his or her manuscript to reflect the best writing. So do the editors. They may make a great many suggestions for revision or just a few, depending on the quality of the manuscript and the editor's critical ability. Whatever the constructive suggestions, the author should accept them with good grace and consider them in a creative frame of mind — and get on with the job promptly. Your book is already tentatively scheduled on the production timetable.

Your editor has the right — and the duty — to *edit* your book. Some of your sentences may be shortened; some words simplified; some cut out altogether. Spelling, punctuation, and grammar may be altered to conform with the publisher's house style.

Among other things, your book title may be changed, if the editor feels it lacks appeal or clarity. A good title should give a clue to what the book is about, without revealing too much. It should not be a label, but a lure.

When questioned about titles, young readers make such comments as the following (and librarians agree with them): "We like the title to tell us what the book is going to be about." "I like a name in the title, so I'll know if it's about a boy or a girl." "It should show if it's an adventure and where . . . or if it's a mystery. . . ."

Your book will require a jacket, and perhaps illustrations, if the story is for younger readers. The artist will be chosen by your editor, although as a courtesy he or she may ask if you have someone in mind. The final choice belongs to the editor, but *if you are a professional illustrator, and your style is appropriate,* you may get the happy job of doing your own book.

Besides art, the jacket needs flap copy. The part that tucks into the front of the book will tell briefly what the story is about. Your editor will take care of that. *Your* job is to provide copy for the back flap — a brief biographical sketch and a few words on how you came to write *this* book. Read some jacket copy on new books and pattern yours accordingly.

Include a good, clear photograph of yourself on glossy paper, with the biographical sketch. It may be a studio portrait or an informal snapshot (as long as your face stands out clearly). Any expenses connected with this publicity picture are tax deductible.

All this, along with working on your new project, should keep you busy. And then, one day, the *galleys* will arrive!

Your original, copyedited manuscript will come with these long galleys.

The same rules apply to the proofreading of galleys as to your typescript: a few pages at a sitting; a sheet of blank paper or a blotter slid under the lines to help you spot errors. Even the most careful printer can make an occasional mistake, so read carefully. "P.E.'s" — Printer's Errors — are no-charge items. Several other people will check the galleys, but you're the most interested party, and you'll hate yourself if mistakes you might have caught slip into the final printing.

Use the standard proofreaders' marks as shown in the sample on the opposite page.

Page proofs may or may not be sent to you. Here changes should not be made except under the most pressing circumstances. Again, proofread carefully and return promptly.

And then at long last comes the day of triumph. The Book arrives! All six, ten, or twelve free copies promised to you in your contract. *Any others you want you'll have to pay for,* but because you're the author, your publishers will give you a 40 percent discount. Do remember these basic economics, even in your initial wild excitement over Your Book's Birthday, and don't rush around giving away copies.

AGENTS — TO HAVE?
OR TO HAVE NOT?

But suppose your manuscript does not follow the happy rainbow course. Suppose it is turned down time and again. Would submitting it through an agent make a difference? No. *An agent cannot sell an unsalable manuscript.*

If you have publishable material for young readers, you do not need an agent to place it for you. I have signed more than fifty book contracts, and I have never had an agent. What's more, I can name dozens of other authors who do not have agents. Anyway, most agents will save you the agony of decision by refusing to handle your work until you've made a name for yourself on your own.

In certain instances an agent can be of considerable value. If you live far from New York, an agent can expedite book submissions, saving you both time and postage. If the agent is also a good critic, you are doubly lucky. If you write

PROOFREADER'S MARKS

MARGINAL MARKS	MARK IN LINE OF PROOF	MEANING
ℒ	Ask note what your country can	Delete
⊙	Ask not what your country can	Reverse
⊂	Ask not what country can	Close up
#	Ask not what your country can	Insert space
¶	for today. Ask not what your	Begin new paragraph
□	Ask not what your country	Indent one em
⊏	L⊐ Ask not what your country	Move to left
⊐	Ask not what your country can ⊐	Move to right
qu?	Ask not why your country can	Query to author
tr	Ask not what your country can	Transpose
country	Ask not what your can do for	Insert
x	Ask not what your country can	Broken letter
no ¶	Ask not what your country can	Run in same paragraph
w.f.	Ask not what your country can	Wrong font
stet	Ask not what your country can	Let it stand
⋀	"Why your country cannot	Insert comma
∀	Ask not what your country's	Insert apostrophe
⧷⧸⧸⧸	Ask not, he said	Insert quotes
=	Your fellow countrymen	Insert hyphen
em	What your country today	Em dash
;	What your country does why	Insert semi-colon
⊙	The country is like this	Insert colon
⊙	This is your country	Insert period
?	Is this your country	Insert interrogation point
l.c.	Ask not What your country	Lower case
rom	Ask not what your country can	Set in roman type
ital.	Ask not what your country can	Set in italic type
caps	Ask not what your country can	Set in capitals
s.c.	Ask not what your country can	Set in small capitals
ld.	Ask not what your country can do for you but what you can	Insert lead between lines

To make several corrections in one line, give marginal symbols in order, separated by slash marks:

cap/ℒ/tr Ask not not what your country can

nonfiction, an agent can be extremely helpful. Frequently, editors have ideas for nonfiction books and contact agents they have worked with to find an author to write the book.

However, in some agencies, the juvenile department is a kind of stepchild, and your book will be sent around without being screened by an expert at the agency. Editors quickly learn which agents actually *know* the quality of the material they are submitting. Thus, some agents' folders sit atop the pile of incoming manuscripts, and some wait their turn at the bottom of the heap. My briefing as a reader for several top publishing houses always included instructions not to be unduly impressed by the fact that a manuscript came in through an agent.

Agents and friends can open doors and sometimes expedite a reading, but they do not influence editorial decisions. Sometimes they prompt a sterner look at material to offset any effects of influence! Publishing a book requires a sizeable investment of cash, time, and highly specialized skills. It can easily cost twelve thousand dollars to produce an unillustrated book. When pictures in color are involved, the cost may go higher than fifteen thousand dollars. It is the editor's job to exercise wise stewardship over his or her employer's money and the company's trust in his or her judgment.

Very short books, picture books, short stories, and poetry are almost never handled by agents in the juvenile field.

HOW TO FIND A GOOD LITERARY AGENT

1. Through the recommendation of an established author who has read your work and found it good.
2. Through the Author's Guild, Inc., 234 West 44th Street, New York, N.Y. 10036.
3. Through some book publishers.
4. The Society of Authors' Representatives, 39½ Washington Square South, New York, N.Y. 10012 has a printed list of its members. Agents are also listed in *Writer's Market.*

TO DO AND NOT TO DO

Do not call on an agent (or publisher) to discuss your work when it has not been read. This will mark you as a nuisance.

If you send an unsolicited manuscript to an agent, he or she may charge for reading it. But if he or she finds the material marketable, or asks to see more of your work, he or she will refund the money.

Agents do not have formal contracts with the writers they represent. It's more of a gentleman's agreement, and may be dissolved by word or letter if either or both parties become dissatisfied. Incidentally, all expenses connected with your agent's fees are tax deductible.

An agent can also help you hook up with a *book packager.* The packagers work with authors, creating books for educational and trade publishers. Staff at the packager will edit the text, find appropriate illustrators if necessary, and present the finished product to the publisher ready for printing.

Unpublished writers have little chance of working with a book packager. However, once you've been published, you may contact a packager with writing samples and be placed in their files. These files are much like those maintained by theatrical casting agencies. Unless the performer rises above the others on file, he or she is likely to remain buried there.

An agent can help you gain notice. Packagers frequently contact agents if an educational publisher needs short stories for an elementary reading text or a series of concept books or a nonfiction collection centered around a specific subject area. Published authors without agents may also contact a book packager with ideas for a fiction or nonfiction series that would interest boy and girl readers of a particular age. Credentials are a must for a writer to impress a packager; an agent is not.

The agent's business is to sell the finished product on a professional basis—at a 10 percent commission of whatever your work earns. Until you reach a professional level in your writing, he cannot afford to handle you on this basis, and you might as well resign yourself to the fact that marketing your material will be a do-it-yourself project.

22
Rejection Lows—
Acceptance Highs

Having read the previous chapters, you must surely realize that when your manuscript is returned by a publisher, it's not because you don't have an agent; it's not because you are an "unknown"; and most assuredly it's not because it was not read.

Everything that comes into a publishing office is *read*. Editors are always on the lookout for new writers. Words may live for centuries, but authors are not so durable. A new crop must be developed, and your chances of being "discovered" are as good as anybody's *if* you can write.

Along with natural attrition, writers have an annoying way (from the losing editor's point of view) of going off to another publisher for one reason or another. This is especially true among those who start in the denominational presses, where editors are more apt to take the time and trouble to train a new author, for just this reason. But because the pay scale in this market is usually low, a writer who begins to sell leaves for greener pastures. Someone must take his or her place—or the magazine must cease publication.

The only advantage the established writer has over you is professional skill, which can be depended upon to produce publishable material. But even professional writers sometimes lose their touch. What the editor hopes for, each time he or she picks a manuscript from the stack on his or her desk, is the enthusiasm and vitality of an up-and-coming author—and so no manuscript is summarily passed up.

"Well then," you might say, "if that's the case, why aren't editors nicer to new writers? They could at least tell us *why* they won't accept a story, instead of just sending a printed rejection slip." But that is just what they *cannot* do, at least not often. Not with the hundreds and even thousands of manuscripts coming into an office run by a small staff. Primarily an editor is paid to edit books or get out a magazine—not to conduct correspondence writing courses at an employer's expense.

Specific criticism is not offered on a book or story unless the editor feels it will make the material publishable. Should you get a personal letter, or even a note suggesting definite changes in a manuscript, it means that the editor is *interested,* even though he or she does not always add, "Let me see this material again." This last could raise a writer's hopes too much, for he or she might think it a definite promise of acceptance, which it is not.

The thing to do *at once* is follow the suggested revision and resubmit the material, with a covering letter. Even if a sale does not result, you will have made a friend. That editor will read your next effort all the more eagerly and make even more specific suggestions, because you have proved yourself receptive and *professional* in your attitude. With any luck at all, you'll *sell* to that market before too long.

Even the briefest message scrawled on the rejection form is a definite sign of encouragement. It means that your material is better than average. Submit to that market again and again to show that you are a producer. They'll notice.

Rejections must not be allowed to send you into the doldrums. Each one is an expression of opinion by an individual publisher, and some other house might be delighted with the story.

If your manuscript comes back from four publishers, read it over carefully. It may be that you'll now see what is wrong with it. Check it against the lists of "musts" in this text and be sure they're *there* in your piece. Then send it out again on a continuing itinerary, or return it to the editors who have rejected it, with a note saying that you have revised the story and perhaps it now will fill their needs. Editors will respect you for the effort.

Some of the publishing houses (magazines) have a printed rejection form that does list reasons for returning a story. While a penciled checkmark is not very communicative, still it is better than nothing.

How are decisions reached? In some larger publishing houses, the editors meet at regular intervals to discuss promising manuscripts—with the manuscripts stacked two-and-a-half-feet-high at times. Some editors, who are basically insecure and terrified of making a wrong decision, consult several reports from paid readers. They line up these evaluations on their desk like a politician checking the latest polls, picking only books likely to mollify everyone and upset no one. In other houses, the editor is in sole command: the responsibility for the department is his or hers, and so are all the final decisions. That's the way I prefer it; but what with all the mergers and less experienced editors taking over after retiring heads, more and more decisions are made in committee.

SUCCESS STORIES

To paraphrase Marcus Aurelius: *Flinch not, nor despair— and don't give up too soon on submitting your material,* as long as you have faith in a particular manuscript. It may well be that all the "experts" are wrong—except you and the publisher who finally accepts your manuscript.

Time and again I get ecstatic phone calls and letters from clients and former students that sound like this:

> Just a note to let you know that my mystery is finally going to be published! After holding it nearly a year, the Big Decision was made—and my editor tells me the book will be out this fall.
>
> It may cheer your class to know that my book was rejected about thirty times and has been going the rounds for over five years. . . . I never would have been so persistent, of course, if you hadn't assured me the book had a chance. . . .

> Sold an article . . . and if you ever need an example of perseverance in marketing for your writing classes, I have it! This article went the rounds off and on *for four years.* I was astounded not only to sell it at all, but to receive a glowing letter about it from the Editor-in-Chief. Have saved same and other correspondence about it, because the letters showed how editors differ. . . .

Of course they do. Editors are people! In checking my own submissions in my 3-by-5 card file, which handily duplicates my folder records, I find that some of my short pieces went out as many as fifteen times!

If you have any manuscripts tucked away in your files, get them out now. Read them over. Revise again and polish, if that's indicated. If the stories seem good to you, retype and send them out again on brand new itineraries based on your study of the *current* markets. Your very next submission may bring you a check instead of a rejection.

THE HARDEST STORIES TO SELL ARE THE ONES YOU KEEP STASHED AWAY IN THE BOTTOM DRAWER OF YOUR DESK. All the others have a chance to be published!

PART II
SPECIAL WRITING PROBLEMS AND PROJECTS

23
Research—Ideas Unlimited

Probably the most frequently quoted rule a writer hears is *Write what you know.* Sensible advice! But *what you know* need not be confined to the scope of your personal experience. You can easily widen that experience, and *you can learn about* anything if you're willing to spend time on concentrated research. Besides being fun, finding out about things you don't know is like tapping an ever-bubbling spring of ideas.

The primary requirement for writing from research is an intense interest in the particular subject. Secondly, you must know how to go about collecting the necessary information on it. Thirdly, you must know how to *organize* the mass of material you collect. You cannot rely on your memory, and a stack of notes a foot high is useless unless you can find what you need *at once.*

TWO KINDS OF RESEARCH
There are two kinds of research: *historical* (period) and *contemporary* (present day).

There is scarcely a time in history that has not been covered in one or more books. In conducting research on a period in history, you should read both fact and fiction. Consult at least three authorities before you accept anything as fact. Fiction should be read not only for additional information (which you can corroborate through the factual sources), but for a sense of place and time. These are universal procedures for writers of period fiction.

A classic example of a perfect period reproduction is *A Tale of Two Cities,* by Charles Dickens. If readers didn't know better, they'd feel certain that Dickens actually *lived* through the French Revolution, so real is every minute detail of people, places, and events. Yet Charles Dickens was born in 1812 and died in 1870, while the Bastille was stormed on July 14, 1789. In preparing to write this book, Dickens read some three hundred books on the subject!

YOUR STARTING POINT

Regardless of the object of research, the library is to the writer what the secret cave was to Ali Baba: an inexhaustible storehouse of riches. And the reference librarian is his or her "open sesame" to all its professionally filed secrets.

Lose no time in getting acquainted with your local library, its reference sources, and its staff. Librarians are interested in authors' projects, and you need never hesitate to ask for help. But because they must serve many others in your community, you should learn to help yourself as much as possible.

Also remember that your local library, no matter how small, has borrowing facilities from larger libraries, and once the material you need is tracked down, it can be borrowed for you (unless it is extremely valuable or irreplaceable). However, long-distance borrowing takes time. Weeks and sometimes months may elapse before the material is in your hands, so plan your writing projects with this possibility in mind.

THINGS YOU'LL NEED
TO KNOW

What you should look for, in preparation for your "period" story, is material that will make you familiar with the days and ways of a time and place: everyday homely details, the speech idiom, the "thinking" of the time, what the people knew, what they strove for: the world as it was *then*.

If you plan to use an actual place, focus your research on the particular country for background detail; then narrow it down to the particular city, even to the streets where the action will take place. Fine detail maps may be available to help you reconstruct the setting accurately. In the United States, local historical societies often prove most cooperative.

You must be able to visualize the homes and the rooms

of the period: their furnishings and even the view from the windows. You must know what children and grownups wore in that day, their manners, the books they read, how they talked, the foods they ate, the toys the children played with. What was the mode of transportation? *What historic events and people were contemporary with the time of your story action?* Make a chronological listing of these. Weave actual happenings into your tale if you can do so without distorting history.

All these facts must seep into your mind as you make notes—until you can feel yourself *there.* Then you will be able to give your reader the proper sense of time and place and identity with an era.

You'll use only a fraction of the information you collect, because your aim is not to teach history but to entertain your reader with a *story.* What you have learned you must use only for the purpose of creating convincing, authentic atmosphere and background for your characters. You are not to take the reader on a sight-seeing tour and point out the historic landmarks. Use only such facts as will forward the action of your plot. Never succumb to the temptation of showing off how much you know.

SOURCE BOOKS
Whatever your project, the first step is background reading. Start in the encyclopedias, adult as well as junior editions. Along with the brief overall information, the articles will also give you a bibliography of other sources. Copy each of these references onto a separate 3-by-5 "bib" (bibliography) card, listing the title, author, and any other pertinent data that may be helpful in locating the item.

PERIODICAL SOURCES
Magazine and newspaper articles are also a fertile field for information. The *Reader's Guide to Periodical Literature* indexes articles, by subject and author, that have been published in more than one hundred general magazines. Bound volumes go back to 1900. Since the *Guide* comes out monthly throughout the year, it is only a matter of a few weeks before the latest articles are listed for reference.

This is only a listing of *where* the articles can be found.

Make a separate listing for each article on 3-by-5 cards. Now comes the legwork. Since your library may not have the magazines in its file, you may have to go to a larger library, or to a backdate magazine source. Consult the librarians on this.

Poole's Index to Periodical Literature lists the contents of thousands of volumes of American and British magazines published between 1802 and 1906. The scope of coverage is breathtaking, with authentic sources for eighteenth- and nineteenth-century social customs; articles written on the War of 1812, the California Gold Rush, the Civil War, etc., by people who lived through these events. Mr. Poole was an American librarian and bibliographer, and the magazines he indexed may be found in the collections of older libraries throughout the country.

The *National Geographic Magazine* is a treasure trove of people, places, customs, and curious facts. Its *Cumulative Indexes* run from 1899 to 1946 in Volume I, and from 1947-1963 in Volume II, with annual supplements published thereafter. Most libraries have an ample stock of back issues.

The *New York Times Index* is published throughout the year. Bound volumes and the microfilm index go back to 1851. The *Index* entries often give a brief synopsis of the story, which can sometimes answer your questions. Microfilm editions of the paper are also available, and if your library has them, locating the information you need is simple. However, if this service is not available, and if what you're looking for is a story of universal interest, chances are it was printed on nearly the same day all over the country. Thus your hometown paper, on file in your library (as part of local history), would probably have it. All you need to do then is find the issue and the page—with the help of your reference librarian.

Incidentally, the *London Times Index (Palmer's Index to the Times Newspaper)* goes back to 1790!—And what a key that is to the life of past eras, not only in the stories, but in the advertisements and the announcements on the microfilmed pages. It can be found in the specialized newspaper collections of the Library of Congress, the New York Public Library, the libraries of other large cities, and in some universities.

PERSON-TO-PERSON RESEARCH

If the time you are interested in is not too remote, you may be able to find old documents, diaries, letters, and even "old timers" whom you can interview. Living witnesses are not always reliable, however. Their memories may be unclear or their feelings strongly prejudiced. For that matter, they may have lively imaginations and lead you off the track altogether! Better check their "memories" against authoritative published material, whether you're working on a fiction or nonfiction project.

MORE AIDS TO RESEARCH

In your search for books on your subject area, consult the other sources in the reference room of your community library, again making individualized listings of titles and authors on 3-by-5 cards. The *Subject Guide to Books in Print* is a hefty animal. Under the alphabetically arranged subject headings are listed the authors and the titles of their works, the year of publication, the publisher — and the price, should you be inclined to buy the book. This *Guide* deals mostly with nonfiction.

Books in Print, also an impressive annual publication, begins with the author index and has the title index in the second half. Obviously, you have to know one or the other to have any success in finding anything. This lists both fiction and nonfiction, currently available for purchase.

The *Cumulative Book Index,* which the librarians call the *CBI,* is usually kept in the librarians' work room. It has been published since 1898. The listings are under author, subject, and editor (or compiler of material). Here you will find listed many books which may be out of print (o.p.), that is, no longer available for purchase through regular trade channels, but probably on library shelves — somewhere. The card catalogue in the reading room will tell you if the titles you want are there; if not, it may be possible to get them through the interlibrary loan system. The *CBI* listing includes books published in English all over the world.

These are but a few reference room aids to your research. The best way to find out how your library can help you is to spend a day or two there and see for yourself just what is available. There are biography indexes; current biography volumes; short story indexes; folklore encyclopedias, reference books on the arts, the sciences, technology, the various *Who's Who's;* lists of specialists in *who knows what* — and it is always heartwarming to discover how graciously the experts agree to help even a budding writer with information. We'll deal with this phase of live research in the next chapter.

Make backgrounds authentic by studying pictures, photographs, and paintings of that period. In order to furnish your period properly and to dress your characters in keeping with their era, begin with books on period furniture and costumes and continue your studies at museums. The Metropolitan Museum of Art in New York City has a splendid Costume Institute, with period costume displays and a library. Other large cities have similar facilities, but if you can't manage to see the real thing, don't despair. With your writer's imagination you can reconstruct what you need to know from books.

YOU AND YOUR RESEARCH

Your research must be exhaustive and *accurate* not only to uphold your own integrity as a writer, but also to foil those carping critics who crouch ready to spring on the mere suspicion of error on your part.

In period stories, beware of anachronisms — using people, places, words, and things out of their proper time. Don't have your characters tugging at zippers before these were invented, or waltzing when they should be dancing the minuet. An Oxford Dictionary is practically indispensable for period story writing, since it indicates when a word first came into use. Running an "Oxford check" on the vocabulary of your story characters will also keep their dialogue consistent with their time.

HOW TO KEEP TRACK OF
YOUR RESEARCH

Of course you will want to take notes on all your reading. You may want to jot things quickly on a stenographer's pad and then copy or type them into your loose-leaf notebook, reserved solely for this purpose. This is my method. On the other hand, if you can read your own writing after a lapse of time, you may want to make the notes directly in your research notebook.

In any event, use a comfortably sized book, not too small and not too large. Put in identifying tabs or dividers for each project to make it easier to store and sort your findings. After the project title, for example, you might have tabs for clothing, food, furnishings, nicknames, or settings. *Use brief notes.* Learn some standard short forms of abbreviations and use them consistently. You might even evolve your own form of shorthand—just be sure you can read it back.

As you do research on a certain historical period, possible characters will flock into your mind to people the setting and to provide action and reaction for you. This approach is better than starting with a complete character already formed in your mind, because the initial research will help you create a character in keeping with his era. He will not then be wearing period-correct clothes and thinking present-day thoughts. *In writing period stories you must keep the characters completely in the mood and under the influence of their time.*

Invariably, as you read—fact, fiction, in the adult and juvenile areas—plot situations will begin to take shape. These you should jot down in your workbook, and as you write in its various sections, the story will grow and develop—until you are really inside your period characters and at home in their era. It is then that you will be ready to write the first draft of your tale.

YOUR BIBLIOGRAPHY

Be sure to keep a list of all the sources you consult—for several reasons. If your project is nonfiction, your editor will expect a bibliography (which may or may not be printed at the back of the published book) to back up the authenticity of your work. If any fact is questioned in your work—whether it be in fiction or nonfiction—you can produce your research authority to prove your point. In preparing to write my very short book *Thanksgiving,* I read more than thirty books on the subject, plus articles and pamphlets, and listed every one of them to present to my editors with the final draft.

Don't worry about "knowing too much" about your subject. You'll never put in even half of what you have learned, but it will be there: a solid background of facts to give you confidence in your ability to carry this project off with colors flying.

24
Contemporary Research –
Open Sesame to the Here and Now

Into this category fall all the present-day things you don't know but would like to write about: people, places, professions, the arts, sciences and even "how-to" procedures it might be necessary for your characters to know. Research begins in general with the steps outlined for historical study and then branches out according to the information you require.

Stories where occupations are used either as background or as career-information romances require a thorough grounding in accurate, up-to-date occupational facts.

HOW TO GET THE FACTS

First read everything you can obtain on the particular field you wish to cover. After you have read both fact and fiction, *in the adult and juvenile fields,* the nebulous main character you've had in your mind will start to materialize into a flesh-and-blood person. However, even if you have given this person a name and a home background, you still do not know enough about the occupation to begin the actual writing. Instead, your next step is to contact someone actually in that occupation and at least one school where its skills are taught. Perhaps a friend – or a friend-of-a-friend – can introduce you to an architect, doctor, model, nurse, engineer, designer, banker, or whatever you need.

Lacking a personal introduction, you can write brief letters to professional people and/or the schools you wish to consult, telling them what you are planning to do. (Someone at the school may send you on to an expert.) List your writing credits, if any. Be honest. Should this effort be your "first," don't worry unduly about getting an interview. If your letter is concise and sensible, the interview will probably be granted.

In order to make the most of such interviews, you must come prepared with leading questions. If you possibly can, find out something about the person you're going to see. *Who's Who* or a professional listing may be helpful. In any case, never sail in with a blithe, "Do tell all about your fascinating work." You are not ready to interview until your reading has put into your mind specific questions that you want to ask.

When your authority discovers that you do know something about his work, you'll get full cooperation and possibly other leads to fill in your background details.

Keep a list of the names and addresses of the people you interview on a page next to the bibliography record in your research book. You'll be able to contact them again, if necessary, and (since they are not paid in cash for the time and information they give you) you can thank them graciously with an inscribed copy of your published book.

THAT SPECIAL TRADE TALK

Each profession, craft, or occupational skill carries with it a special vocabulary characteristic of itself. This is often the hardest thing to worm out of the authority you are interviewing. His special vocabulary is a part of his daily life and he no longer recognizes it as such. But a little persistence and gentle prodding will elicit a few catch phrases to add authenticity to your story and make your reader feel "in the know."

Never neglect to get his private trade talk into your research. Even if you're not working in a given field, jot down whatever "backstage terminology" you encounter in conversation, in reading, or in a movie, and file it under the proper heading, such as medical talk, theater jargon, astronauts, musicians. It may save you lots of time in the future. What's more, some word or phrase may even spark a story idea or catchy title.

OCCUPATIONS — THE
SAME — BUT DIFFERENT

Some occupations, though basically the same, have important differences in different countries. For example, to refer to something I know well: ballet in America and ballet in England are approached in an entirely different way, and in France there are differences not common to either one. If I had used British or French sources exclusively in the beginning of my writing, I would have given an entirely wrong slant on the subject to my American readers.

In consulting published material on your subject, note the date of publication. Things change with the passage of years. Also note the country of origin, especially in the case of books. We import a great many translations, so be sure the locale or occupation you're reading about is really the one you need for your story.

Always check the acknowledgment and the bibliography in each book you use for reference. These may be timesaving leads to other sources.

In writing the career or occupational story, make your hero or heroine novice to the business so that as he learns about it, the reader also learns, in a natural course of story events. Readers of fiction do not want to be jolted out of the story by a block of exposition or barrage of statistics. They just want to be *there,* where the story people are, and to live their life with them.

HOW TO MAKE AND DO

If your story people need to build a boat, tie fisherman's flies, make a telescope, climb a mountain, conduct scientific experiments, do magic tricks or get themselves involved in any of a zillion projects *you* don't know a thing about, what do you do? Look it up, of course. There's probably a fine clear book on how to do it, and all you'll need to do is follow instructions. It's as simple as that—and fun!

THE OPEN ROAD—USING
TRAVEL BACKGROUNDS

Should you be planning a trip in this country or abroad, consider utilizing some place that you'll be visiting in a story or a book. But don't expect the plot to come to you on location, without prior preparation on your part. Prepare a channel for ideas to flow toward you by reading about the area you plan to visit. The nucleus of the story may begin to form right then. Whatever ideas you get jot down for future consideration.

When you reach your destination, you will see it with the knowing, selective eye of the writer in search of definite story material. You'll recognize characters as they walk past you, and background and atmosphere will soak into you. You'll be able to accumulate enough of both in a few days to make your story come alive, because of your preparation to be receptive and responsive. *Take lots of photographs—* of people, streets, alleys, houses, particular objects—to stimulate your memories and bring your notes to life when you get back to your workroom. Make notes of the strange sights, sounds, colors, foods, smells, even the climate and how it affects the scene around you.

And don't overlook a visit to the local library or school! The librarians or teachers will probably be delighted to meet you, for writers are considered rather special people by them. If you do not speak the language, someone in the community is sure to know at least a little English. Through the good offices of your new-found friends you may be able to get much more than the tourists' view of the area, and learn of local customs and legends which you can later utilize.

Here, too, advance preparation will pay off. The leading questions you ask will show that you already know something of the area and its people—a compliment to them.

Many places have historic sites carefully preserved or reconstructed. If your story is to be a period piece, be sure to visit these and let your imagination and your prior reading take you back to the time you'll be writing about.

The secret of success in utilizing brief travel research is to write from a non-native viewpoint. Do not select a native boy or girl as your viewpoint character. You cannot know enough to write from inside such a character with any depth. A magazine feature, a picture story, or a book for very young readers may come off successfully from a short jaunt to Italy or India, Africa or Thailand, but for older readers you need to know the thinking and ethnic culture of these people much more intimately. Plan to use an American hero or heroine, and view the foreign scene through his or her eyes. In that way your story can be plausible and convincing.

In planning regional stories of our own country based on a short visit, use a main character with whose viewpoint you're familiar, and transport him or her to the area that will be strange to him or her. The character's reaction to everything that is new and different will be natural, and the reader will see the area and learn about it through his eyes.

STORY TAKE-OFF FROM THE HOME PAD

If you cannot pay an actual visit to the site of your story, there are other ways of getting a look at it. If you should be writing about North American deserts, as I did in several of my novels, then visit a natural history museum. The one in New York City was a tremendous help to me in visualizing my setting, complete with flora and fauna. As to how it "felt" — imagination, stimulated by my reading, took care of that. The zoo helped too with its camels and ostriches and other creatures, for whose habits and appearance I was already prepared. A writer must not go out into the field for "live" research until his or her head is crammed full of facts and details compiled through reading. Then he or she will see much more and absorb particulars that might otherwise be missed.

State and local chambers of commerce will send you packets of valuable material. Tourist maps range from the general to the particular, with fine layouts of towns and cities and streets. Local historical societies can also provide interesting details. Getting to know an area can be greatly helped through a subscription to a local newspaper. A few weeks of faithful reading will make you feel like a native.

With such concentrated study you can be *there* in no time, and take the reader with you. When I was writing my California stories, even the weather reports for the Imperial Valley were of the utmost concern to me — at my desk in New Jersey. After all these years I still feel a kinship with that area and remember with delight a review on one of those books. The critic said that I wrote of the desert "with the affection and enthusiasm of a native"!

LAUNCHING FOREIGN SETTINGS FROM THE HOME PAD

If you plan to use a foreign setting, basing all you know about it on research, there is one other source open to you besides those already described: the foreign embassies. Do not write to U.N. Missions, for most of them are under-staffed and have no facilities for answering your questions. Instead, write to the cultural attaché in Washington, D.C., of whatever foreign embassy you want to contact. State your queries clearly and you will usually get a generous response.

As a common courtesy, include a stamped, self-addressed envelope with any requests you make by mail.

RETURN WITH INTEREST ON YOUR RESEARCH TIME

Extensive research can be costly time-wise, but there are ways to make it pay off. You can use the same research for several books, stories, and articles, and possibly cull it for anecdotes with which to enliven the interviews and book talks you'll be bound to give, once it becomes known in your area that you are a "real live author."

There you are: *Write what you don't know — but find out all about it first!* Whichever way you've come by the background knowledge, your reader should feel convinced that you know it all first hand.

There's magic in "found out" material. It's all fresh and new — and tremendously exciting. The "finding out" has led me into strange and fascinating places: into a lion's cage with a frisky young two hundred eighty-pound lioness in it! And into a Hawaiian party shop — where I learned how to make an orchid salad. It has taken me up a narrow, cob-webbed, winding stairway into a Norman-Gothic tower, where I discovered an imaginary dragon, and into the Oriental Room of the New York Public Library, where I learned about Chinese water clocks and time sticks.

"Choose backgrounds with which you are familiar. . . . Write what you know. . . ." Pooh! If the "rules" of writing were hard and fast, maybe the craft would be easier to practice. On the other hand, people like Jules Verne and Edgar Rice Burroughs would have been complete failures; certainly the one never traveled *20,000 Leagues under the Sea;* and the other was never closer than three thousand miles to Africa when he wrote *Tarzan of the Apes.*

The one thing to remember about research is that no matter what fascinating material it reveals, the human elements, the problems, the conflicts—*the story*—must be your first and foremost concern. Your research, just like your background, should make itself part of the plot.

25
Mystery Stories and Novels

Along with all the other elements that go into a well-crafted story, *a mystery must be mysterious.* It must have some important secret that cannot be easily discovered or readily explained. The enigma, riddle, puzzle, or special problem must involve the story actors to such a degree that they immediately set off to track down one clue after another, despite all obstacles. So much suspense should be generated that even reluctant readers are compelled to move along at a pace never before achieved "to find out what happens next." Most boys and girls like mysteries regardless of their reading skills, and that is why librarians are always searching for bafflers aimed at all ages.

The writing of mysteries for children and teenagers can be rewarding on many counts, but you should not attempt them unless you enjoy that type of story yourself. A lively, inventive imagination is a must, as well as a mastery of the writing craft. You cannot plunge in at the first glimmer of an idea, for the course of a mystery must be charted every step of the way.

Before you try this kind of writing, get the feel for good, currently published mysteries. Your community library is a perfect resource center. Back copies of children's magazines are usually kept on file so you can check through to see how mysteries are handled for particular age groups. The librarian will tell you which books are the most popular with the young crowd. Take an armful home and familiarize yourself with plots and suspense devices used for each age group.

WHAT IS A MYSTERY?

When you encounter this question, you may wonder why it's even posed. Everyone knows what a mystery is!

Or do they?

Here is a true incident. The Edgar Award is given each year by the Mystery Writers of America (MWA) for the best juvenile mystery published in the previous calendar year. Recently, an author, having been presented with an Edgar, whispered to the chairperson of the MWA Juvenile Awards Committee: "Don't tell anyone. But my book isn't a mystery."

Obviously, the YA novel was a mystery even though the author viewed it as an adventure yarn with plenty of suspense and excellent characterization. The novel was eligible for the MWA award because the antagonist was able to prevent the illegal deed and capture the culprit. Although the tale was not one where the main character sought to unmask the unknown villain, the story did depict the law-abiding against the lawbreaker, the age-old battle of good against evil.

There's a lesson to be learned from this author's puzzlement upon winning the honor. A mystery first and foremost is a story with in-depth characterization and a series of events that illuminate some facet of life. Reading that statement, you immediately think those requirements fit any story or novel for youngsters. True. However, some mystery writers mistakenly discount these vital needs—appealing characters and a thoughtful, convincing plot—of juvenile and teenage fiction, assuming the mystery and suspense elements will carry the story. Even if a mystery is filled with eerie, heart-stopping scenes, a magazine or book publisher will not be interested unless the framework supporting that puzzling story contains the substance that any quality story must possess. The editor will label those would-be mysteries as "thin" and return them to the author.

Another insight into the mystery genre that can be learned from the award-winning author's confession is that mysteries—like the villains therein—come in all guises. In the cited incident, the award went to a survival story filled with overtones of mystery. Other published mysteries can be classified as science fiction, romance, fantasy. Don't forget humor in your search for suspense. Think how Alfred Hitchcock introduced humor into his films. The problem is for the author to weave the elements of mystery and suspense throughout whichever type of story he or she wants to write.

PLANNING A MYSTERY

Every writer evolves his or her personal method for planning a story or novel. Intending to write a mystery does not force you to work out the puzzle first and then drape the remainder of the story around it. Many authors who specialize in suspense tales take the opposite tack.

Proceed precisely the same way as for any other fiction. If you select a certain setting, then create characters that will fit into it (or act like square pegs and provide instant conflict). As characters emerge, consider some human situation in which they might be involved — something that will pose a problem, provide opposition, engage the reader's sympathy for the hero and antagonism toward the villain.

Because you'll want boys and girls to read your story, have both taking active part in everything that happens. Read over the chapters in this text that deal with conflict, opposition, suspense. Check over the chapter on characters and see to it that yours have contrasting personalities and drives.

All the time, your basic framework is taking shape. Keep in the back of your mind the idea of injecting some mysterious adventure into the lives of your characters — a puzzle so important that it becomes the focal point of the story, complicating and aggravating the lives of the people in it.

When you really know your characters and setting, let your imagination soar. Have strange events take place, people do or say inexplicable things — all realistically motivated by the characters' personality makeup. The reasons may not be evident to the hero or heroine. Keep in mind the opening sentence of this chapter. *A mystery must be mysterious.*

Be sure to involve your main character personally, so that the solving of the mystery is of utmost importance to him or her and the character actively takes part in everything that happens. He or she might even cause some of the happenings. Never allow your lead to be a mere narrator, watching and reporting what others do. A Dr. Watson can't be the main character (and is no longer popular with editors or readers). The hero-sleuth must be a *doer*, and even though he or she blunders now and then, the character must be an interesting, likable person who carries the reader to the end.

Something has to be happening all the time. Red herrings must be interlaced with real leads to clues. There should be one main mystery that will be solved at the very end after a hair-raising climax. But there should also be minor happenings which send the main character off in the wrong direction, have him or her jump to the wrong conclusion. Smaller mysteries can be explained along the way while the big one still eludes solution.

Planning is ultraimportant to mystery fiction. Foreshadow something here, withhold information there—for a while. However, never base a mystery on some misunderstanding that could have been cleared up if two characters took the time to sit down and have a discussion.

Do not use false clues or place undue emphasis on anything that is not eventually revealed or used. According to Chekhov, "The gun on the wall must be fired." Never create false suspense by focusing on an item or event that is meaningless and has no importance in the story. Things may have a momentary sinister appearance. A spot of red liquid on the kitchen floor may seem to be blood. But if that's ketchup, the true explanation had better be discovered within a few sentences or, at the most, several paragraphs after the sighting. Should several subsequent scenes be motivated by the main character desperately searching to find the cause of the blood stain only to learn the harmless truth, reader frustration will be strong.

But there is no reason to resort to cheap tricks just to bolster the feeling of suspense you want to develop and maintain. It's all in the planning.

MIX AND STIR WELL: THE INGREDIENTS OF A MYSTERY

The Setting.

Settings are very important to a mystery, but not in the way that new writers may assume. An editor of children's books at Alfred Knopf rejected an eight-to-twelve mystery novel with this comment. "Haunted houses have been done to death." That was in 1969. The situation has not changed.

Settings need not be inherently mysterious. Authors are not forced to seek out dilapidated houses, graveyards, darkened buildings with thunderstorms rattling the window panes and torrential rain beating on the roof. Mysteries can happen in classrooms which have brightly decorated bulletin boards and equally revealing fluorescent lighting. Skullduggery can occur on a sun-bathed beach of white sand loud with the gleeful screams of children frolicking in the cool waves. A fast food store, summer theatre, or high school basketball court scrutinized by hundreds of cheering fans could all be used. The environment need not be dark; the motivations and deeds of the antagonist should provide the somber notes to the story or novel.

Recently, one of my students abandoned a mystery novel she planned to write. She concluded unhappily: "No one wants to read a mystery that takes place in the San Joaquin Valley of California! Nothing strange happens here."

My terse answer was: "*Make* something happen."

In this case, the author was wrong. The San Joaquin Valley would be an exciting location for a story laden with mystery. First, it's specific. In years past, juvenile and teenage fiction was justly accused of too often being set in a vague Middle American town that had an all-white population of families who would be prime candidates for the "Good Citizen of the Year" award. Fortunately, writers have emigrated from these idealized and often nonexistent settings, seeking the greener pastures of individualized, realistic locales. This is true of mystery writers, too. Authors also no longer belive they must travel to Zurich, Kyoto, or London to find appropriate backgrounds. They have peered out their windows and realized they can employ their homes, their towns, as the site for nefarious goings-on.

Also a specific location will give you specific personalities. Thus, your cast of characters is figuratively or even literally knocking on your door. We are all influenced by our environment. This is especially true for people who have lived for many years in one area. Think of the variables involved, the influences on us all: financial needs, familial history and goals, the questionable future and what it may or may not

hold, the personality conflicts, the internal doubts and re-
criminations we suffer. These motivational factors are directly related to the world around us. Emotional drives and
buffeting social forces are different in the Adirondack
Mountains, Key West, or the San Joaquin Valley.

The Hero and the Villain.
The word *characters* leads us to two more vital ingredients
of our mysteries: hero and villain. They are inexorably
bound plotwise and of equal intelligence, drive, and physical prowess—with the hero having a slight edge over the
villain.

In other types of fiction, writers sometimes fall into the
trap of not having a main character who is relentless in striv-
ing for a goal. Something about the mystery genre usually
helps writers eliminate this plotting and characterization
weakness. Even the newest writers recognize they must
have a main character who works to solve the puzzle. The
entire plot hinges on his or her efforts to clear away the
mists of confusion. The one precaution to keep in mind is
to avoid having your hero or heroine a younger version of
Superman or Wonder Woman. All human beings have their
flaws, blind spots, less-than-desirable traits. Yes, even our
mystery/suspense protagonists.

And all human beings have a positive facet to their personality—small and not easily recognized as it may be—
even villains. So don't select one too quickly. Don't create
a character so arch that she or he would feel at home in a
melodrama, and keep a watchful eye peeled lest your villain
become a more interesting character to the reader (and
you) than the hero or heroine.

When choosing your villain, avoid people of a particular
national, racial, or religious heritage or any individual who
has a severe physical or emotional abnormality. First, doing
so gives the impression that you are categorizing an entire
group as unsavory. For example, too many children in the
United States are growing up today with the frightening
misconception that every Moslem is a potential or actual
terrorist. We do not want to perpetuate any misconceptions
about segments of our population. Also, vigorous attempts
are being made today to guide youngsters toward an understanding of and a compassion for the physically and emo-

tionally handicapped. Fiction for children and teenagers certainly does not need villains who are escaped residents of a mental health facility, have amputated arms or legs, or are horribly scarred. Fortunately, editors are alert to any negative character who may taint innocent members of a larger group with his or her reputation.

The Crime.
In the mystery short story, you are more limited in your choice of crimes than in a novel. Due to the word length, you are almost forced to keep your main character in a familiar setting: home, school, playground, shopping mall. The crimes he or she encounters are ones that a child would reasonably experience in everyday life. A competitor for a school honor might attempt to discredit a rival. There can be classroom thievery or minor vandalism or stealing of personal possessions. For teenagers—whose social environment is wider—the crimes suffered can be more serious ones involving drug use or felonies such as arson or grand larceny. Except for teenage magazines that accept stories of 2,000 words or more—and there are only a few—murder is not a subject to be tackled.

The short story crime occurs in the opening lines or paragraphs, and the villain is usually a person of similar age and known to the main character before the story begins. This doesn't mean the main character necessarily views his or her suspect as an unpleasant individual before the crime's solution. The crime can also be motivated by self*less* drives. A friend may play tricks on a pal because the second person is continually doing that to those around him or her. The aim of the "crime" is to teach the jokester that his or her deeds are not always funny.

The Title.
Still another ingredient for a mystery is the title. Don't underestimate the importance of this baited hook. Just as the story or novel itself should contain clues to the final solution, the title should have clue words that immediately alert the suspense-greedy reader that here is a delectable meal.

Once upon a time, mystery titles *had* to contain words like: mystery, secret, case, riddle, puzzle. Everyone believed that mystery readers were attracted to such titles like magnets of opposite poles. And they were right.

Something has changed—especially in the book field. While it is true that young readers of all age groups are still attracted to titles like "The Mystery of—" and "The Secret of—", editors claim that this is not true for the eight-to-twelve reader and the young adult suspense fan. The editors prefer titles which are more obscure, some novels even bearing titles that smack of literary pretentiousness.

Let us consider the titles that editors will place on their companies' products.

In the short story field, the famous "clue" words are still used at all age levels. We can add to the alluring ones already given nouns and adjectives like treasure, ghost, mysterious, haunting. In the book field, we are coming in contact with those editors with lofty aspirations. Up to the nine-to-twelve level, the traditional title may be employed. Only a few publishers of nine-to-twelve mysteries (but no editor of YA novels) will have "The Case of . . ." or "The Mystery of . . ." on their spring or fall lists.

Listed below in alphabetical order are recent titles of suspense and mystery novels for these two age groups. Each was nominated for a MWA Edgar and the starred ones were winners:

Bury the Dead (Peter Carter)
Clone Catcher (Alfred Slote)
The Island on Bird Street (Uri Orlev)
Night Cry (Phyllis Reynolds Naylor)
The Other Side of Dark (Joan Lowery Nixon)
Taking Terri Mueller (Norma Fox Mazur)
Through the Hidden Door (Rosemary Wells)
The Twisted Window (Lois Duncan)
We Dare Not Go A-Hunting (Charlotte MacLeod)

The Plot.

Thinking about your plot can help you make several important decisions. It will help you determine whether your mystery is appropriate for a story or novel and what age group is best. Can the crime be solved in two or three scenes? This would make it a short story. The example cited above concerning practical jokes is one that would be handled in short fiction. There are not sufficient twists and turns or complexity of character motivation to stretch this minor mystery into a book except in a picture book mystery.

Yes, Virginia, there are picture book mysteries. Dig into any of Robert Quackenbush's Detective Mole books to see a perfect example of mysteries for the youngest reader.

FITTING THE MYSTERY TO THE AGE GROUP

Let's look at how the age group you choose affects your mystery.

Picture Book Mystery

Miss Nelson Is Missing! (Harry Allard and James Marshall), the worst-behaved class in an elementary school suddenly has a long-term, witch-like substitute teacher because their wonderful, albeit too lenient, Miss Nelson has mysteriously vanished. The children are so threatened by the harridan, the class becomes the *best* one in the school. Clues are scattered throughout the story—both in the text and the illustrations—as in any ethical mystery. Several students engage in sleuthing, trying to locate and rescue their beloved Miss Nelson.

Even from this brief description, you may have guessed the solution, but the answer is rarely obvious to the youngest reader who becomes totally immersed in the story. This mystery with a well-meaning culprit was a nominee for the Best Juvenile Mystery Edgar.

The Seven-to-Ten Mystery

Moving into the seven-to-ten book, there is much more leeway for types of crimes and settings. Again, the scope widens as the amount of available wordage to an author grows. The crimes involve more detailed detection: clues, red-herrings, mysterious characters, and even adult criminals.

In Mary Blount Christian's *The Maltese Feline* for this age group, Fenton and Gerald stumble upon a mystery when they encounter a stray cat. In this same scene, an intrusive girl their age, Mae Donna, and her dog, Stew, arrive on the scene to provide contrasting personalities and conflict.

I bent down and stroked its head. Then I pulled out the leftover half of my sandwich and broke it into little pieces. The cat sniffed quickly, then choked down the tuna, leaving the pickles.

Suddenly the cat bristled, its orange eyes flashing like the lights on a patrol car. I looked up to see Mae Donna and Stew coming toward us fast. Stew must have spotted the poor cat, and was barreling down on it. Mae Donna's eyes were all bugged out like a frog's, and she was holding onto Stew's leash with both hands, pulling with all her might. But the dog was dragging her along easily.

I moved to throw myself between the dog and the cat, but the cat would have none of that. Instead, it swelled up like a blimp, its fur standing out stiff and straight. Its claws sprang out like daggers. *Pfffttt!* it spat angrily.

Stew did a quick U-turn and skittered around behind Mae Donna's legs, peering out, his eyes glassy with fear.

Mae Donna started yelling. "Stew, didn't you hear me tell you to heel? Shame! Shame!" I figured she was madder at her dog for being such a coward than for chasing a cat.

I swelled with pride. That kitty had bluffed Mae Donna's big old dog. What a tough cat! Maybe all that fat was pure muscle! And it was obviously lost, poor thing. Why else would it follow a couple of strange kids — make that *unknown* kids. "I guess the least I can do is to take you home with me until I find out who you belong to," I said.

I scooped the cat into my arms, and that was when I noticed the collar it was wearing. It was really fancy, with colored glass cut to look like rubies and diamonds. The glass stones were fixed in a flower design so it seemed like the cat had a wreath of daisies around its neck. And then I saw something stuck in the collar — a rolled up piece of paper.

I pulled it out and unfolded it. Scribbled in red crayon was a note that said, *Help me, please!*

Notice how this common occurrence of finding a stray animal introduces a puzzle that is minimal at first but will take on more sinister overtones.

There are several reasons authors intending to write mysteries for this age group should read *The Maltese Feline*. True, the young reader might not catch the humorous rewording of a well-known adult mystery title, but with so many old movies being shown on television these days, who knows?

The style of writing is perfect for the seven- to ten-year-old; lively, filled with humor. Christian uses another plotting device that works well with juveniles and adult readers. *A reader enjoys knowing something the main character does not*. In this particular story, the information involves Mae Donna's father and Gerald's perception of his occupation.

The ending is worthy of study if you are considering whether your youthful detectives should help capture the criminal. It's unfair to disclose an author's devices when discussing suspense novels and whodunits, but the climax of the story where Gerald and his buddies help to physically apprehend the villains is believable as well as exciting.

The Nine-to-Twelve/Ten-to-Fourteen Mystery.
This category permits an even wider choice of settings. Yes, it is possible to use foreign settings at this level, but note that word — possible. It is not essential. The major requirement of a setting is that the author can make it come alive for the reader.

In books for this age group, the crimes become more serious; the culprits more heinous. Also, the skillful use of mystery techniques by the author has to be raised to an even higher level. The complex techniques for developing suspense, providing clues while at the same time obscuring them, and building steadily toward an exciting climax and quick wrap-up are required for this reader as much as for an adult mystery fan.

Related to that last ingredient, the device utilized in many, now-dated adult mysteries of having a detective collect all the suspects in a room and indulging in an endless, moment-by-moment, clue-by-clue explanation of the crime and how he or she so cleverly unravelled the mystery is strictly *verboten*. Present day young readers will not endure such wordiness. And there is no reason they should. The responsibility rests on the author to plan the flow of his or her mystery so the various strands of plot will be explained before the climactic moment. In that Big Scene, the question to be answered is either "Who?" or "How will our hero or heroine win?" Or both.

The author for this age reader should have a thorough understanding of the average youngster clearly in mind — his or her sophistication, desires in terms of reading material, grasp of the realities of life. In the early 1960s, a nine-to-twelve mystery novel centered on the disappearance of a diamond ring. One hundred and twenty-eight pages later, the reader learned the dastardly thief was the crow living in the apple tree. The bird had stored the jewelry in its nest. A young reader's reaction today to such a trivial puzzle dragged out into a book-length story would be a laugh of derision or a word that you would probably not use in a mystery for this age. Be aware. Youngsters today do not want to waste their time with inconsequential mysteries that should be relegated to the slag heap reserved for old-fashioned reading matter.

And to keep your novels contemporary, the plots may concern the important issues of the day and how they affect the young main character, his or her friends, and family. Nine-to-twelve mysteries have had story lines dealing with racial or religious bigotry, child abuse, and the problems of single-parent families. Obviously, the young person featured in the story cannot solve these social problems but he or she can develop an awareness of them and combat their ramifications at his or her level. This is simply an option open to you, not something to be flung into your story to give it a modern feel.

Most important, don't underestimate this reader. Mysteries for the six-to-nines and seven-to-tens have plots that adults can figure out long before the conclusion. Don't assume such elementary plots will do for the nine-to-twelver. You will have to be at your best to keep them guessing until the end. The moment you think, "Oh, they're not sharp enough to figure that out," you have lost. *Really* lost. The youngster will close your book and seek out one that offers a challenge.

The Young Adult Mystery.
Challenge is the keyword for young adult mysteries. The following statement is not an exaggeration. *The average young adult mystery book is better written than the average adult mystery book.* This generalization does not include authors such as Martha Grimes, Dick Francis, or P. D. James—but then they're not average—but does include many authors whose adult hardcover mysteries have sold thousands of copies and their paperbacks, millions.

There may be several reasons for this fact of publishing life. (A) Young adults are more discriminating in their mystery tastes than adults.

(B) Young adult writers are more skillful than many writers for the adult market.

(C) Young adult novels more frequently break the mold of genre writing.

Pick one of the above.

(Actually, all three have degrees of truth in them.)

Any crime, criminal, or mode of detection that is used in a book for grown-ups can be utilized in a young adult mystery. Any line of dialogue that a writer of adult material would use can be employed in a young adult novel. The major requirement is that the main character of a young adult mystery must be a male or female in his or her late teens or early twenties. And, as already stated, *quality*, spelled in blazing capital letters.

Patricia Windsor is an outstanding author of young adult mystery and suspense novels — outstanding in a field where excellence is the norm. Her novel, *The Sandman's Eyes*, winner of MWA's Best Juvenile Edgar, opens with teenager Michael Thorne arriving in his hometown of Monrovia Park.

> I had come back from being away a long time. I stepped off the train, put my suitcase down, and looked at the town. It looked the same as when I left. The big iron Kornkill sign still hung crazily from one hinge and the red neon letters still spelled BUD in the window of the Station Diner. Even the smell of the place was the same: a sour tang from Krackmayer's sausage factory mingling with the brooding river's fishiness. I was home.

As the story unfolds, we learn Michael is returning from a center for disturbed youth where a court had sent him for treatment. Sitting alone that first night, he is beset by memories and fears.

> Suddenly I have to sit up and feel my chest. Getting the can't-breathe feeling. Don't panic. I think: Dr. Painter. He'd give me a tranquilizer. There's aspirin and Tylenol in the bathroom cabinet. The idea of walking all the way to the bathroom is overwhelming. A hundred miles. I can't do it.
>
> I'm not going to get scared. It's stupid. But there are no doctors here. It's a funny thing, but I never thought of it. They let me out and now there are no more doctors. They sent me home without a doctor. What am I going to do, living here without a doctor?
>
> "Let yourself flow with it," Dr. Kline used to say. "Don't fight the truth if it wants to reach you."
>
> So what's the big truth that wants to reach me now, here in my own bedroom?

Flow, flow, breathe steadily. You can breathe. It's automatic. Your body takes care of breathing all by itself. You only think you're in charge of breathing but you have nothing to do with it at all.

Dark shadows loom around me and wind rushes past my face. I'm trying to flow with it, but I don't think I like this particular moment of truth. I'm high up, standing at the top of the wall, looking down. Something's crumpled at the bottom. I saw it fall, arcing like a bad dream that can't change its mind; a nightbird flailing its wings as it soared downward. Did I hear the thud or just imagine it?

A screen door bangs shut in my mind. The light comes back. The shadows retreat, the wind stops blowing. I'm sitting on my bed holding a copy of Nietzsche and I'm breathing, I'm still alive. But the taste of the memory is sour.

What are the large questions Windsor poses in this mystery? For starters, the double-barreled one of "What is sanity and reality?" Like beauty, concrete definitions of those two conditions exist only in the mind of the beholder. Luigi Pirandello, the Italian playwright, spent his life in the theatre struggling to answer that question, as did Eugene O'Neill in *The Iceman Cometh*.

The setting of *The Sandman's Eyes* is a small town. We've all learned that life in such a closed, firmly stratefied environment is not what we see in a Norman Rockwell painting. For that matter, that magazine cover art may merely be fantasy-fulfillment, something the viewer desperately wants to believe pre-suburban life was like "back then." Writers such as Shirley Jackson in her adult short story, "The Lottery," have revealed the darker side of small town existence.

Other questions are raised in Windsor's novel. Was there a murder or a tragic accident? Who seems to be trying to prevent Michael from learning the answers to his questions? Do the evil conditions surrounding the death exist only in Michael's mind?

If there was a crime, then Michael was the sole witness. Internal forces demand he determine the facts. But a mathematical ratio is set up: the more clearly the teenager understands what actually occurred, the more desperate the killer becomes. Peace of mind for one can only create frantic fears for another. A nightmarish relationship is established until one person will be declared the victor.

Such is the stuff that mysteries are made of.

26

Writing for the Earliest Ages — Picture Books

The term *picture book* is both a perfect group name and a murky one. What makes it so appropriate is that all the books in this category are indeed *picture* books, ranging from those that have only illustrations to the books in which the drawings and words share the responsibilities. What clouds the issue is that many companies use the term to signify only that collection of material printed for the five-to-seven-year-old.

As a result, you may learn that Publisher X seeks "picture books" but still be uncertain exactly what the editor wants. This is why market study is an author's best friend. Send for a free publisher's catalogue which is revised twice a year — spring and fall — and see what type of picture books a company publishes. The age groupings will be given in the blurb for each book. You will notice that publishers separate picture books into three types: (1) babies to two-year-olds, (2) three- to five-year-olds (3) Five- to seven-year-olds.

Before we examine each subdivision individually, let's see what you need as a writer if you wish to enter this wide-ranging category of children's books.

YOU AND PICTURE BOOKS

At one time or another everyone tries to write a picture book. But though many are called, few get published. Why? Because the writing of picture books is a specialized art in a highly specialized field.

Know thy reader. This motto should be on the desk of every would-be picture-book writer. Not knowing one's reader is probably rejection cause number one for those aspiring to write for the baby-to-seven age group. It is responsible for stories which are much too long, too involved, full of grownup ideas children "ought to like," and sugarcoated sermons written dotingly to some imaginary "perfect" child or to an equally nebulous "naughty" one.

The first step in producing a suitable story for this age is to get to know little children as intimately as possible. If you don't have youngsters, or the ones you do have are not the right age for this kind of study, become an honorary aunt or uncle to some nearby small fry, and observe the tricycle set from the closest range possible. Tell them stories; read to them.

When did you last read with a child? Or better still, with two or more children on either side of you and the picture book in your lap? When they are not passive listeners but participants encouraged to interrupt, exclaim, comment and discuss, children can be led to tell you what kind of stories they like and don't like and why. Gradually they can be trained to comment even on your own efforts without being overly polite.

The writer for this age group needs eyes and ears to see and hear all the small sights and sounds of the child's world, as well as the great big obvious ones. Get down to the child's eye-level—physically—squat, kneel, sit, lie down on your back or your stomach, and see as he does: objects, towering grownups, pets, toys, grass, bugs. Remember how high ceilings were when you were very small? How big all the rooms? How deep the shadows? *How tall* your Christmas trees? A heart that feels, or perhaps remembers, the terrific impact of infant joy, tragedy, and triumph is essential, too.

Visits to a nursery school, a kindergarten, a first grade— where you can observe the infinite variety of small, uninhibited personalities asserting themselves, displaying their interests and their skills, and sounding off on their own big ideas—may also prove valuable, if the youngsters forget you're there and act naturally. Be sure to discourage the grownup in charge from introducing you as that "nice writer who is going to do a story all about us!" This will ruin everything and you might as well go home. *No* introduction is much better. Be in the room before the children arrive, and sit out of the way pretending to occupy yourself with something that looks like an uninteresting report or checklist. Soon the children will forget you're there and you can tune in on them.

Playgrounds are another fertile field for observation — and story ideas. Listen to the children talk, watch how they play, note their favorite games, their favorite "pretend" characters, the causes for their laughter and their tears.

If, back in your study, you still have difficulty in visualizing a child of the age you need — either as a story actor or story listener, here is a trick that has helped my students. Clip from magazines pictures of likely looking young children and use them as prototypes and as "audience" for your tales. Look straight at them as you write and later read your material. If these pictured youngsters become real to you, you will not condescend to them from your superior adult world. You will not sermonize, you will not dash off adult whimsy under the impression that you are writing for children. *You will write directly to the child of his or her own world, in his or her own language.*

Get to know the product by collecting an armful of picture books from your community library. Study them thoroughly. You will find that the publications average 25 to 1,000 words. For those of the toddler to three-year-old and the five- to seven-year-old, a simple plot begins to enter in, with three or four exciting little incidents brought to a satisfactory conclusion. The books usually run thirty-two to forty-eight pages, including those allotted to front matter: title pages, copyright, etc. The five- to seven-year-old requires a bit more plot — and possibly a sixty-four page book, with not quite so many illustrations.

Your best method for getting the *feel* of a picture book may be to select several you especially like and type out the texts, word for word. Seeing the books in typescript will give you a clearer impression of the amount of text that is acceptable, and also of how text and pictures are balanced.

For submission, however, editors advise writers to type their stories straight through, triple-spaced or double-spaced twice between the lines. Do not type a line or two to a page.

Editors also suggest that in the planning stage you dummy up your story. That is, imagine the picture and place the text with it, so that you will not run over the usual length of such a book, or underestimate it. When your first draft is ready, mark off the possible pictures, drawing a pencil lightly between the lines of text. Then count off the number of *different* pictures you have. Variety of scenes or character groupings and action is a must.

A fairly equal amount of text for each page is preferred, rather than a line or two on one page and a solid block of type on the next. And remember, *in a picture book the pictures must carry about half of the text; descriptions are cut to a minimum, if not altogether.* The final layout and picture-text matching will be done in your editor's office. Do not send detailed notes on what the pictures are to be. However, where clarification is definitely required, brief notes, single-spaced between lines of text, may be made in parentheses. Don't overdo the suggestions; editors come equipped with lively and well-trained imaginations.

And now let's examine the scope of the picture book market.

THE THREE TYPES OF PICTURE BOOKS

At one time, editors viewed picture books as only those volumes that now come under the five-to-seven age classification. They did label some as "younger" and "older" picture books, but that is as far as their subdivisions extended. Bookstore and public library demands have opened a market that trade book editors never knew existed. Relatives enter bookshops, requesting books aimed at babies and toddlers, and "Toddler Corners" are being set up in public libraries. In an effort to cash in on this lucrative market, some editors are classifying their books inappropriately. You can be more knowledgeable than many editors, however. Here is an accurate profile of each age group.

Babies to Three-Year-Olds:

Because this age group has special needs, it is not open to the average writer of juvenile literature. Typical children in this age bracket are totally self-involved, and their world extends little beyond that which they can see. They have to learn what a book is and that you proceed consecutively from the front pages to the back. A book is an adjunct of their toys in that it has to develop visual perception and eye-to-hand coordination, and aid motor development. All this means that books that are truly appropriate for the baby-to-three-year-old group should be written by experts in child psychology and edited by people with an in-depth awareness of the very young child.

Although there are publishers who claim that certain of their books are suitable for these readers, many trade books cited as being for babies to three-year-olds are actually for toddlers to five-year-olds. The problem lies in the fact that most editors have not been trained in recognizing the stages of physical and emotional development of the very young child. In fact, some may look down on child experts as "educators" and feel these people do not know literature. While this may be true in a few instances, these "educators" *do* understand children and writing and editing books for this age group require that special knowledge.

An excellent example of a book that recognizes the special needs of the youngest readers is Rod Campbell's *Buster Gets Dressed,* a book with activities for physical development and a text that will appeal to children who are mastering the task of dressing themselves. By flipping half pages, readers add clothes to Buster's still form. The articles of clothing are labeled, and details pointed out: "Buster's overalls have buttons."

Another title worth studying is *Lost and Found* by Martha Whitmore Hickman, who received training in child psychology at Mount Holyoke College in Massachusetts. Even for extremely young children who exist in a confined environment, objects can be lost. Or the family dog may become lost. And, if a parent or protecting adult is out of the room for too long, the youngsters can experience the emotional trauma of being lost—aloneness, no one to provide for them, a feeling of being unwanted, deserted. In *Lost and Found*, the everyday situations depicted will entertain but also comfort the readers.

The best books for this age group are offered by publishers specializing in educational materials. The books are prepared in-house, which means they are conceived and written by full-time employees of the company. The authors are highly attuned to a child's physical and emotional needs and therefore better suited for the creation of this material than the average writer and the (too-often) unaware trade book editor.

Toddlers to Five-Year-Olds.
Take heart! If you are not the ideal candidate to write for the youngest segment of the picture book audience, you may well be perfect for this group. If you have ever been a parent, numerous ideas are in your head just waiting to be plumbed.

Books for this age reader are deisgned to be read, not manipulated like jigsaw puzzles, and meant to acquaint the child with his or her widening world as well as provide an esthetic experience. They are also intended to be a springboard for the adult reader to develop the book's contents into a larger event for the child listener, a true time for generation sharing.

Let's determine what is unique to the toddler to five-year-old. The breadth of his or her world increases by the day. True, babies to three-year-olds are taken shopping by their parents or accompany other adults on family outings, but the external scenery to those youngsters is like a motion picture film where the time sequence has been speeded up. Places and people flash by in a blur. The older child is noticing locations and individuals, and, while not consciously seeking to do so, is trying to fit into that expanding vista. Both reluctant to leave an existence where he or she is the center of attention, yet eager to explore one where he or she is part of the larger world, the child is struggling to relate to the increasing variety of faces and places. The young person's perception of objects is that they are no longer hands-on toys but things that provide a service. The labels the younger members of this age group attach to these objects may amuse or confuse parents when the known word is applied to the unfamiliar. The family car may be called a house. "Are we going to ride in the house today?" The child realizes his mother or father refer to that giant metallic container as a "car" but to him or her it provides almost everything a home does with the addition of motion.

The author must not only explain objects and experiences that the toddler to five-year-old is encountering but help the child to see him/herself in relation to this ever-widening inventory. To facilitate the education, the *concept book* has evolved. Concept books — fiction or nonfiction — promote an understanding of what is happening in the child's world. The published volumes can deal with solid objects or intangible subjects such as time, but for this age, the emphasis is on *experiential* books for the child: a stormy night or a walk through the park or caring for the family pet.

While the illustrations and brief text are an entity unto themselves, the wise adult reader expands the book-sharing into a larger experience where the grown-up and child exchange memories and feelings. These books are not meant to put a child to sleep. (Is it any wonder that fewer children read today when their first perception of a book is something that a parent carries into their bedroom and reads in order to put the youngsters to sleep?) Concept books are designed to awaken the children's imagination and provide an even wider knowledge of their place in the broader scheme of life. And they may be used as reference books of sorts. The book about a stormy night may be utilized a few days after the initial reading when an evening thunderstorm moves into the area. The intelligent parent sits with the child as the wind roars and thunder crashes, recalling the book, but the grown-up and youngster now open themselves even further to reveal deeper reactions.

And this is why I said earlier that if you have ever parented, you may be a natural as a writer for the toddler to five-year-old. Dredge up memories of what intrigued or dismayed your child at that age: the first awareness of falling snow on his face, the first jet flight to visit grandparents, sharing her toys with a visiting child. (If you want a story with *conflict*, try that situation as a basis for a fictional account.)

You might employ the free association method, sitting alone with a pad and pencil and just letting memory fragments flow, jotting *each* down no matter how insignificant. Later you can investigate them for their book potential. Just allow those warm and sometimes chilling mental images to surface. Accept the ordinary because what's usual to us can be of major significance to a toddler to five-year-old. Author Margery Facklam wrote two concept books for this age: *I Go to Sleep* and *I Eat Dinner*. At first glance, you may think,

"How commonplace." Exactly! A second evaluation makes you realize what important rituals these are to a child whose days pass in a series of seemingly unexceptional (to adults) routines. Once you've let your reminiscences pour forth, examine each idea.

Many concept books are sensory experiences. For example, let's consider that walk through a park mentioned earlier. The combination of text and illustrations will bring the five senses alive, recreating them in the child-listener: odors, tastes, sounds, visual images as well as the sense of touch.

Or the concept book draws a connection between the child's experience and a larger one existing in the world. Facklam's *I Eat Dinner* makes a point that the book's narrator eats dinner in only one way that is different from ducks, cats, and other familiar animals. The child uses a table and a spoon and enjoys *dessert*. Although not overtly stated, the book's message reveals that humans are members of the animal kingdom, and, thus, must eat. The illustrations show a youngster that a boy will assume is a boy and that a girl will think is a girl. The pictures also depict what is not explained in the written text: details about how each animal eats.

Once you've selected an idea and have decided whether it's a sensory experience for the reader or an informational one that will help the youngster place him/herself into the total picture, the time has come to check the competition.

Has the concept been explored in book form for the toddler to five-year-old?

Your school or public librarian will help you answer that question as will publishers' catalogues. You, of course, cannot send for a listing from each company, but you can check a publication that features ads for the major juvenile publishers. Each February and July, *Publishers Weekly* has an issue laden with announcements for the next season's books. Titles (very direct for this age group) as well as specific age levels are provided. Most children's librarians of public libraries keep these children's book issues on file.

After studying the ads and learning what is already in the library, your first reaction may be, "But *everything's* been done!" Not so. Each year new titles are published, and they do not rehash what has already seen print. It is true that the most obvious ideas have appeared in book form. The examples cited in this section—snow, storms, a park stroll—have been utilized. All that remains is for you to dig deeper, bring forth the less obvious facets of the child's world. They are there, and you will unearth them if you view each day through a young child's eyes. And that's the key to success. Become a child when writing a book.

And let's keep that technique in mind as we make the selection of what should appear in your book. Return to our example of a visit to the park. It would be possible to list down hundreds of sights, sounds, and odors that a person encounters while strolling along the paths or lake shore. You will have only thirty-two pages, however. Keep thinking what would impress a child during that park adventure. An adult might spot the litter baskets overflowing and often ignored altogether, the homeless asleep on the benches, a romantic teenage couple embarrassingly physical for a public place. The child might react to the warmth of the sun compared to the coolness of the shade, or the ice cream vendor with a silvery, refrigerated pushcart, or the gray squirrels that will run right up to you and take food from your fingers.

When it comes to the writing, use *one fact per page*. If you decided to let your main character feel the sun's heat and savor the elms' shade, you cannot do that on a single page. The toddler to five-year-old can absorb only one impression at a time. A page would be devoted to the blazing sun, another to the dim shade.

In your first version, let *everything* appear on the pages. Don't let your imagination become doubled-over with cramps because you're trying to edit as you put the first words on paper. That is your job as you work on the second version and the third version. Those are the times the "fat" is lopped until the "meat" remains. Here is Margery Facklam talking about writing her companion volumes *I Eat Dinner* and *I Go to Sleep*.

> Actually I sent my editor a longer version, one book that incorporated the idea of both books and some additional information about animals. But the editor kept telling me to cut and trim, which I thought was impossible because I was already writing shorter than I usually do in nonfiction. (I seem always to be in the teaching mode, and you know how long-winded teachers can be.)

It wasn't long before I became addicted to cutting, and it became almost a contest with myself to see how much I could say in the fewest words.

And now for a sample of toddler to five-year-old writing. We've already discussed the format for *I Eat Dinner*. The same organization was employed for the same reasons in *I Go to Sleep*—the narrator compares his or her sleeping habits to animals. In the sample below, each line represents a page in the printed book.

> I go to sleep,
> but not like a bunny in a burrow,
> or a mole in a hole
> or a bear in a den,

And what is the difference? The young main character goes to sleep . . .

> after a story and a hug.
> Good night.

Five to Seven-Year-Olds.

The reader has grown older and less self-centered, striking out on his or her own—for brief periods of time. At the upper end of the age bracket, they trek to school each day, leaving the security of home and parents behind. Their tastes in reading have broadened along with their horizons. While concept books are still offered, new categories appear: contemporary stories, folktales, fantasies, and the perennial animal stories.

You studied the brief example from a concept book for the toddler to five-year-old audience. Here is a sample from *The Goodnight Circle* by Carolyn Lesser, written for the oldest of the picture book set. Again, the concept is animals sleeping, but now there is no need to constantly relate it to the reader's life. He or she will do that during the reading. Merely the information about the creatures is presented. Note also the writing is fuller, even poetic, for this older age group. The line indentations duplicate the actual page format, and the extra spacing between the two sections indicates separate pages.

> The goodnight circle begins, as the setting sun turns the sky orange. The warm spring air cools. Mother deer nudges her

fawns into a bed of soft, fragrant pine needles. The fawns
nestle close to mother deer, as she lovingly licks their fur.
Good night, pretty deer.

It is scold and chatter, all day, as the noisy squirrels show
their ten babies where to find nuts. At last evening comes.
All the babies are safe in the cozy nest, high in the hollow
tree. Mother squirrel ducks into the hole and snuggles with
her babies. Good night, busy squirrels.

The line arrangement is shown only because you may
spot odd designs in printed books as you study them. When
you type your manuscript, do not worry about doing this.
Simply arrange each page in a paragraph. Once the book
goes into production, the art department of the publisher
will determine artistic placement of the print.

As for the other types of five-to-seven picture books, you
must have a story to tell. This means a story with a pattern,
with growth and a climax. Too many beginners get a character in mind and sail off in a welter of cute sentences, some
rhymes, and possibly an initial cunning situation. Without
a carefully thought-out plan, they soon dissolve into no-
story or an inconclusive little incident. Stories of that type
are legion—and very hard to sell. Occasionally they do get
a benign nod, but only because some novel twist caught the
editor's attention, or she knows just the artist to bring this
particular little piece to life.

In general, even the simplest picture book must have a
story, in the sense of a beginning, a middle, and an end.
Events must occur in a logical sequence that leads to a logical—or perhaps to a surprising—*happy* conclusion.

The child from three to seven is *read* to. You need not
confine yourself to the "easy reading" vocabulary of some
200 to 500 words.* Nevertheless, you still want to choose
simple, rhythmic, expressive words a child can understand.
A pattern of repetition can be a successful attention-keeper
for the very young, who cannot follow a wandering plot.
The repeated words become a pleasing, familiar landmark.

---

*Some educational researchers claim that four's and five's understand from
1,500 to 2,300 words but use only about one-third of them. Their attention
span is short—fifteen to twenty minutes. The six-, seven-, and eight-year-olds
have a listening vocabulary of about 24,000 words, a speaking vocabulary of
some 2,500, and a reading vocabulary of only a few hundred.

For this age, plot should be the simplest plan of cause and effect: because of this, that happened.

PLOT MATERIAL

There is ample plot material for the picture story. Everyday happenings in play activities, family fun, home adventures make good subjects when given a fresh, unhackneyed treatment. Pets, toys, all sorts of possessions can furnish springboards for lilliputian adventures.

The child's inner world can be delved into also. Although his or her fears must be treated carefully, they offer fine story material. Fear of the dark, swimming, playmates, or animals can be dealt with and *resolved*. And the universal needs: to be safe and secure — home, mother; to be loved; to achieve; to belong; to know — all these are also good material.

FANTASY — THE WORLD
THAT IS BUT NEVER WAS

Fantasy has its place in plot material for the very young — and more of it is published now than a few years back. But making the unreal seem real, the impossible plausible, and writing straight-faced, endearing nonsense requires not only a bumper gift of special talent, but also the ability to make of it a polished art. Such polished writing is not usually within the scope of the newcomer to the field.

Still, you may be a "natural" at the fantastic, able to write it with a precious kernel of truth — like Dr. Seuss. Only you must not write *like* Dr. Seuss, Maurice Sendak, or Shel Silverstein. You must write like *you*, revealing the uniqueness of your imagination through your own individual conceptions and style. Neither imitation nor rehashed old favorites are wanted by the editors — unless they are retold, translated, or adapted folk tales.

Stories which will get serious consideration from editors must be well conceived and competently presented. Stories of personified animals, like the little badgers in Lillian and Russell Hoban's *Frances* concoctions: *Bedtime for Frances, A Birthday Party . . . A Baby Sister . . . Best Friend for Frances*, and so on. Each one is amusingly tender, childlike, and "real" — and each has a smidgen of universal wisdom to impart painlessly to the reader. The rules of good plotting and planning are always observed in stories that really endure.

Imagined experiences—as long as they are not dreams—like trips into space or backward and forward in time or into the ocean depths as in Jane Yolen's *Greyling* are good subjects. Great suspense is created when Greyling must decide if he should rescue his "father" who is drowning. If he goes into the sea, however, he will revert to a seal. This is contrasted by the "mother's" agony as she watches her husband floundering, yet does not want to lose Greyling. Science fiction for the younger reader, imaginatively laced with a background of facts, will get an eager reading if its entertainment value is high. There is no dearth of subjects!

So, although fantasy is far from easy to bring off acceptably in today's competitive market, it can be done. I am not going to discourage you from attempting it—just warn you again of the rocky road ahead. Editors are swamped with bad fantasy (and awful picture books), but a gem will always shine through—and I assure you, every manuscript that comes in is sampled by that hopeful "first reader." A "discovery" is such a triumph!

Maybe the triumph will be yours.

STORIES IN VERSE

These are troublesome. Over and over editors have told me:

> . . . we have found children's books written in verse extremely difficult to sell. This is true, amazingly enough, even with poetry of well-known authors. As a result, we have to be extremely wary about undertaking this type of project unless we are thoroughly convinced that it has a very special spark and charm which gives it lasting appeal—and a sound, sure sales potential.

But stories in verse *do* get published, and if you're one of those whom nothing will discourage, you will continue to tell your stories in rhyme. There are people who have a natural flair for this; the words seem to bubble over in them spontaneously. But like writers in prose, they too have blind spots and on occasion, tin ears. One reason why verse stories fail to come off is that lines are forced, contrived to rhyme. The reader stumbles over them and the whole effect falls flat.

Picture books, especially verse, must always be tested by reading aloud. Try each line, couplet, rhyme. Substitute a word or phrase. Sometimes juggling the lines will do the trick; sometimes altering the position of the stanzas. It's painstaking labor. You must read—change—read again, *listen*.

Years ago, my husband had the rare privilege of observing Jasha Heifetz select a violin for his concert work. The artist played classic Guarnari, Stradivari, Amati, and finally made his choice. When someone in the group around him asked why he chose that particular instrument, he replied simply: "It sings to me."

Your verse should sing to you. Until it does, don't send it to an editor.

THE FIVE SENSES

Remember, children love the texture of things, the smells, the tastes, the color, the sounds of things: plan to use as much sensory detail as possible in your stories. But it has to be an integral part of the story, not just words thrown in at measured intervals. As a writer for the young, train yourself to gather these impressions not only in grownup words, *but in words a small child might use*. Listen to the living sources of a vitally expressive vocabulary running about your house or neighborhood, or chattering in the seat behind you on the bus. Your eyes and ears must always be open, and the impressions you collect should be kept at the tips of your wits to garnish whatever tale you concoct.

> . . . not even Anderson . . . can match the inventiveness of the small child, who hears the grapefruit juice going *dupple, dupple* from the can, the waves making a *suchsush* against the ship, the rain coming down in *dlocks*. . . .
>
> [The child] listens to those who speak his language. It is a language of action, of sensory images, a language telling of the touch of things, and their colors, odors, sounds. It has movement, pace, rhythm. For the child is not a static creature. Out of his reservoir of sensory responsiveness come rushing up words that move with the rhythm of this thought: galloping, bumping, coasting, swinging words. . . .

This is from Dr. Claudia Lewis's book, *Writing for Young Children*, in which she has made a scientific as well as an artistic study of children's language, showing how it reveals what is going on inside of them.

AND THE FINISHED PRODUCT

Whatever a beginner's blithe ideas may be about writing "those cute little books," they soon undergo a change if he or she sincerely tries to carry such a project through. The picture book is one of the hardest things to write. It requires brevity and therefore the sternest discipline and testing of writing skill—not a word wasted, rewriting time and again—four, five, ten times, for the desired effect.

Dr. Seuss estimated that he wrote and drew more than 1,000 pages for each sixty-four-page book *he* completed. Whenever you grow weary and permissive on rewriting, think of that.

Walter de la Mare said: "Only the rarest kind of best in anything can be good enough for the young." So the picture book writer must be a perfectionist, for the production of a children's book of lasting value is a highly demanding art. And once beloved, a book will be read and re-read to thousands of children, possibly for generations!

27
Writing the Easy-to-Read and Hi/Lo Book

With publishers actively seeking material to satisfy the ever-hungry market for easy-to-read and hi/lo books, authors who have perfected their storytelling craft might well investigate this field. You do not need a background in teaching, although such training would be helpful. Some publishing houses provide word lists; others merely want the author to write the story as simply as possible, and an educational consultant hired by the publisher adapts the text to the low reading level. Unfortunately, some editors are so eager to jump aboard the trend they are labeling any book that appears simple as an easy-to-read. Perhaps they do not realize that those three words have a specific meaning for teachers and librarians who purchase the book and assume they are obtaining an authentic easy-to-read—one written at a specified reading level.

Before deciding that you want to write either type, be sure to read an armful of either kind of book. A librarian will help you find such novels and nonfiction.

EASY-TO-READ BOOKS
Of the two types, there is a stronger potential for you to sell the easy-to-read book because so many more are being published than hi/lo books. Study them by reading each book several times—at least once aloud. Type a few pages from a published book so you get a feel for the simple sentences. Now you are ready to write *your* story. And that's what you do—write the story without thinking about vocabulary, sentence length, or whether it's easy or hard to read. Worrying about those elements during the creative stage will merely block your ideas and cripple the story. When

you have polished the story so that the tale can stand on its own, you will change the text to fit the requirements for this category.

You will notice that most easy-to-read books are written in the *ragged right* format. This means paragraphs are not indented, and a printed line is a natural word group or a complete sentence in itself. Also, each line usually contains about six to eight words. Here are the opening paragraphs of *Tall Corn—A Tall Tale* by Dorothy O. Van Woerkom. (The space between what appears to be merely three paragraphs actually indicates the page breakdown.)

> The corn in Texas grows mighty tall.
> And that corn can grow mighty fast.
> Mighty tall farmers live in Texas too.
>
> One mighty tall farmer
> had a mighty tall wife,
> three mighty tall boys,
> and a short little girl named Alice.
> One day the farmer said
> to his three sons, "Let's go out
> and plant some tall corn."
>
> At noontime Ma said to Alice,
> "Alice, it's time for lunch.
> Take the lunch basket to
> your pa and your brothers."
> Alice took the lunch basket
> out into the cornfield.

Van Woerkom has shared with us her memories of how this easy-to-read book came into existence. Note what she says about her idea file. A recurring theme through this text has been that authors keep idea files. We all have the same general headings: plot incidents, themes, characters, settings. But we must individualize these files. What excites one writer's imagination may leave another cold. Here is what Van Woerkom recalls about *Tall Corn—A Tall Tale*.

> The editor asked me to do a tall-tale story for readers at the second-grade reading level. She wanted a child character, single viewpoint, with a plot that showed the child hero resolving a story

problem through the child's ability to think something through and to make a right decision. I keep a file of ideas, themes, sayings, etc., and in my "Tall Tales" file I found this one-liner: THE CORN GREW SO TALL, THE SUN POPPED IT RIGHT OFF THE EARS.

So in effect the editor gave me the idea and theme, the one-liner gave me the vehicle to explore them through. I love one-liners.

Page breakdown is your first step toward getting your story into the required form. Generally, easy-to-reads are about forty-eight pages in length. Leaving a few blank pages for the front and back matter in the book, you should plan your story in thirty-eight pages.

Re-read the story that you have written, breaking it into thirty-eight segments. While you are doing this, keep in mind that these pages will carry illustrations. Does each section of your story contain a new scene to be illustrated? If you have three consecutive pages where two characters are merely talking, the artwork will become repetitive. So—get action into that story wherever too much conversation occurs. The illustrator—hired by the publisher—needs help in creating exciting pictures for the book.

The next step is to take each of the thirty-eight parts and mold them into the easy-to-read style. Let's use an example and see how it evolves into a more simply written version.

Debbie stared at the seashore shell in the store window. Other purple shells and yellow shells surrounded this special one. But Debbie's favorite shone as if it had a pink light inside. Perhaps Mom would buy the shell for her birthday.

The paragraph as it now stands is written at about a fourth-grade level and is too difficult for an easy-to-read to be used by first, second, and third graders. We have to begin to simplify the writing. The first step is merely to shorten the sentence length. See if we can provide the same information for the reader but in shorter sentences. Basically, the reader has to know that (a) Debbie is peering into a store window (b) there are many shells in the window (c) one is her favorite and it is pink (d) her birthday is coming (e) she hopes her mother might buy it for her birthday. Since she does not wish for her mother *or* father to buy the shell, we suspect there is no father in the family. Let's see if we can put that information in shorter sentences.

> Debbie stared into the store window. There were purple shells and yellow shells. She especially liked the bright pink shell. Her birthday was coming. Perhaps Mom would buy the shell.

Merely by cutting the length of the sentence, you have taken a major step toward meeting the demands of an easy-to-read book. Next, we have to check the vocabulary. What words might be difficult for youngsters in grades one through three? *Stared* and *especially* are the only two in this segment. Replace them with *looked* and *really*. Now—for the final step. We will arrange the material in a ragged right format. Be sure that each line is a complete phrase in itself. For example, don't end a line with the word *and*, because that leaves the reader hanging. Begin a new line with the word *and*. Here is our segment in the ragged right:

> Debbie looked into the store window.
> There were purple shells
> and yellow shells.
> She really liked the bright pink shell.
> Her birthday was coming.
> Perhaps Mom would buy the shell.

And there you are—ready to move on to the next segment. What you might have considered to be a painful chore is not so tedious at all. Just remember the basic steps: (1) divide your story into thirty-eight segments; (2) shorten the sentences; (3) simplify any hard words; (4) arrange in the ragged right format.

When the entire story is an easy-to-read, put the material away for a month and work on another project. You will need time for that writing to cool so you can look at it objectively. Working on another story or article will also help place distance between you and a piece of writing. When the month in solitary confinement is over for the manuscript, retrieve it from the file drawer and check through it again. Does the material read smoothly even though it is written simply? Can you visualize an illustration for each page? (Don't give your ideas to the editor, however!) Will your book not only be easy but fun to read? If all your answers are yes, then type the manuscript for submission. Do not use a separate sheet of paper for each page. Type the pages double-space and leave about eight spaces of white to indicate where your page breakdown occurs.

HI/LO BOOKS

The publishers releasing hi/lo books are searching for exciting stories—mystery, sports, science fiction—and interest-grabbing nonfiction topics for the junior and senior high school students who are their audience.

Because hi/lo books are purchased mainly by schools, explicit sex or undue violence is avoided, as is "realistic" language. At best, a *damn* or *hell* might slip into the text, but the beginning writer of hi/los should avoid even that.

Just as the new writer of easy-to-reads should study the published books in that field, so should the potential author of hi/lo books. Here are samples of how fiction and nonfiction are written at the hi/lo level. First, a few paragraphs of *Felina*, a novel written by Mary Blount Christian at the second-grade reading level.

> The alarm didn't go off the next morning, and Joe ran late—too late to stop for Felina.
> He slid into his seat just as the late bell rang. He looked toward Felina's chair, but she wasn't there. Joe began to worry when she wasn't in any other classes that day, either. What if something was wrong? She might be sick, or even worse! He didn't trust that old woman; she might really be a witch. Maybe there are such things after all, Joe thought.

And now read nonfiction written at the same grade level in Arnold Madison's *Great Unsolved Cases*.

> The facts are simple. Between August 31 and November 9, 1888, five women were murdered in London. There were other killings at that time, also. But these five persons were all murdered by the same killer. After the fifth murder, there were no more killings by this person.
> No one knows who did the murders. Or why the women were killed. Or even why the murderer stopped. Almost a hundred years have gone by since the crimes. The answers are still unknown.

Examining the two samples provides clues to the requirements of writing hi/lo books. First, the sentence length must be kept short. A good length should be about ten to twelve words. But interspersed among those sentences should be shorter ones of about five to seven words. Notice how familiar verbs are used: *ran, looked, knows, are, were*. The fiction example reveals another technique. Little description is given to the reader, only action and dialogue and the thoughts of the main character. The reason is that publishers of hi/los generally use photographs as illustrations to provide the "scenery" for the reader. Also, description slows the pacing of a story, and hi/lo readers need fast-paced stories or they lose interest.

The method of writing a hi/lo book is the same as writing any other juvenile or teenage novel. The characters and plot must be meticulously worked out. Don't skimp on your preparation because you think these readers do not need the best. In fact, this is what they do need: the most skillfully drawn, believable characters and a tightly knitted plot. The story should build steadily toward a dramatic climax with character growth resulting for the main character. And — just before you are ready to begin the actual writing — check to be sure each chapter ends with a strong "hook" — something that makes the reader want to turn that page immediately.

And that is the main purpose of both easy-to-read and hi/lo books: getting the youngster to read and *keep* reading.

One junior high school teacher reported an anecdote about an eighth grader named Tom B. Tom had never read a book in all his eight years of schooling. Then the librarian directed him to *Dead-Start Scramble* by Chet Cunningham, an Action Book. Tom read the book that night, and carried the novel around with him for the next five days. He read and re-read the story about motorcycles. Not only did he enjoy the story, but Tom had the tremendous satisfaction of knowing he had read a *book*. Giving a child such a lift in his or her self-image provides an author with rewards far greater than mere financial income. And that pleasure can be yours, too.

28
Writing Nonfiction

Too often prospective writers of juvenile and teenage material overlook the rich field of nonfiction in both magazines and books. There are several reasons for this attitude. First, the books they remember best from their young years were fiction. *Nonfiction* to them meant school texts written in the driest, most boring style. Also, the author may be thinking back to high school and college, where writing nonfiction meant writing tedious term papers, while the fiction he or she wrote in creative writing courses was fun, uplifting, and satisfying.

But writing juvenile and teenage nonfiction can and should involve those same three qualities. Young people today read nonfiction for fun. The sports novel has almost died out because youngsters want nonfiction books about their favorite sports heroes or specific techniques for various sports.

MAGAZINE ARTICLES

Magazine nonfiction is written for different age levels, just as fiction is. And for the new nonfiction and fiction writer alike, the magazine field is the wisest beginning place. First, you will develop your nonfiction writing skills on short pieces rather than investing much time in preparing a book. Also, whether you realize it or not, you probably have articles in your mind just waiting to be written.

What do you know that youngsters would like to read about?

More than you realize. Do you make holiday decorations to give your home a festive air? If so—study the magazines. You will see that many juvenile and teenage magazines use craft pieces of all types and complexity. Do you engage in any sports or outdoor activities? Boating? Backpacking? Share your excitement for the sport with the young reader and allow him or her to benefit from your experience. What about nature? A majority of the magazines seek nature-related articles whether they are on a particular animal that may be in danger of extinction or how to make a leaf collection. Science is another area with great potential. There is no need to be a science teacher, but, if you are, you already have many experiments to offer. They should be simple and *safe*. Crossword puzzles and games as well as articles on historical sites, careers for teenagers, and biographies of outstanding people both historical and contemporary appear in magazines. The number of ideas is endless. Your problem may be a delicious one: finding time to write all the articles for which you have ideas.

Selecting a topic is a two-pronged effort. First, as indicated above, you may already have knowledge about some activity or experience that you can use as a basis for an article. But before you launch into writing the piece, you must check the markets. Visit the children's room of your library and read through a pile of different magazines to see the type of nonfiction material used.

Here is a general list of subjects which magazines mention in their writers' guideline sheets:

Adolescent Problems	Natural Science
Animal Care	Nutrition
Biography	Outdoor Activities
Career Information	Personal Experiences
Contemporary Issues	Personality Pieces
Crafts	Photo Essays
Crossword Puzzles	Physical Fitness
Electronics	Puzzles
Health	Recipes
History	Safety
How-to Projects	Self-Help
Hygiene	Service Projects
Inspirational Essays	Sports
Mood Pieces	Travel

The types are extensive, but even further market study is

necessary before you decide on your article subject. Take "recipes." Magazines for six-to-nines would use different kinds of recipes than an eight-to-twelve publication. A teen magazine would seek still another sort of food-preparation project. Once you've narrowed the possible nonfiction piece to a definite age range, still more work awaits you. *A writer of fiction and nonfiction must study sample copies of magazines. Anything less is foolhardy and self-defeating.*

Three teen magazines that announce in their editorial requirements sheet that they seek "recipes" may want totally different kinds. One may offer its readers health-food ideas while another uses party snacks and the third prints only holiday-related pieces. By sending your recipe to a magazine that does not publish your sort of recipe, you will waste time and postage. Also, you will have alienated the editor by announcing that you are a lazy writer who does not do his or her homework. The editor will figure you are the sort of individual who cannot handle a simple task such as sending for a sample copy. Therefore, he or she will doubt how carefully you have prepared and written the nonfiction piece. Unfortunately, editors seem to store the names of such writers in their long-term memory banks.

You will see that the writing style is definitely not pedantic but rather informal, breezy and, if possible, filled with glints of humor. Your personal interest in the subject should shine through. Here are two samples of nonfiction writing. First, read this paragraph from an article for a Boy Scout troop designed to train the youngsters to deal with emergencies — "Blindfolded Obstacle Race" by Dick Pryce.

> Plunged suddenly into total darkness, an average person may have trouble finding his way. And what's merely difficult for one may be almost impossible for a group. Think it isn't so?

And study this section from the book, *David Ben-Gurion* by Herma Silverstein.

> The passengers sweltered from the hot sun as the caravan wedged its way through the traffic on Rothschild Street. The sixty-two-year-old man in the lead car dabbed his handkerchief across his cheeks, tanned and leathery now from living so many years in the desert. Finally the caravan stopped in front of the Tel Aviv Museum of Art. The man got out of the car, and hundreds of Jews

crowding outside the museum burst into cheers. He waved, then went inside and joined his colleagues behind a dais in front of the auditorium.

Nonfiction writing, whether for articles or books, must have punch, an aliveness. The personal interest of the two authors above shines through in their material. The degree of excitement you bring to your writing project will be evident in the final product.

Now—what do you do if you have an interesting topic and have studied the magazines, finding one that uses the type of material you will submit? First, if the article is short— under 500 words—write the piece, type the material in the format shown for fiction in this text, and submit the piece with a stamped, addressed envelope for its possible return.

If the article is going to be longer, the professional writer first writes a *query letter*. A query letter is merely one that describes the article you intend to write and asks the editor if he or she would like to read it. This is the most efficient way to sell your work. You will not be wasting postage to send an article to a magazine that has no use for the piece, nor will you invest time in writing an article that may never find an interested editor. Obviously, you will devote tremendous time and effort to this letter because that is the first sample of your writing that an editor sees. Sloppy writing such as spelling errors or poor English will kill the sale, as will a messy-appearing presentation with cross-outs and inked-in words. A sample query letter appears on the next page. Notice how certain basic facts are given to the editor so the person can make an intelligent decision of whether or not to read the full article:

a general description;
length;
at least a working title that might be changed;
the availability of photos;
and a bit about the writer's publishing record—if there is one. Of course, do not mention the fact that you are unpublished.

Notice the last sentence of Ms. Jackson's letter. The phrase *on speculation* is most important. This means that should the editor suggest sending the article, the magazine

Ms. Deborah Smith
Features/Fiction Editor
<u>YM</u>
685 Third Ave.
New York, NY 10017

Dear Ms. Smith:

Each year the number of young people entering the ranks of treasure hunters grows larger. Metal detectors, the basic tool of treasure hunters, are inexpensive, and many of your readers may now own one. Merely holding an activated detector, however, does not guarantee success. Too often the girls in their early teens fail to find coins or jewelry because they have not developed the proper technique of using the metal detector.

Would you be interested in seeing an article of about 1000 words on the proper method of handling a metal detector? Points such as walking and swinging the detector would be explained as well as how to "interpret" the sounds emitted or the dial readings on the detector. I think the article should have a simple, direct title such as "Using Your Metal Detector." I can provide B&W photos depicting girls using this electronic device as well as close-ups of the controls.

Perhaps you would like to know a bit about my background. I have had articles published in <u>Boys' Life</u> as well as <u>Bread</u> and <u>Current Science</u>.

Do let me know if you would like to read the full article. I understand I would be submitting the piece on speculation.

Cordially,

Martha Jackson

is under no obligation to purchase the article. If they like the article, they will buy the rights: but if, for some reason, the article does not meet the promise shown in the query letter, the piece will be returned.

Be sure to include a stamped, addressed envelope with your query.

An important rule: *Send only one query per article at a time.* What would you do if two editors wrote back to say they were "definitely interested in reading" your piece? "Please send it along when it's completed. Meanwhile, we will keep your letter on file." And if they respond positively, they often keep the query on file.

NONFICTION BOOKS

The same procedure should be followed in preparing a nonfiction book. Study the market to see the wide variety of nonfiction being published. Find a topic that has not been explored. Then query the editor. The process will require more time than an article simply because more research, planning, and writing will be needed.

Again — visit the library and ask the children's librarian to suggest a variety of nonfiction books for various ages. You will want to study them for style, subject, and length.

The breadth of the categories may impress you. From simple science experiments to the latest medical discoveries to involved psychological studies are explored and analyzed as well as world events from prehistoric times to the present day. If biographies interest you, approach that type of nonfiction with care. As late as the 1970s, biographies were a mainstay of any nonfiction publisher. Today, that is not so. Some biographies are sought, but they tend to be about contemporary people, especially those in the minorities. Also, biographical studies that can be heavily illustrated with black-and-white photographs are in demand. Whatever your choice of topic, study books for all age levels in that general area.

Now — you have to begin searching for an idea, but the hunt will be comparatively easy. Ideas are all around you. Possibly, as in the articles field, you have an interest or skill that can be used as a basis for a book. Or else you might spot a newspaper article about the high number of serious accidents involving skateboarders, and you would like to do a book on the whole subject including the safety aspect. Arnold Madison was distressed by the amount of vandalism in his community and decided to investigate the subject. As a result, *Vandalism: The Not-So-Senseless Crime* was born. Then, using another method for obtaining ideas, Madison discovered through his research that vandalism caused many people to form vigilante groups. Thus, *Vigilantism In America* came into existence. This second book gave birth to a third because the author became intrigued with the most famous vigilante of all—Carry Nation. A young adult biography appeared in print two years later.

Remember—you do not have to be an expert in order to write a book about a subject. You will *become* an expert through intensive research. In fact, a writer coming to a topic cold can often do a better job in writing a juvenile or teenage nonfiction book than an expert. Those too familiar with a subject may have trouble selecting the most important points to be covered and may produce a rambling text that bogs down in minor technicalities.

Once you have struck what you think is gold, you still have to do a bit more digging. Check *Subject Guide to Children's Books in Print*, which is available in most public libraries. Think of all the possible general headings your idea might be listed under and see if any juvenile or teenage book has been released on that subject within the last three years. Be sure to check the ages of the reader. Should you be planning a teenage book on skiing, and the only skiing book listed is for the eight-to-twelve reader, that does not compete with your book. If, however, you find one aimed at the same age level as yours, the chances of interesting an editor in your idea are rather slim unless you've come up with a completely different angle. Most editors have *Subject Guide* on a nearby shelf and will check the listings while considering your book proposal, so do not assume you can sneak a topic already in print past the editor.

When you have a subject that fires your interest, meets the demands of the readers, and is not currently in print, you can begin preparing the *package* or *proposal,* which is a detailed outline and generally two or three sample chapters. If the editor likes the idea, the outline, and the way you have written the chapters, a contract is usually offered. This is one of the great benefits of writing a nonfiction book.

You do not invest the time to write the entire book before obtaining a contract. In fiction, you must write the full novel before an editor will accept the manuscript.

First, do general, overall research. Get a full picture of your subject. Even at this beginning stage, however, keep notes on resources so you do not have to backtrack later. When you have a clear view of the total scope of the topic, you can begin breaking the material into chapters. See how bits of information naturally group together. An important rule in nonfiction is never to repeat the same information in several sections of an article or book. Collect all the facts about one topic in one section. Thus, you are already starting the outline to be submitted to a publisher.

One doubt that may plague you is that since only surface research has been done at this stage, it is too soon to commit yourself to a final outline. Be aware that the editor will not expect the outline to be an exact, unchanging plan of the final book. He or she understands that deeper research might create new chapters or different interpretations. In fact, editors prefer to work with authors who leave themselves open to unexpected leads as they are writing a book. On the other hand, however, be careful not to have gaps in your outline. For example, don't write a chapter description in the outline that reads, "Not sure what will go in here. Maybe I'll find something when I do more research."

The best form for an outline is a chapter-by-chapter plan. First, you will find it helpful to think in chapters right from the beginning. Also, as you make a list of the exact chapters, you will usually spot any holes in the book before an editor does. Another plus is that the chapter outline is not written in full sentences, but merely phrases announcing what will be covered in a particular chapter. Nor is it organized in the form you may have used in high school where capital letters clashed with Arabic numerals.

Here are a few examples from actual outlines of published books. The sample from *Surfing: Basic Techniques* by Arnold Madison will show how a chapter description is written:

> Chapter Four: ON THE SAND. Carry the board with safety in mind for yourself and other people on the beach. (Boards break if dropped on rock or pavement.) Be constantly aware of the jutting skeg (fin). Waxing the board—or if too little wax, waxing your

feet. Deciding where to launch the board. Check shoreline: rocky or sandy? A drop into deep water? Sea creatures? Breaking waves which might wash the board back?

Editors will want to know how you plan to research the subject so, at the end of the outline, devote a small section to the available sources. This also shows the editor that you know where and how to find the information through a wide variety of means. Here is the research portion of the outline of *Suicide and Young People* by Arnold Madison.

> *Research:* Secondary research will be varied. *Books In Print* lists almost one hundred adult titles devoted to the general topic though none deal specifically with youthful suicide. In addition, readings will be made in the categories of education, anthropology, young people, problems of the minorities, and behavioral sciences. Newspaper and magazine articles will be consulted, also.
>
> The primary research is equally important—actual interviews with those who work in suicide prevention and with the people who have been forced to actively consider suicide as well as their friends and family.

One final item to be included in your outline is ultra-important in a juvenile or teenage nonfiction book. This part is called *back matter* and generally appears in the printed books as *Other Sources of Information*. Editors are very concerned about how much information you can provide for this section because there is a direct influence upon the book's sale. Librarians seek books that the young readers can use as a springboard to more detailed facts on a related subject.

Track down any free materials the reader might send for or governmental publications that can be obtained free or for a nominal fee. Are there educational films? If so, youth groups may want to order them for a monthly meeting to spur a discussion. Have your facts as specific as possible: names, addresses (including zip code), and telephone numbers, if applicable. The newspaper and magazine articles that you researched as well as the books will be listed in a separate bibliography, so there is no need to include those in the back matter.

Once the outline has been prepared, it is time to work on the sample chapters. At least the first two chapters of the book should be sent so the editor can see if you can get the book moving, capturing the reader's interest immediately.

Then, as the third sample chapter, you can either choose the next one in the outline or a chapter from deeper in the text. Perhaps chapter eight is an interview with an authority in the field, while the first two were merely informational. You might be wise to include chapter eight to demonstrate how you can handle different types of writing. Your sample chapter section should be about twenty to thirty pages. Remember—a decision to accept or reject a book will be made on the basis of these chapters. They must be the best possible writing that you can produce. The words should *sing*. If they do, and if your outline shows that there will be plenty of good material to fill a book, you will be rewarded with a contract.

PUTTING PEN TO PAPER

A full discussion of all nonfiction techniques cannot be detailed in a single chapter. Although the next pages will deal with the most-asked questions by new writers, there are other sources to assist you in honing your skills. First, read the texts devoted to nonfiction writing listed at the end of this book and others you might find in your library. *The Writer* and *Writer's Digest* frequently publish pieces about articles and nonfiction books for young readers. Each one can teach you needed techniques.

The Opening.

Just as the first paragraph of fiction must capture the reader's interest immediately, the beginning of an article or nonfiction chapter has to serve the same function. There is a variety of openings, but let's discuss the three most popular: statement, question and answer, anecdotal.

The statement beginning is the most often used—which does not mean it is the most effective. You "state" a general or specific fact about your subject and then immediately explore the topic point by point. For examples of statement openings re-read the first sentence of this chapter as well as Chapters Two, Four, and Five. In fact, most chapters in this book employ statement openings.

The question-and-answer introduction is another favorite. If someone asks us a question, we are inclined to answer it. In the Q&A beginning, however, the reader need not reply because the second sentence provides the answer. Here are two examples.

From a teenage magazine article titled "Preventing Suicide":

> What should you do if a friend or relative threatens suicide?
> Something.
> The cardinal rule in suicide prevention is "Do Something" even if you believe the threat is an idle one or designed to evoke sympathy.

Check this question-and-answer beginning from a ten-to-fourteen book on surfing. The chapter is "Launching Your Surfboard."

> How does a person feel, grabbing his/her surfboard, running down an untried beach, and flinging the board and his/her body into the water?
> Sorry. Very, very sorry.
> The first step in preparing to launch your fibre-glass board is to explore the beach and offshore water for hidden rocks and . . .

The anecdotal opening is fun to write and the most effective in snaring a reader. The article or chapter starts like a dramatized scene in fiction. The attraction is that we all are caught up in a story.

The opening of this book's Chapter 29 has an anecdotal opening, as does Teri Martini's article on the Statue of Liberty—"Freedom's Lady"—published in *Five/Six*.

> Everyone in Paris was talking about the lady. Again and again her ocean voyage had been postponed, but she showed no sign of impatience or disappointment. Tall and proud she stood in Monsieur August Bartholdi's courtyard in Paris to receive the thousands of visitors who had wanted to wish her well. To all she appeared gracious and dignified.
> "She is very beautiful," whispered a shopgirl to her friend, "but she does not belong here. She was never meant to stay in France."
> "No," replied a young carpenter, "and yet without money, without the proper place to stay, she cannot go to America. Perhaps Monsieur Bartholdi can do something more for her."

Warning: an anecdotal opening goes on for only a few paragraphs. Then you switch to a straightforward nonfiction style. Dramatized nonfiction is rejected by editors, who dislike articles where one knowledgeable person explains something to an uneducated individual. We are bombarded with that deadening technique in television commercials.

The Body.
Once you are into the article, there are vital considerations to observe. Avoid sexism, racism, and religious prejudice so that unintentional slurs do not worm their way into your writing.

Keep your nonfiction nonsexist. The editorial *he* has fallen into disgrace. *He* is only employed when referring to the male animal. Otherwise *he and she, person,* and *him or her* are employed. There are a few language purists who claim this creates clumsy writing. These same people prefer the candle to the electric light bulb. Be sure to change any sexist terms describing general groups: salesmen, chairmen, paper boys.

The same awareness of people's sensitivities should be present when referring to ethnic groups: Latinos, Native Americans or Amerinds, and Oriental-Americans or Amerasians are all designations that are accepted as respectful.

Inadvertent religious discrimination may arise if the author assumes that everyone is of the Judeo/Christian heritage. Unthinking use of a phrase like "a good Christian" (unless that person *is* a Christian) or implying a person is a decent individual and therefore must be observing the Ten Commandments will insult members of the other major religions. Moslems and Buddhists, for example, have their own codes of behavior that are equally positive. If, however, you are writing for a denominational publication, you would slant your phrasing to that readership.

Another problem facing you is how to insert quotations. We know that quotes add authority to our nonfiction and that readers want to learn not only what the writer thinks but what the experts know. These quotations come from either printed matter or interviews.

Up to fifty words may be quoted without permission unless you are citing *brief* materials like poetry or song lyrics. A line from a poem, for instance, might be 25 percent of that literary effort. Music companies are extremely protective of their properties, and you will be expected to pay a fee for using copyrighted lyrics. A charge of one hundred dollars for six to ten words is not unusual. Illustrations or photographs from printed, coyrighted material can't be employed unless you have written permission. To obtain permission, send a letter of inquiry to the magazine or book publisher.

Most facts cannot be copyrighted, however. But if you are using data that a person or team gathered through investigative means, then you should credit the source even if you are not quoting the exact words. In July, 1988, author John Hersey was forced to make a public apology to fellow-writer Laurence Bergreen, because Hersey used information from Bergreen's biography of James Agee in an article for the *New Yorker*. Although the material was paraphrased rather than being quoted exactly, Hersey admitted he should have credited the published work from which he drew his facts. Fortunately, the lawyers for both parties agreed that a public apology would be sufficient so the case was never brought into court.

Now let's see about incorporating quoted material into our writing providing proper credit. No juvenile or young adult article or nonfiction book uses footnotes. But that's a plus factor. Footnotes draw the reader's attention from the text, and we certainly don't want anything to do that. The readers would be like people who attend a foreign movie with English subtitles and get so distracted that when they leave the theatre, they don't remember anything about the performances. We want our readers to remember our writing! Therefore, the source of the information is woven into the same paragraph as the quotation. Here are some examples.

1. *Paraphrased information:*

> In January 1977, *Newsweek* magazine claimed that arson is the fastest-growing crime in the United States.

2. *Longer quotation with credit:*

> "Today 2,739 children will be seriously hurt by adults," reads a letter sent out by the National Committee for Prevention of Child Abuse. "Today, more than thirteen children will die a slow and needless death. These children are victims of *child abuse*."

3. *Lengthy quotes:* For inserting a quotation of more than three or four sentences, state the source and then leave four spaces, shrink the margins, and single-space the quote. This method is used throughout this book. (For those selections that have no credit, the author of the excerpted material agreed that none need be given.)

The Ending.
Every article or nonfiction book chapter should have a wind-up sentence or paragraph. If this is lacking, there's an incomplete feeling to the piece. The reader is left dangling in the air, waiting to be grounded. Bring him or her firmly down to earth with a few words that sum up the point of the nonfiction piece. With book chapters, several words or sentences can perform the same function (see the final paragraph of this chapter) or lead the reader into the next chapter. For examples of a lead-in for the next chapter, read the conclusions of Chapters One, Two, and Three. Also, check other chapter endings to see if you can spot those that have a carry-over. And with that last bit of advice, it is time to end this chapter.

Investigate juvenile and teenage nonfiction. There is a whole world out there, from crossword puzzles to career articles, or a book on rabbits for the younger reader to a serious investigation of being gay in a homophobic society aimed at young adults.

29
Plays, Plays, Plays

We are sitting in the theatre. All around us, people shift positions expectantly: programs crackling, seats creaking, shoes scraping the floor. The houselights dim. Anticipation surges within us.

When the curtain opens, we will be transported from a mundane existence to another place, another time. Our lives will mesh with those of persons we've never met before. And we are willing to go wherever the playwright will lead us as long as the author has done his or her job well.

Picture yourself, the playwright, sitting in the rear row. For the last tense minutes, you've been crushing the play-script into an ever-tightening scroll. You've sat through the rehearsals, watching a cast who executed their roles perfectly and a few actors, who, though they tried valiantly, could not bring the character to life.

And now, the auditorium lights fading, the realization comes that you have an opportunity to experience what a poet, short story writer, or novelist is rarely permitted. You will see your creation come alive. Even more unmatched is the privilege of observing your intended audience during the moment it first experiences your work. Will they lean forward nervously as the dramatic moment is reached? Will laughter shake the walls when they hear the clever line that came to you at three o'clock one morning?

"The play is the thing," Shakespeare told us, and how right he was.

Amazingly, few, *very* few, people who want to write for children or teenagers ever consider creating a play. Possibly you are among that large group.

But why discount a route to sales and publication and

possibly the thrill of seeing your work performed?

First, you may say that you have no interest in writing a play. Then—even if you did—you have no idea how to go about writing one. And, lastly, if in some burst of inspiration, you did pen a play, what in the world would you do with the thing?

Let's look at your objections. You say you have no interest in writing a play. Okay. But your lack of incentive may well be tied to your other doubts. No skill. No market.

But you do have the skills! If you feel confident enough to tackle a short story, then you obviously have faith in your ability to plot, characterize, and write dialogue. Bring those same techniques to writing for the stage. And, mind you, markets exist. Some are even starved. Several juvenile magazines no longer list plays on their market lists because no one submits any. From the short play, which is basically one or several scenes, to the more complex full-length script, there are magazines that buy plays as well as companies that specialize in the publication of one-acters and longer works.

There is still one more factor which may be working against you without your awareness—a misconception about what a play for children or teenagers is.

Do you picture a fantasy: kings and queens and fire-breathing dragons? Or a script depicting the origins of St. Valentine's Day? Possibly a short skit about Lincoln reading by the firelight. In one sense, you are right. All these are examples of the plays written for youngsters and young adults. But the field is as varied and complex as that of fiction for the same age groups. There are mysteries, comedies, realistic dramas. Science fiction plays are sought as well as musicals and even American-written versions of foreign theatre such as the Japanese Noh drama. Retold folktales and adaptations of classical drama such as Shakespeare or Ancient Greek plays penned for young audiences are wanted. Let's examine the marketplace a bit more closely to see where you would fit.

THE MARKET

The picture of available markets is so multi-faced that deciding where to enter it can be perplexing. Let us break the complex picture into its components.

1. *Plays Written for Children to be Acted by Children.*

This category is equivalent to the short story and novel for the pre-schooler, primary grade child, and youngsters nine to twelve years old. For children under nine, plays are rarely written only for reading. Therefore, magazines solely devoted to plays or companies whose only business is the publication of theatrical projects are the only markets open to you. The nine-to-twelve child will either read the play or perform it—if only in a classroom production. The plays appear in weekly religious publications and more general magazines such as *Cobblestone* or *Plays*. And, of course, publishers of playscripts will purchase quality plays.

Here is a sample of topics for plays—short and long—of interest to this age division:

Adaptations of classics
Adventure
Biographical (Generally childhood incidents revealing the traits that will become dominant when these youngsters become adults)
Contemporary home or school situations
Customs of the minorities
Dramatized folktales, myths, and legends
Ecology
Fantasy
Historical (Especially the Revolutionary and Civil wars)
Holidays and special occasions
Humor
Mysteries
Perennially favorite character types: ghosts, pirates, evil spellcasters, and good-natured youngsters who unwittingly create chaos
Puppet plays
Science fiction
Westerns

2. *Plays Written for Children to be Acted by Adults*. All of the above types are fodder for this hungry classification. These works are labelled "Children's Theatre." Many communities or school PTAs form children's theatre groups where the productions are mounted and performed by adults but intended for a young audience. Children are included in the cast only if a role demands a younger person.

One-acters are popular, but even more longer plays are sought. The plots are more complicated than in Category #1, as are the acting roles. For example, a character's speech may be longer because adult actors can maintain a characterization through several sentences whereas young performers are best equipped to handle phrases or one-sentence lines.

The publishers for this play type are those that print play-books. Check out the requirements and writers' guidelines for companies such as Baker's Plays or the Dramatic Publishing Company.

3. *Plays Written for Teenagers and/or Adults to be Acted by Teenagers and/or Adults.* This is a subdivision of wide extremes, ranging from ultra-conservative plays to Broadway caliber scripts. The producers are high school drama clubs as well as community, college, and professional regional theatres.

The one strand that is typical of most of these plays is that the main character must be a teenager or a young adult. And contemporary settings are certainly preferred.

Let's break this category down even further. The first grouping is those plays aimed at communities that are rigidly moral. The scripts contain no swearing, smoking, or sex. Teenagers may peck each other on the cheek or hold hands, but nothing more demonstrative should be shown onstage or implied to be happening offstage. Consumption of alcohol by any character—other than the town drunk—is strictly forbidden. If a person suffers the shock of terrible news, his or her companion may get that individual a cup of "strong, black coffee." But that's only in the case of extreme emotional trauma.

The young characters seem to be refugees from the 1940s radio show "Henry Aldrich" or the Andy Hardy movies. Any resemblance to today's teenagers is purely coincidental. There are stock characters who appear repeatedly. The overweight girl whose gargantuan appetite is a constant source of laughs; the high school jock—usually a football player—who is heavy on brawn but light on brains; the teen female with the Southern accent that sounds like a bad imitation of Scarlett O'Hara, her lines constantly filled with "Ah" rather than "I." In mysteries, there is often the male character who is not the person he claims to be. All characters, whether teenage or adult, observe the strict roles mandated for each sex while Queen Victoria ruled the British Empire.

The plays have titles like these: *A Midsummer Night's Scream* (teenagers rehearsing Shakespeare's play in a "haunted" nineteenth century theatre), *Mummy Sea, Mummy Do* (set on a tramp steamer bearing a cargo of Egyptian mummies), and *Hillbilly Weddin'* (described in the publisher's catalogue as a "three-act hillbilly farce").

As unrealistic as the characters and plots of these plays are, there is a large audience for them—especially in the Midwest, which is where most of their publishers maintain headquarters. One reason for their popularity is the fact that they are paced quickly. The action and plot developments zip along so quickly that the audience is carried through each act. Also, the plays are easily acted by the inexperienced thespian. The lines are short—generally a word or two or a complete sentence—which adds to the machine gun pace of the production. And, most important, there is nothing contained in the show that will ruffle any feathers.

Authors who ascribe to the inherent values set forth by these scripts or who are able to adapt their philosophies to this sort of theatrical fare will find receptive editors and rapt audiences.

At the opposite end of the spectrum are those productions of Broadway successes and plays of equal depth. Again, the must factor is that the main characters are teenagers or people in their early twenties who are dealing with realistic problems. Student or adult casts appear in *Biloxi Blues* (Neil Simon), *Child's Play* (Robert Marasco), and *Tea and Sympathy* (Robert Anderson). Although these are former Broadway hits, you do not have to be a name playwright to write plays for this knowledgeable audience. In fact, most authors of such dramatic material have never had an off-Broadway or Broadway production. You must, however, possess insight into the pressures of today's world, a thorough understanding of young people, and have solid skill in basic playwriting techniques.

Reading those requirements, you can see this play classification is the theatrical twin of the young adult novel. The characterizations are complex, the dialogue skillfully wrought, and the plots set in realistic settings. The authors should consider not only submitting their scripts to publishers but also to college and regional theatre competitions, which offer a cash prize and frequently an expense-paid opportunity for the author to attend the rehearsals and performances of the winning play. Even the prestigious Eugene O'Neill Theatre Conference, which encourages playwrights by giving readings and stages productions of new works each summer is an avenue open to the authors of this category of plays.

And it's only appropriate the organization does so. Eugene O'Neill, who helped mold and advance the realistic theatre movement, began by writing one-acters, which were first staged in a fishing shanty in Provincetown, Massachusetts, and in a converted stable in Greenwich Village, New York City. Is writing plays for children and teenagers any less humble?

THE CREATION OF A PLAY

"You can't learn playwriting at your desk. You have to go to plays and, even better, act in plays—to understand the needs of the theatre. Reading plays helps, but words on a page and live theatre are remarkably different."

Sage advice from playwright Sandra Fenichel Asher, who also writes juvenile and teenage novels under the name of Sandy Asher.

Actual contact with an audience develops an instinct for what "works" with those people out front. What holds their attention, fascinates them, touches their deepest feelings. You will learn the simplest things such as to repeat vital information several times because who can predict when an audience member may cough or a screaming fire engine might pass the theatre. You will also acquire a sense for how long a scene may go on before boredom envelops the audience. There is a means for you to gain this valuable experience. All community theatres seek new blood. Active participation in any production is truly the first step in the creation process, enabling you to begin planning your own theatrical piece.

The genesis of a play is a process similar to that of a short story or novel. From initial idea to outline to completed manuscript, the author moves along step by step.

The Idea.
Although the seeds for stories and plays come in all forms, most playwrights agree that their first glimmer came in the form of a situation. Nameless, faceless characters are confronted with a predicament. Neil Simon's *The Odd Couple* may well have arisen from the author's curiosity about what would happen—dramatically speaking—if he forced a fastidious individual to share an apartment with a slob. So add potent situations to your idea file.

A playwright, as any author, keeps files of plot situations, characters, settings, and titles. Edward Albee found the title for his prize-winning drama scrawled on the wall of a New York City subway station.

"Who's afraid of Virginia Woolf?" asked an unknown graffiti artist.

When a basic situation has been conceived that excites you with its possibilities, the time has come to develop a cast.

The Characters.
There is something about playwriting that can undercut your drive to fully characterize each person who walks upon the stage. It's the realization that a human will be up there, doing your work for you. True, the author need never describe his or her characters (except in production notes) but each character must have a distinct personality with drives and a life before the curtain rose and usually one that continues after the curtain falls.

An actor prepares for a role by visualizing all facets of the character so that his or her knowlege will surpass what is depicted in the script. The author, too, must explore the character and become that person while writing. Merely putting a robe on a man, a scepter in his hand, and a crown on his head will not make that man a living, breathing king. Monarchs come in all sizes and shapes with flaws and positive qualities in their emotional makeup. We all do.

The Plot.
The story line of a one-act play is similar to that of a short story just as the plot for a full-length play is equivalent to a novel.

In the one-acter, the main character is usually onstage

when the curtain rises. His or her problem is introduced in the first line or certainly within the first few exchanges of dialogue. For a full-length play, hints about the central plot problem may be discussed in the opening lines. This same dialogue may prime the audience for the main character's appearance if that individual is not already onstage. In both the short and long dramatic work, the audience may become aware of the story problem before the main character.

Once the protagonist begins working toward his or her goal, you are into the middle of the play. In a one-acter, this can happen by the second or third line of dialogue. In a full-length play, the middle might be delayed a few pages. A short play almost always moves in chronological order. The hero or heroine works to find success. Stumbling blocks thwart his or her progress, each more serious than the one before. In a full-length play's middle, novelistic techniques can be employed. There might be flashbacks — scenes dramatizing incidents that occurred before the play's beginning. Subplots involving the secondary characters should intertwine with the main character's story.

All plays generally have a "black moment" as do short stories and novels. The main character, however, draws upon inner resources or external means and effects a successful completion to the plot problem. The unhappy ending is extremely rare in theatrical offerings for children and teenagers. Failure at the end of fiction says to the reader that there is no point in struggling because unhappiness will be the end result. There have been great tragedies written for the stage, but in those dramas, the audience finds inspiration from the heroic main character who, faced with insurmountable odds, continues to fight. The theme then becomes one that stresses it's not whether the battle is lost or won, but how one fights.

Once the plot has been resolved, have a solid, dramatic line for the main character — a curtain line — and then ring down the curtain. Those final words often come to the playwright during the planning stage when he or she is compiling a scenario.

The Scenario.

Professional playwrights complete a scenario — a fully detailed outline — before committing a word to paper. They don't worry about the scenario crimping their creativity. Instead, they praise the scenario, realizing a well-executed one facilitates the actual writing. This thorough planning also eliminates *much* rewriting further along in the creative process.

Short story writers and novelists would be amazed at the minute details a well-written scenario contains. In fact, they should be motivated to make their own outlines equally full. Not only is each encounter between characters planned, but the specific topics are outlined for each stage conversation and are listed in the *exact order they will flow.* In order to produce this highly desirable aid to your writing, a knowledge of a play's parts is needed.

An *act*, the largest division of a play, may be divided into *scenes*, which end to signal a passage of time or to highlight an important plot event. Both acts and scenes are indicated in the manuscript. Not marked are the smaller sections: segments and beats.

Scenes are divided into *segments*, which are verbal exchanges between a character and him/herself (monologue) or between two or more characters. Even professional theatre people may mistakenly call these scenes. But, as explained, a scene is much larger and noted on the manuscript pages. Segments begin by the curtain opening to reveal characters onstage, a person entering, two more characters left alone by another individual, or a telephone or doorbell ringing. The play moves from segment to segment until the scene or the act has ended.

Each segment is composed of one or more *beats*. A beat is the smallest fragment of a play. In fact, it may be only a sentence long or continue for several pages. The simplest definition for a beat is a *topic of conversation.*

Let's say that Beth and Mary have a phone discussion during Act One. That will be a segment, starting when Beth answers the phone and ending when both parties hang up the receiver. But the telephone segment is separated into beats. First, the women exchange pleasantries (Beat #1). Then they discuss the community theatre tryouts that night (Beat #2). Next, they decide where to go shopping that day so Beth can buy a dress for the audition (Beat #3). The mail carrier rings Beth's doorbell so both parties bid hasty good-byes (Beat #4).

In your scenario, that is the way you will list the events:

ACT ONE:
Segment A.   Telephone Conversation—
Beth and Mary
Beat #1: Pleasantries
Beat #2: Tryouts that night
Beat #3: Where shopping?
Beat #4: Mail carrier—
good-byes
Segment B.   Beth and mail carrier
Beat #1: Mail carrier needs
signature for registered let-
ter
Beat #2: Beth suggests
mail carrier audition that
night

And so on through every moment of the play.

Beats are literally the heartbeats of a play. Therefore, let's take a closer look at the two types of beats, using the above telephone conversation.

THE BEAT, BEAT, BEAT OF THE . . .

Plot beats provide exposition or prepare the audience for some event that will happen later in the play.

BETH: The Little Theatre's tryouts for *Streetcar Named Desire* are at seven tonight. I'm going.

or

MARY: Grayson's is having a sale this week. You can probably find just what you want there.

or

BETH: Didn't the director of *Streetcar* handle our production of *Hair* two years ago?

Character beats offer clues to the personality of the speaker or another individual being discussed. They can detail likes and dislikes, motivations for past or future actions, and provide insight into a person's feelings and thoughts. Character beats are an excellent means of creating conflict.

> MARY: Yes, but what color dress? Don't be offended, but I really don't think brown is your color. It does terrible things to your complexion.

or

> BETH: I get so nervous at these auditions. The others seem to take it in their stride, but I fall apart.

or

> MARY: I see you more as Stella than Blanche. Stella is so . . . earthy.

Beats are not always clumped purely by one type or the other. In a conversation—even one of just a few lines—you can have a mixture of plot and character lines. But in any grouping of lines, one type of beat usually predominates; giving an organized feeling about what's happening onstage.

Consider *Fox Boy's Night Vision* by Anita Gustafson. The full-length play, a semi-finalist at the Eugene O'Neill Theatre Conference, is based on Native American tales and would fit our market category of *Plays Written for Children to Be Acted by Adults*. The action and dialogue are highly stylized and truly create a magical world for the audience. Here is a portion of the opening segment of Act One.

Late afternoon on a forest trail.
Forest sounds are heard.

MOTHER:
(Off) Little boy fox! Hurry!

FATHER:
(Enters, calls back) Fox Boy! Hurry up!

(MOTHER enters. MOTHER and FATHER wear Indian clothes of no specific tribe. They are laden with packs.)

(Looking back) *Now* where is he?

MOTHER:
Speak gently, my husband.

FATHER:
Gently! It is long after noon, and soon time to set up a trail camp. And how can we do this when we must go back and forth like hobbled animals to find him? (Calling) Fox Boy!

MOTHER:
There never was a time when a boy's first journey did *not* go slowly.

FATHER:
Have I not taught him the trail-walk? How to move rapidly and silently and easily through the forest?

MOTHER:
This you have done.

FATHER:
Then *what* is he doing?

MOTHER:
There is much to see when the trail is strange and the boy young.

FATHER:
Too young.

MOTHER:
No, my husband. The little boy fox will soon go alone on his vision-quest and see the path he must take through life. He will soon grow up. It is time he traveled.

FATHER:

Bah! Even before my vision-quest, I knew to keep up on a journey. He is too young by far!

MOTHER:

Have patience.

FATHER:

Patience! I have been patient for twelve years and still he is a child.

MOTHER:

Come, sit with me. (Sitting) We'll wait for him.

FATHER:

(Sitting) He'll *never* grow up—that's the way it looks to me! Put on your mocassins we had to tell him this morning! (Mimicking) "I won't put them on!" Stamping his feet and waving his arms! "I won't put them on!" A fine case of snits to begin his first journey!

MOTHER:

He had the snits from excitement. It is only natural.

FATHER:

Well, I won't have it! (Rising, stamping his feet, waving his arms) I WON'T HAVE IT!

MOTHER:

And you, too, seem to be having the snits, my husband.

FATHER:

What?

MOTHER:

It is true.

FATHER:

I won't have this! First I must wait for him, and then— THEN!—I am told I am having the snits. Never was a time when I must have this!

MOTHER:

(Soothingly) Have patience, my husband.

FATHER:
He must keep up with us or return to sit in our home camp. I have spoken.

MOTHER:
Send him home? Alone? When it is late and time to make a trail camp? And what will that do?

FATHER:
It will teach him to keep up!

MOTHER:
He will catch up.

FATHER:
It will teach him to *grow* up!

There are many good points to note about this segment. Go back and classify each line of dialogue as either a character or plot beat. You will notice that what you've read is primarily a character beat of the larger segment. The playwright wishes to create not only a picture of the offstage immature Fox Boy but also the relationships of the impatient father and over-indulgent mother to the youth as well as to each other. But see how the author has also provided the facts of "where" and "when" as well as foreshadowing events to come. These are plot beats. You probably wonder, why include information about where the scene is taking place and the time of day when that information would be printed in the program. Never trust an audience to read the playbill.

The action is even more effective because the information is provided in a conflict scene. Whether playwrights are offering plot clues or hints of characterization, they must do it in a way that holds the audience's attention.

Song of Sixpence by Sandra Fenichel Asher fits into the same market category as Gustafson's play, but the one-acter can also be acted by students in the sixth grade through high school for a younger audience. Thus it can be a *Play Written for Children to be Acted by Children*.

Inspired by the nursery rhyme "Sing a Song of Sixpence,"

in which blackbirds are baked in a pie, the play is peopled with original characters. Asher worked on the premise of "what if. . . ." What if the blackbirds revolted? And, indeed, they do by initially attacking the King's maid while she is doing the laundry.

Here is a segment where Weedling, a servant, and Gallop, his talking horse, relate the drastic news to Queen Mathilde and King Hempleworth the Hopeful. (Check how that personality trait of "hoping" is *shown* to the audience.)

WEEDLING: The point is, Your Majesties, the servants are all running away. They say it's too dangerous to stay here. We've been under attack for nearly a week.

KING: Yes, I know. You informed me the moment it began, Weedling.

WEEDLING: I'm always ready to serve in any way I can. Humble, faithful and reliable. That's me. (Hand out and ready) You've always been good enough to reward me, Your Majesty.

KING: What? Yes, of course. Here, an ancient penny from my collection. It's very valuable. It has King Rufus Stubblecheeks on it. They say it's a good likeness.

WEEDLING: Thank you, Your Majesty. You're too kind to your humble, faithful and reliable servant.

KING: Probably.

QUEEN: You've known about those blackbirds for a week and haven't done anything about it?

KING: Um—ah—yes.

QUEEN: But why?

KING: I kept hoping they'd go away.

QUEEN: Oh, no.

WEEDLING: Begging your pardon, Your Majesty, but this penny is worthless.

KING: Worthless? But there's King Rufus Stubblecheeks right on it.

WEEDLING: We've never had a King Rufus Stubble-cheeks.

KING: Uh-oh, I was afraid of that.

QUEEN: You mean, you knew your pennies were worthless, but you didn't do anything about it?

KING: Well, I *thought* they might be worthless, but I kept hoping I was wrong. Somehow, *somewhere* there could have been a King Rufus Stubblecheeks, couldn't there?

QUEEN: They don't call you Hempleworth the Hopeful for nothing, do they?

WEEDLING: They ought to call him Hempleworth the Hopeless. Come on, Gallop, let's get out of here. (GALLOP doesn't move) Here's your penny, Your Majesty. Rufus Stubblecheeks, indeed! Well, let's go, Gallop. (GALLOP doesn't move) Giddyap!

GALLOP: I have to leave, Your Majesty. I'm terribly sorry. If you ever get rid of those blackbirds, I'll come right back. We'd all like . . .

WEEDLING: Whoa, Gallop, you neighing ninny. The point is, Your Majesty, we quit.

KING: Whatever happened to old humble, faithful and reliable?

WEEDLING: The same thing that happened to King Rufus Stubblecheeks. Giddyap, Gallop!

As you analyze this scene segment, you notice that it is composed mostly of character beats with touches of plot beats here and there along with *humor*. And exactly the sort of humor that young children will appreciate. Socrates said, "Know thyself." For playwrights, the motto should be "Know Thy Audience." Asher certainly knows that theatre audiences — just like readers of fiction — need conflict to hold their interest. In this short exchange we have conflict between Weedling and the King, the King and the Queen, and minor conflict between Gallop and Weedling.

For a last example to help you study the beats of a play, here is a total segment from a *Play for Teenagers and/or Adults to be Acted by Teenagers and/or Adults.* Kevin Shaw's *Locker Room* was the winner in a national play competition in which there were more than 200 entries. The story develops on two levels. As the drama opens, seventeen-year-old Mark enters the locker room of his new high school for the initial basketball team practice. A few minutes into Act One, Scene One, a second story level is revealed in the first of several flashbacks that weave throughout the play — a mystery that occurred in Mark's former hometown. It is this "memory" segment that we see here, where Mark remembers a conversation with the Sheriff, but that mental exchange is played out for the audience to see and hear. A flashback in drama is no different than a flashback in literature.

(An armchair with a law enforcement officer standing beside it. SHERIFF is short, pot-bellied, and in his mid-forties. His rubbery face is grim and even when he smiles, the expression seems forced.)

SHERIFF: Sheriff MacDougal. Rocky Cove Police. (Without being asked, SHERIFF plops into the armchair) Just tryin' to get some things straight about last night. Terrible thing. That accident.

MARK: Yeah.

SHERIFF: And the victim, Todd Walters, arrived here around seven-thirty.

MARK: Right.

SHERIFF: Why?

MARK: Why?

SHERIFF: (Pausing) You do understand this isn't an official investigation. You won't sign a statement or anything . . . yet. It's just to help me figure out the e-vents. (Makes two words of the one) That is clear to you, isn't it?

MARK: Yes.

SHERIFF: Good. Now why'd Walters come here? He must've had a reason.

MARK: Just to stop over. We did it all the time. No special reason.

SHERIFF: Um-huh. And your father was here.

MARK: Yes.

SHERIFF: He was home all night, too. Right?

MARK: Definitely. Both of us.

SHERIFF: Neither of you used the pickup that was involved in the hit and run.

MARK: Not last night. No.

SHERIFF: And the Walters boy left about nine-fifteen.

MARK: Around that.

SHERIFF: And he was going to walk to his house about five blocks from here. A ten minute walk.

MARK: That's right. We always walked to each other's houses.

SHERIFF: Yet the people in the houses at the scene say they heard the tires squeal and the thud around ten o'clock. Where was Walters for forty-five minutes?

MARK: I don't know. Maybe stopped to visit someone. Or bought some cigarettes at the Seven-Eleven.

SHERIFF: I checked there. No one with his description came in last night.

MARK: Then I have no idea where he went after he left.

SHERIFF: Okay. When he left, you didn't see that your pickup was missing?

MARK: No.

SHERIFF: Okay, son, let's talk about the victim. You don't mind, do you?

MARK: Why should I?

SHERIFF: Well, I've been hearing things about your buddy. (MARK stares, stonefaced) From what people say, he was queer. I mean honest to god queer.

MARK: Maybe.

SHERIFF: Maybe? He wrote a letter to the school principal asking if he could bring a 'guest' to the senior prom. (MARK nods) And this guest was going to be another guy. Wouldn't you call that queer?

MARK: Gay.

SHERIFF: Whatever name you want. Did he tell you about this letter before he wrote it? (MARK nods) What did you say?

MARK: (Crossing away a few steps) I told him it wasn't a good idea.

SHERIFF: Why?

MARK: I told him the guys at school would be after his ass.

SHERIFF: After his ass? Is the whole goddamn school queer?

MARK: (Facing SHERIFF) Make jokes about him. Pick fights. Make his life miserable.

SHERIFF: And did they?

MARK: Kind of. Not as bad as I thought they would.

SHERIFF: Can you give me any names of the people who were 'after his ass?'

MARK: Todd never mentioned any.

SHERIFF: What did he *mention*?

MARK: Just things people said to him in the hall. And guys avoiding him in the locker room after gym. Obscene phone calls. Threatening letters.

SHERIFF: And you didn't think that was bad?

MARK: I guess I expected guys beating on him.

SHERIFF: These threatening letters. Did they arrive in the mail?

MARK: Sometimes Todd found them stuffed into his locker. I think some were delivered by mail.

SHERIFF: That's a Federal offense.

MARK: I guess so.

SHERIFF: Guess so? Now this is just sup-po-sition, but do you think one of those letter writers could have stolen your daddy's truck and run down Todd Walters? And then abandoned the pickup down by the beach?

MARK: Why steal *our* truck?

SHERIFF: Someone used it. Your buddy was on the sidewalk. The truck, your daddy's pickup, swerved from the road and went up on the sidewalk. Almost like on purpose. But maybe the driver was drinking. Did you and Walters have anything to drink while he was here last night?

MARK: No.

SHERIFF: Drugs?

MARK: We weren't into shit.

SHERIFF: Well, we're waiting for the autopsy report. We'll see what shows up. (SHERIFF shifts positions as if to stand but remains seated) I guess that's about all. You and your father were home for those important forty-five minutes?

MARK: I was in my room. He was watching TV.

SHERIFF: Did your father come up to your room? (MARK shakes his head) Did you come downstairs?

MARK: No.

SHERIFF: Then how does he know you were in the house?

MARK: I told him I was going upstairs to watch my small TV.

SHERIFF: But you could've sneaked down the stairs and out the back door.

MARK: Why would I do that?

SHERIFF: I don't know. And if your daddy didn't see you, then you didn't see *him*.

MARK: That's right.

SHERIFF: He might've used the truck.

MARK: I would've heard it start. My bedroom faces the driveway.

SHERIFF: He could've pushed it to the street.

MARK: Our driveway slopes down to the garage. You would need at least two people to push the truck up to the street.

(SHERIFF sits silently, staring at MARK, who becomes uneasy.)

Is there anything else you wanted to know?

SHERIFF: When your buddy Todd came here, did you two ever fool around?

MARK: Fool around?

SHERIFF: You know. Engage in sex-u-al activities?

(MARK advances upon the SHERIFF. Blackout)

Unlike the excerpts from *Fox Boy's Night Vision* and *Song of Sixpence*, this segment is composed of only one type of beat: plot beats. Again, the information must be presented dramatically. Tension exists because there is something inherently threatening about the red-neck Sheriff and, as the facts are revealed, a puzzling factor about Mark's involvement with Todd. Mystery fans are already asking questions. Did either Mark or his father use the pickup to run down Todd? Was it one of those guys bothering Todd? And the really astute mystery buff is wondering if the playwright is trying to mislead the audience by giving the impression the murderous driver was male. Could the villain be a female? Yet, while the exposition is being performed and the audience's interest piqued, the two characters onstage must reveal facets of themselves through their choice of words as well as their actions and reactions.

THE INITIAL ENCOUNTER
WITH PLAYWRITING

Short story writers and novelists who experiment with playwriting the first time are pleased by two unexpected reactions. First, they find that while writing the play, they are more fully gripped by a total involvement with the characters and their problems — more so than when writing other types of fiction. The external world fades, and the writer truly feels onstage with his or her characters. This happens because playwrights deal with the meat of a story — dialogue. There isn't a need to write setting description or detail the actions of a character (except in brief stage directions) — nothing to pull you from the interaction of the story people.

Another realization forms when it's time to revise the first draft. Rewriting is never simple, but it is easier when revising a play because you can isolate more quickly the parts that need changing or where additions should go. You can read through the script and realize that there are not enough character beats to fully create a person or certain plot beats can be eliminated because a character is describing too fully a segment that the audience has already witnessed.

But new playwrights may encounter a minor problem. Manuscript format. You have examples of the two acceptable ways to type a playscript. Use either the format employed by Anita Gustafson in her tale about Fox-Boy or the one used in Kevin Shaw's *Locker Room*. The only variation between the two is the placement of the character's name when noting who is speaking. Either style is fine with publishers and play producers.

TRY IT. YOU'LL LIKE IT.

Theatre is exciting for the audience and an adventure for a writer. Don't let a lack of experience intimidate you. Take a short scene from one of your stories and "play around" with it. Try writing the sequence as a play segment. You may be surprised at how you'll instinctively make changes in the dialogue to accommodate the needs of the stage. It is easy enough to educate yourself to the more intricate demands of playwriting. Magazines like *The Writer* and *Writer's Digest* publish articles on playwriting, and there are numerous textbooks available. Market lists will guide you toward either print or performance. Or both. Trust me. You'll like it.

30
Further Reading . . .
Reference Sources at Your Elbow . . .
Other Annotated Aids

For further reading and study here is a selection of annotated material from my own shelves. To a truly good textbook you can return again and again for inspiration, stimulation, and additional knowhow. Such a book grows in value and helps you grow as a writer.

Whatever texts you choose to read, do so a little at a time, not in great indigestible gulps. And remember, *all* the advice is not for you. Accept it if the ideas fit your own thinking on writing. Some material you may not appreciate now, but will recognize as pure gold later on. Other material may never be of use to you, even though I have found it helpful.

These are the books (listed in order of importance under each category) I recommend to my classes and to you:

REFERENCE ITEMS ON MY BOOKSHELVES
Roget's Thesaurus of Words and Phrases. A *must* for every writer. Published in several editions, hardcover and paperback.
Webster's Elementary Dictionary. For children from the fourth through the sixth grade, including some words for seventh graders. Some editors advise: "If it's not in the *Elementary Dictionary*—don't use it!" (Merriam.)
Webster's New Collegiate Dictionary. When you really need to know *all* about a word. (Merriam.)
Finding Facts Fast: How to Find out What You Want and Need to Know. Alden Todd. The title tells it all. Nonfiction authors should purchase. Paperback. (Ten Speed Press.)

SOME TEXTBOOKS FROM MY SHELVES
Writing, Illustrating and Editing Children's Books. Jean P. Colby. An overall view of the field by an editor-writer who knows first-hand all the aspects of our trade. (Hastings.)

Writing Juvenile Stories and Novels. Phyllis A. Whitney. A foremost authority who practices what she preaches. Enormously successful in both the juvenile and adult fields. (Writer.)

Writing for Christian Publications. Edith Tiller Osteyee. Excellent, especially for this special field. (Judson Press.)

The Art of Dramatic Writing. Lajos Egri. Definitely! (Writer.)

Modern Fiction Techniques. F. A. Rockwell. Don't miss her chapter on titles. Best I've ever read. (Writer.)

Techniques of the Selling Writer. Dwight V. Swain. You'll probably have to grow up to this one—as a writer—but keep it in mind. Indexed. (University of Oklahoma Press.)

From Childhood to Childhood: Children's Books and Their Creators. Jean Karl. A book by one of the most distinguished children's book editors, who is now retired. (John Day Co.)

Writing Mysteries for Young People. Joan Lowery Nixon. A well-known author reveals her secrets for creating suspenseful mysteries. Excellent. (The Writer.)

How to Write a Children's Book and Get It Published. Barbara Seuling. This author, illustrator, and former children's book editor shares a wealth of insights and professional knowledge to help beginning authors publish successfully. (Scribners.)

Playwriting: The Structure of Action. Sam Smiley. The most comprehensive text on playwriting available. (Prentice-Hall.)

The Children's Picture Book. Ellen E.M. Roberts. The best text about this active market. (Writer's Digest Books.)

How to Write Plots That Sell. F. A. Rockwell. Recommended for writers of eight-to-twelve and young adult fiction. Paperback. (Contemporary Books, Inc.)

Three Genres: The Writer of Poetry, Fiction, and Drama. Stephen Minot. Contrasts the three types of writing. General, but helpful. (Prentice-Hall.)

Mystery Writer's Handbook. The Mystery Writers of America. Writers of eight-to-twelve and YA suspense should add this volume to their personal library. A must. (Writer's Digest Books.)

Writing the Modern Magazine Article. Max Gunther. Not to be missed! Eight-to-twelve and young adult article writers should study this text. (Writer.)

Writing Short Stories for Young People. George Edward Stanley. Examines the major categories of short stories. Entire stories accompany several of the story types. (Writer's Digest Books.)

Guide to Fiction Writing. Phyllis A. Whitney. Although aimed at writing adult fiction, this is a helpful text for authors of older children's fiction. (Writer.)

Writing and Selling a Nonfiction Book. Max Gunther. Not for the concept book author but extremely helpful to the eight-to-twelve and YA nonfiction author. (Writer.)

Nonfiction for Children. Ellen E.M. Roberts. The stress is on writing nonfiction books from the picture book age to young adult. (Writer's Digest Books.)

Writing Young Adult Novels. Hadley Irwin & Jeannette Eyerly. An overall picture of this important market. (Writer's Digest Books.)

FOR THAT STAMP OF PROFESSIONALISM

Elements of Style. William Strunk and E.B. White. A classic in guides to good writing. Seventy-one pages of text—a must! Available in paperback. (Macmillan.)

ABC of Style. Rudolf Flesch. A splendid guide to plain, *effective* English. In dictionary form. Never out of my reach. (Harper.)

The Art of Readable Writing. Rudolf Flesch. Will help to rid you of a lot of cluttery, fluttery words. Also available in paperback. (Harper.)

A Manual of Style. More trade talk and sound advice. At every book editor's elbow. (University of Chicago Press.)

MAGAZINES FOR WRITERS

Writer's Digest, 1507 Dana Avenue, Cincinnati, Ohio 45207.

The Writer, 120 Boylston St., Boston, Massachusetts 02116.

The Horn Book (book reviews and articles on children's literature), 585 Boylston St., Boston, Massachusetts 02116.

School Library Journal (book reviews and articles), R.R. Bowker Co., 1180 Avenue of the Americas, New York, New York 10036.

Writer's Yearbook (an annual published by Writer's Digest.)

MARKET LISTS

Writer's Market. Complete, annotated market coverage. Listings include agents, publishers, editors, specific manuscript requirements, contracts, rates paid—everything the working writer needs at his fingertips when he is ready to market his material. (Writer's Digest Books.)

Literary Market Place. Suited more to professionals than to newcomers in the field. (Bowker.)

31
Bon Voyage!

To learn *about* writing you must read. Yet no book can *make* a writer of you. I have done my best to point you in the right direction, but the journey you must make yourself.

Writing is never easy. "I was amazed to learn that there was so much *to* it," an earnest student told me once. There is indeed. I cannot promise you that after the joyous miracle of the first sale — or the tenth, or twentieth — it will be easier.

But writing is a vocation so compelling that even after you know all the hard work involved, there is still nothing else you'd rather do. You cannot give it up — at least not for long. There's heady stuff in being a maker and shaker of worlds of your own creation. You can *be* anything and anyone in any time or place or occupation. And, when you are writing for the young, you are doubly blessed because you form the habit of viewing everything around you with the fresh eyes of youth. Yours is always a big, wide, shining world — regardless of the headlines.

What *you* think and say in your books and stories is far from inconsequential, for everything a child reads becomes a part of him and her, and quite possibly an influence upon his/her future life and thought.

Emerson said: "The crowning fortune of a man is to be born to some pursuit which finds him employment and happiness, whether it be to make baskets or broadswords, or canals, or statues, or song."

I hope you too will find in your writing *employment and happiness,* for to the committed writer, profit is only the by-product of his or her work. Happiness is the chief product.

INDEX

More Great Books for Writers!

Ten Steps to Publishing Children's Books—Get published in the popular genre of children's books! You'll discover vital tips from successful writers and illustrators to help you polish the skills necessary to make your dream come true. Plus, the input of editors offers a unique perspective from the publishing side of the industry. *#10534/$24.95/128 pages/150 illus.*

The Children's Writer's Word Book—Even the most original children's story won't get published if its language usage or sentence structure doesn't speak to young readers. You'll avoid these pitfalls with this fast-reference guide full of word lists, reading levels for synonyms and much more. *#10316/$19.99/352 pages*

Writing and Illustrating Children's Books for Publication: Two Perspectives—Discover how to create a good, publishable manuscript in only eight weeks! You'll cover the writing process in its entirety—from generating ideas and getting started, to submitting a manuscript. Imaginative writing and illustrating exercises build on these lessons and provide fuel for your creative fires! *#10448/$24.95/128 pages/200 b&w illus., 16 page color insert*

How to Write and Illustrate Children's Books and Get Them Published—Find everything you need to know about breaking into the lucrative children's market. You'll discover how to write a sure-fire seller, how to create fresh and captivating illustrations, how to get your manuscript into the right buyer's hands and more! *#30082/$24.99/144 pages/70 color, 45 b&w illus.*

The Very Best of Children's Book Illustration—Feast your eyes on this wonderful collection of the best in contemporary children's book illustration. You'll see nearly 200 full-color illustrations sure to spark your creativity. *#30513/$29.95/144 pages/198 color illus.*

How to Write and Sell Children's Picture Books—Learn how to put your picture book on paper and get it published—whether you're retelling a wonderful old tale or spinning a splendid new yarn. *#10410/$16.99/192 pages*

Grammatically Correct: The Writer's Guide to Punctuation, Spelling, Style, Usage and Grammar—Write prose that's clear, concise and graceful! This comprehensive desk reference covers the nuts-and-bolts basics of punctuation, spelling and grammar, as well as essential tips and techniques for developing a smooth, inviting writing style. *#10529/$19.99/352 pages*

The Writer's Essential Desk Reference—Get quick, complete, accurate answers to your important writing questions with this companion volume to *Writer's Market*. You'll cover all aspects of the business side of writing—from information on the World Wide Web and other research sites, to opportunities with writers workshops and the basics on taxes and health insurance. *#10485/$24.99/384 pages*

The Writer's Digest Dictionary of Concise Writing—Make your work leaner, crisper and clearer! Under the guidance of professional editor Robert Hartwell Fiske, you'll learn how to rid your work of common say-nothing phrases while making it tighter and easier to read and understand. *#10482/$19.99/352 pages*

How to Write Attention-Grabbing Query & Cover Letters—Use the secrets John Wood reveals to write queries perfectly tailored, too good to turn down! In this guide-book, you will discover why boldness beats blandness in queries every time, ten basics you must have in your article queries, ten query blunders that can destroy publication chances and much more. *#10462/$17.99/208 pages*

The Writer's Digest Sourcebook for Building Believable Characters—Create unforgettable characters as you "attend" a roundtable where six novelists reveal their approaches to characterization. You'll probe your characters' backgrounds, beliefs and desires with a fill-in-the-blanks questionnaire. And a thesaurus of characteristics will help you develop the many other features no character should be without. *#10463/$17.99/288 pages*

The Writer's Digest Character Naming Sourcebook—Finally, you'll discover how to choose the perfect name to reflect your character's personality, ethnicity and place in history. Here you'll find 20,000 first and last names (and their meanings) from around the world! *#10390/$18.99/352 pages*

Writer's Encyclopedia, 3rd Edition—Rediscover this popular writer's reference—now with information about electronic resources, plus more than 100 new entries. You'll find facts, figures, definitions and examples designed to answer questions about every discipline connected with writing and to help you convey a professional image. *#10464/$22.99/560 pages/62 b&w illus.*

Creating Characters: How to Build Story People—Grab the empathy of your reader with characters so real—they'll jump off the page. You'll discover how to make characters come alive with vibrant emotion, quirky personality traits, inspiring heroism and other uniquely human qualities. *#10417/$14.99/192 pages/paperback*

The Writer's Digest Guide to Manuscript Formats—No matter how good your ideas, an unprofessional format will land your manuscript on the slush pile! You need this easy-to-follow guide on manuscript preparation and presentation—for everything from books and articles, to poems and plays. *#10025/$19.99/200 pages*

Beginning Writer's Answer Book—This book answers 900 of the most often asked questions about every stage of the writing process. You'll find business advice, tax tips, plus new information about online networks, databases and more. *#10394/$17.99/336 pages*

Make Your Words Work—Loaded with samples and laced with exercises, this guide will help you clean up your prose, refine your style, strengthen your descriptive powers, bring music to your words and much more! *#10399/$14.99/304 pages/paperback*

Voice & Style—Discover how to create character and story voices! You'll learn to write with a spellbinding narrative voice, create original character voices, write dialogue that conveys personality and make the story's voices harmonize into a solid style. *#10452/$15.99/176 pages*

Getting the Words Right: How to Rewrite, Edit & Revise—Reduction, rearrangement, rewording and rechecking—the 4 Rs of powerful writing. This book provides concrete instruction with dozens of exercises and pages of samples to help you improve your writing through effective revision. *#10172/$14.99/218 pages/paperback*

Freeing Your Creativity: A Writer's Guide—Discover how to escape the traps that stifle your creativity. You'll tackle techniques for banishing fears and nourishing ideas so you can get your juices flowing again. *#10430/$14.99/176 pages/paperback*

30 Steps to Becoming a Writer and Getting Published—This informational and inspirational guide helps you get started as a writer, develops your skills and style and gets your work ready for submission. *#10367/$16.99/176 pages*

How to Write Fast (While Writing Well)—Discover what makes a story and what it takes to research and write one. Then learn, step by step, how to cut wasted time and effort by planning interviews for maximum results, beating writer's block with effective plotting, getting the most information from traditional library research and online computer databases and much more! Plus, a complete chapter loaded with tricks and tips for faster writing. *#10473/$15.99/208 pages/paperback*